DATE DUE

MR 1 3'01			
AP 2 6 03			

DEMCO 38-296

BRETT ASHLEY

Major Literary Characters

THE ANCIENT WORLD THROUGH THE SEVENTEENTH CENTURY

ACHILLES
Homer, *Iliad*

CALIBAN
William Shakespeare, *The Tempest*
Robert Browning, *Caliban upon Setebos*

CLEOPATRA
William Shakespeare, *Antony and Cleopatra*
John Dryden, *All for Love*
George Bernard Shaw, *Caesar and Cleopatra*

DON QUIXOTE
Miguel de Cervantes, *Don Quixote*
Franz Kafka, *Parables*

FALSTAFF
William Shakespeare, *Henry IV, Part I, Henry IV, Part II, The Merry Wives of Windsor*

FAUST
Christopher Marlowe, *Doctor Faustus*
Johann Wolfgang von Goethe, *Faust*
Thomas Mann, *Doctor Faustus*

HAMLET
William Shakespeare, *Hamlet*

IAGO
William Shakespeare, *Othello*

JULIUS CAESAR
William Shakespeare, *Julius Caesar*
George Bernard Shaw, *Caesar and Cleopatra*

KING LEAR
William Shakespeare, *King Lear*

MACBETH
William Shakespeare, *Macbeth*

ODYSSEUS/ULYSSES
Homer, *Odyssey*
James Joyce, *Ulysses*

OEDIPUS
Sophocles, *Oedipus Rex, Oedipus at Colonus*

OTHELLO
William Shakespeare, *Othello*

ROSALIND
William Shakespeare, *As You Like It*

SANCHO PANZA
Miguel de Cervantes, *Don Quixote*
Franz Kafka, *Parables*

SATAN
The Book of Job
John Milton, *Paradise Lost*

SHYLOCK
William Shakespeare, *The Merchant of Venice*

THE WIFE OF BATH
Geoffrey Chaucer, *The Canterbury Tales*

THE EIGHTEENTH AND NINETEENTH CENTURIES

AHAB
Herman Melville, *Moby-Dick*

ISABEL ARCHER
Henry James, *Portrait of a Lady*

EMMA BOVARY
Gustave Flaubert, *Madame Bovary*

DOROTHEA BROOKE
George Eliot, *Middlemarch*

CHELSEA HOUSE PUBLISHERS

Major Literary Characters

DAVID COPPERFIELD
Charles Dickens, *David Copperfield*

ROBINSON CRUSOE
Daniel Defoe, *Robinson Crusoe*

DON JUAN
Molière, *Don Juan*
Lord Byron, *Don Juan*

HUCK FINN
Mark Twain, *The Adventures of Tom Sawyer, Adventures of Huckleberry Finn*

CLARISSA HARLOWE
Samuel Richardson, *Clarissa*

HEATHCLIFF
Emily Brontë, *Wuthering Heights*

ANNA KARENINA
Leo Tolstoy, *Anna Karenina*

MR. PICKWICK
Charles Dickens, *The Pickwick Papers*

HESTER PRYNNE
Nathaniel Hawthorne, *The Scarlet Letter*

BECKY SHARP
William Makepeace Thackeray, *Vanity Fair*

LAMBERT STRETHER
Henry James, *The Ambassadors*

EUSTACIA VYE
Thomas Hardy, *The Return of the Native*

TWENTIETH CENTURY

ÁNTONIA
Willa Cather, *My Ántonia*

BRETT ASHLEY
Ernest Hemingway, *The Sun Also Rises*

HANS CASTORP
Thomas Mann, *The Magic Mountain*

HOLDEN CAULFIELD
J. D. Salinger, *The Catcher in the Rye*

CADDY COMPSON
William Faulkner, *The Sound and the Fury*

JANIE CRAWFORD
Zora Neale Hurston, *Their Eyes Were Watching God*

CLARISSA DALLOWAY
Virginia Woolf, *Mrs. Dalloway*

DILSEY
William Faulkner, *The Sound and the Fury*

GATSBY
F. Scott Fitzgerald, *The Great Gatsby*

HERZOG
Saul Bellow, *Herzog*

JOAN OF ARC
William Shakespeare, *Henry VI*
George Bernard Shaw, *Saint Joan*

LOLITA
Vladimir Nabokov, *Lolita*

WILLY LOMAN
Arthur Miller, *Death of a Salesman*

MARLOW
Joseph Conrad, *Lord Jim, Heart of Darkness, Youth, Chance*

PORTNOY
Philip Roth, *Portnoy's Complaint*

BIGGER THOMAS
Richard Wright, *Native Son*

CHELSEA HOUSE PUBLISHERS

Major Literary Characters

BRETT ASHLEY

Edited and with an introduction by
HAROLD BLOOM

CHELSEA HOUSE PUBLISHERS
New York ◊ Philadelphia

to (1929) of Lady Duff Twysden (the model for Brett Ashley). *inset:* Title page from the first edition of *The Sun Also Rises* (New York: Scribner's, 1926). Courtesy of Charles Scribner's Sons, an imprint of Macmillan Publishing Company.

Chelsea House Publishers

Editor-in-Chief Remmel T. Nunn
Managing Editor Karyn Gullen Browne
Picture Editor Adrian G. Allen
Art Director Maria Epes
Manufacturing Manager Gerald Levine

Major Literary Characters

Senior Editor S. T. Joshi
Associate Editor Richard Fumosa
Designer Maria Epes

Staff for BRETT ASHLEY

Picture Researcher Patricia Burnes
Assistant Art Director Noreen Romano
Production Manager Joseph Romano
Production Coordinator Marie Claire Cebrián

Printed and bound in the United States of America

First Printing

1 3 5 7 9 8 6 4 2

Library of Congress Cataloging-in-Publication Data

Brett Ashley / edited and with an introduction by Harold Bloom.—1st ed.
p. cm.—(Major literary characters)
Includes bibliographical references (p.   ) and index.
ISBN 0-7910-0951-2.—ISBN 0-7910-1006-6 (pbk.)
1. Hemingway, Ernest, 1899–1962. Sun also rises. 2. Hemingway, Ernest, 1899–1962—Characters—Brett Ashley. 3. Hemingway, Ernest. 1899–1962—Characters—Women. 4. Ashley, Brett (Fictitious character)
5. Women in literature. I. Bloom, Harold. II. Series.
PS3515.E37S922 1991
813'.52—dc20
90-25244
CIP

CONTENTS

THE ANALYSIS OF CHARACTER

Harold Bloom

"Character," according to our dictionaries, still has as a primary meaning a graphic symbol, such as a letter of the alphabet. This meaning reflects the word's apparent origin in the ancient Greek *charactēr*, a sharp stylus. *Charactēr* also meant the mark of the stylus' incisions. Recent fashions in literary criticism have reduced "character" in literature to a matter of marks upon a page. But our word "character" also has a very different meaning, matching that of the ancient Greek *ēthos,* "habitual way of life." Shall we say then that literary character is an imitation of human character, or is it just a grouping of marks? The issue is between a critic like Dr. Samuel Johnson, for whom words were as much like people as like things, and a critic like the late Roland Barthes, who told us that "the fact can only exist linguistically, as a term of discourse." Who is closer to our experience of reading literature, Johnson or Barthes? What difference does it make, if we side with one critic rather than the other?

Barthes is famous, like Foucault and other recent French theorists, for having added to Nietzsche's proclamation of the death of God a subsidiary demise, that of the literary author. If there are no authors, then there are no fictional personages, presumably because literature does not refer to a world outside language. Words indeed necessarily refer to other words in the first place, but the impact of words ultimately is drawn from a universe of fact. Stories, poems, and plays are recognizable as such because they are human utterances within traditions of utterances, and traditions, by achieving authority, become a kind of fact, or at least the sense of a fact. Our sense that literary characters, within the context of a fictive cosmos, indeed are fictional personages is also a kind of fact. The meaning and value of every character in a successful work of literary representation depend upon our ideas of persons in the factual reality of our lives.

Literary character is always an invention, and inventions generally are indebted to prior inventions. Shakespeare is the inventor of literary character as we know it; he reformed the universal human expectations for the verbal imitation of personality, and the reformation appears now to be permanent and uncannily inevitable. Remarkable as the Bible and Homer are at representing personages, their characters are relatively unchanging. They age within their stories, but their habitual modes of being do not develop. Jacob and Achilles unfold before us, but without metamorphoses. Lear and Macbeth, Hamlet and Othello severely modify themselves not only by their actions, but by their utterances, and most of all through *overhearing themselves,* whether they speak to themselves or to others. Pondering what they themselves have said, they will to change, and actually do change, sometimes extravagantly yet always persuasively. Or else they suffer change, without willing it, but in reaction not so much to their language as to their relation to that language.

I do not think it useful to say that Shakespeare successfully imitated elements in our characters. Rather, it could be argued that he compelled aspects of character to appear that previously were concealed, or not available to representation. This is not to say that Shakespeare is God, but to remind us that language is not God either. The mimesis of character in Shakespeare's dramas now seems to us normative, and indeed became the accepted mode almost immediately, as Ben Jonson shrewdly and somewhat grudgingly implied. And yet, Shakespearean representation has surprisingly little in common with the imitation of reality in Jonson or in Christopher Marlowe. The origins of Shakespeare's originality in the portrayal of men and women are to be found in the *Canterbury Tales* of Geoffrey Chaucer, insofar as they can be located anywhere before Shakespeare himself. Chaucer's savage and superb Pardoner overhears his own tale-telling, as well as his mocking rehearsal of his own spiel, and through this overhearing he is emboldened to forget himself, and enthusiastically urges all his fellow-pilgrims to come forward to be fleeced by him. His self-awareness, and apocalyptically rancid sense of spiritual fall, are preludes to the even grander abysses of the perverted will in Iago and in Edmund. What might be called the character trait of a negative charisma may be Chaucer's invention, but came to its perfection in Shakespearean mimesis.

The analysis of character is as much Shakespeare's invention as the representation of character is, since Iago and Edmund are adepts at analyzing both themselves and their victims. Hamlet, whose overwhelming charisma has many negative components, is certainly the most comprehensive of all literary characters, and so necessarily prophesies the labyrinthine complexities of the will in Iago and Edmund. Charisma, according to Max Weber, its first codifier, is primarily a natural endowment, and implies a primordial and idiosyncratic power over nature, and so finally over death. Hamlet's uncanniness is at its most suggestive in the scene of his long dying, where the audience, through the mediation of Horatio, itself is compelled to meditate upon suicide, if only because outliving the prince of Denmark scarcely seems an option.

Shakespearean representation has usurped not only our sense of literary character, but our sense of ourselves as characters, with Hamlet playing the part of the largest of these usurpations. Insofar as we have an idea of human disinterestedness, we tend to derive it from the Hamlet of Act V, whose quietism has about it a ghostly authority. Oscar Wilde, in his profound and profoundly witty dialogue, "The Decay of Lying," expressed a permanent insight when he insisted that art shaped every era, far more than any age formed art. Life imitates art, we imitate Shakespeare, because without Shakespeare we would perish for lack of images. Wilde's grandest audacity demystifies Shakespearean mimesis with a Shakespearean vivaciousness: "This unfortunate aphorism about art holding the mirror up to Nature is deliberately said by Hamlet in order to convince the bystanders of his absolute insanity in all art-matters." Of *Hamlet*'s influence upon the ages Wilde remarked that: "The world has grown sad because a puppet was once melancholy." "Puppet" is Wilde's own deconstruction, a brilliant reminder that Shakespeare's artistry of illusion has so mastered reality as to have changed reality, evidently forever.

The analysis of character, as a critical pursuit, seems to me as much a Shakespearean invention as literary character was, since much of what we know about how to analyze character necessarily follows Shakespearean procedures. His hero-villains, from Richard III through Iago, Edmund, and Macbeth, are shrewd and endless questers into their own self-motivations. If we could bear to see Hamlet, in his unwearied negations, as another hero-villain, then we would judge him the supreme analyst of the darker recalcitrances in the selfhood. Freud followed the pre-Socratic Empedocles, in arguing that character is fate, a frightening doctrine that maintains the fear that there are no accidents, that overdetermination rules us all of our lives. Hamlet assumes the same, yet adds to this argument the terrible passivity he manifests in Act V. Throughout Shakespeare's tragedies, the most interesting personages seem doom-eager, reminding us again that a Shakespearean reading of Freud would be more illuminating than a Freudian exegesis of Shakespeare. We learn more when we discover Hamlet in the Freudian Death Drive, than when we read *Beyond the Pleasure Principle* into *Hamlet*.

In Shakespearean comedy, character achieves its true literary apotheosis, which is the representation of the inner freedom that can be created by great wit alone. Rosalind and Falstaff, perhaps alone among Shakespeare's personages, match Hamlet in wit, though hardly in the metaphysics of consciousness. Whether in the comic or the modern mode, Shakespeare has set the standard of measurement in the balance between character and passion.

In Shakespeare the self is more dramatized than theatricalized, which is why a Shakespearean reading of Freud works out so well. Character-formation after the passing of the Oedipal stage takes the place of fetishistic fragmentings of the self. Critics who now call literary character into question, and who proclaim also the death of the author, invariably also regard all notions, literary and human, of a stable character as being mere reductions of deeper pre-Oedipal desires. It becomes clear that the fortunes of literary character rise and fall with the prestige of normative conceptions of the ego. Shakespeare's Iago, who wars against being, may be the first deconstructionist of the self, with his proclamation of "I am not what I am." This constitutes the necessary prologue to any view that would regard a fixed ego as a virtual abnormality. But deconstructions of the self are no more modern than Modernism is. Like literary modernism, the decentered ego came out of the Hellenistic culture of ancient Alexandria. The Gnostic heretics believed that the psyche, like the body, was a fallen entity, mechanically fashioned by the Demiurge or false creator. They held however that each of us possessed also a spark or pneuma, which was a fragment of the original Abyss or true, alien God. The soul or psyche within every one of us was thus at war with the self or pneuma, and only that sparklike self could be saved.

Shakespeare, following after Chaucer in this respect, was the first and remains still the greatest master of representing character both as a stable soul and a wavering self. There is a substance that endures in Shakespeare's figures, and there is also a quicksilver rendition of the unsettling sparks. Racine and Tolstoy, Balzac and Dickens, follow in Shakespeare's wake by giving us some sense of pre-Oedipal sparks or drives, and considerably more sense of post-Oedipal character and personality, stabilizations or sublimations of the fetish-seeking drives. Critics like Leo Bersani and René Girard argue eloquently against our taking this mimesis as the only proper work of literature. I would suggest that strong fictions of the self, from the Bible through Samuel Beckett, necessarily participate in both modes, the sublimation of desire, and the persistence of a primordial desire. The mystery of Hamlet or of Lear is intimately invested in the tangled mixture of the two modes of representation.

Psychic mobility is proposed by Bersani as the ideal to which deconstructions of the literary self may yet guide us. The ideal has its pathos, but the realities of literary representation seem to me very different, perhaps destructively so. When a novelist like D. H. Lawrence sought to reduce his characters to Eros and the Death Drive, he still had to persuade us of his authority at mimesis by lavishing upon the figures of *The Rainbow* and *Women in Love* all of the vivid stigmata of normative personality. Birkin and Ursula may represent antithetical and uncanny drives, but they develop and change as characters pondering their own pronouncements and reactions to self and others. The cost of a non-Shakespearean representation is enormous. Pynchon, in *The Crying of Lot 49* and *Gravity's Rainbow*, evades the burden of the normative by resorting to something like Christopher Marlowe's art of caricature in *The Jew of Malta*. Marlowe's Barabas is a marvelous rhetorician, yet he is a cartoon alongside the troublingly equivocal Shylock. Pynchon's personages are deliberate cartoons also, as flat as comic strips. Marlowe's achievement, and Pynchon's, are beyond dispute, yet they are like the prelude and the postlude to Shakespearean reality. They do not wish to engage with our hunger for the empirical world and so they enter the problematic cosmos of literary fantasy.

No writer, not even Shakespeare or Proust, alters the available stock that we agree to call reality, but Shakespeare, more than any other, does show us how much of reality we could encounter if only we retained adequate desire. The strong literary representation of character is already an analysis of character, and is part of the healing work of a literary culture, which implicitly seeks to cure violence through a normative mimesis of ego, *as if it were stable*, whether in actuality it is or is not. I do not believe that this is a social quest taken on by literary culture, but rather that we confront here the aesthetic essence of what makes a culture *literary*, rather than metaphysical or ethical or religious. A culture becomes literary when its conceptual modes have failed it, which means when religion, philosophy, and science have begun to lose their authority. If they cannot heal violence, then literature attempts to do so, which may be only a turning inside out of the critical arguments of Girard and Bersani.

I conclude by offering a particular instance or special case as a paradigm for the healing enterprise that is at once the representation and the analysis of literary character. Let us call it the aesthetics of being outraged, or rather of successfully representing the state of being outraged. W. C. Fields was one modern master of such representation, and Nathanael West was another, as was Faulkner before him. Here also the greatest master remains Shakespeare, whose Macbeth, himself a bloody outrage, yet retains our imaginative sympathy precisely because he grows increasingly outraged as he experiences the equivocation of the fiend that lies like truth. The double-natured promises and the prophecies of the weird sisters finally induce in Macbeth an apocalyptic version of the stage actor's anxiety at missing cues, the horror of a phantasmagoric stage fright of missing one's time, of always reacting too late. Macbeth, a veritable monster of solipsistic inwardness but no intellectual, counters his dilemma by fresh murders, that prolong him in time yet provoke him only to a perpetually freshened sense of being outraged, as all his expectations become still worse confounded. We are moved by Macbeth, however estrangedly, because his terrible inwardness is a paradigm for our own solipsism, but also because none of us can resist a strong and successful representation of the human in a state of being outraged.

The ultimate outrage is the necessity of dying, an outrage concealed in a multitude of masks, including the tyrannical ambitions of Macbeth. I suspect that our outrage at being outraged is the most difficult of all our affects for us to represent to ourselves, which is why we are so inclined to imaginative sympathy for a character who strongly conveys that affect to us. The Shrike of West's *Miss Lonelyhearts* or Faulkner's Joe Christmas of *Light in August* are crucial modern instances, but such figures can be located in many other works, since the ability to represent this extreme emotion is one of the tests that strong writers are driven to set for themselves.

However a reader seeks to reduce literary character to a question of marks on a page, she will come at last to the impasse constituted by the thought of death, her death, and before that to all the stations of being outraged that memorialize her own drive towards death. In reading, she quests for evidences that are strong representations, whether of her desire or her despair. Such questings constitute the necessary basis for the analysis of literary character, an enterprise that always will survive every vagary of critical fashion.

EDITOR'S NOTE

This book brings together a representative selection of the best criticism that has been devoted to Lady Brett Ashley, heroine of Ernest Hemingway's classic novel *The Sun Also Rises.* I am grateful to Richard Fumosa for his skilled assistance in editing this volume.

My introduction centers upon Brett's image as a destructive muse, akin to Walter Pater's interpretation of Leonardo's Mona Lisa. A selection of extracts from the criticism of Brett follows, tracing much of the history of her reception. Included are such crucial novelists as Hemingway himself, Scott Fitzgerald, Virginia Woolf, and our prolific contemporary, Joyce Carol Oates.

Eleven critical essays give us something like a full survey of Brett's complexity as a major literary character, starting with Robert W. Lewis's invocation of her as a Circe, transforming her lovers into swine. Jackson J. Benson, a touch kinder, sees Brett as dominated by mere self-pity, while Bertram D. Sarason examines her relation to her prototype, Duff Twysden.

In Carole Gottlieb Vopat's judgment, Lady Brett Ashley loses control of Jake's passion for her, even as the novel concludes. The image of Brett found by Sam S. Baskett is almost a pagan fertility goddess, around whom her lovers dance in self-deluded reverence. A rather more mercantile reading is given by Patrick W. Morrow, for whom the all-consuming Brett is an emblem of "the Bought Generation."

Linda Wagner-Martin's Brett restores the semi-stoic heroine closer to Hemingway's apparent intention, while Roger Whitlow's estimate gives us a self-destructive figure, not a cruel one. Circe, as an allegorical image, returns in Milton A. Cohen's essay, at once a tribute to Brett's energy and a shrewd warning as to the temporal limits of its reign.

Brett's problem, as analyzed by Wolfgang E. H. Rudat, is that she cannot evade her destiny as a tragic protagonist. In this book's final essay, and perhaps its best, Mark Spilka explores the literary contexts most relevant to the subtle displacements of gender that occur between Brett and Jake. Spilka's Brett is very nearly as much an Odysseus as a Circe, which takes us back full circle to my comparison of Brett to Pater's Mona Lisa in my "Introduction." A new Brett begins to emerge, at once a Fatal Woman and a High Romantic quester, seeking tragically for what cannot be found.

INTRODUCTION

Lady Brett Ashley, the heroine of Ernest Hemingway's superb novel *The Sun Also Rises* (1926), was termed by Carlos Baker a Circe-like enchantress, a kind of fatal witch. As such she seems, two thirds of a century later, only a grand period piece, rather than a fully achieved literary character. This nymphomaniac and alcoholic aristocrat roaring through the Twenties, devouring bullfighters, is scarcely more persuasive a representation of reality than is her immediate forerunner, the Daisy of F. Scott Fitzgerald's *The Great Gatsby,* which Hemingway had read only a month or two before beginning the composition of *The Sun Also Rises.* But there is more inwardness to Lady Brett than there is to Daisy, if we begin by putting aside the vision of Hemingway's heroine as a Circe.

Circe is out of place in a Biblical vision, and rather more than just the style of *The Sun Also Rises* suggests that Hemingway is founding himself upon Biblical Wisdom literature. His title and epigraph, from Ecclesiastes, sums up the ethos of Lady Brett Ashley:

> One generation passeth away, and another generation cometh; but the earth abideth forever . . . The sun also ariseth, and the sun goeth down, and hasteth to the place where he arose . . . The wind goeth toward the south, and turneth about unto the north; it whirleth about continually, and the wind returneth again according to his circuits. . . . All the rivers run into the sea; yet the sea is not full; unto the place from whence the rivers come, thither they return again.

On so dark a view of repetition, it is not just the generation of Lady Brett that is lost. All flesh is grass, and the true subject of *The Sun Also Rises* is a stoic immersion in mortality and change. Solomonic wisdom, whether in the Proverbs or in Ecclesiastes, is a stance neither of belief nor of despair. Hemingway's prose is Biblical both in style and in sensibility, and conveys the wisdom of acceptance, acceptance of human limits and of the incommensurateness between the human condition and human aspirations. The surrogate for that acceptance is Jake Barnes, who owes something to the Nick Carraway of *The Great Gatsby* but more to their common source in Marlow, Conrad's favorite narrator, particularly the Marlow of *Lord Jim* and *Heart of Darkness*. Like Jake and Nick, Marlow is detached, cut off from much of male aggressivity and desire, and vitally concerned with the morality that makes someone else "one of us."

Brett necessarily is always mediated for us by Jake, who is in love with her, but that love seems rather more historical than present, and for reasons that transcend Jake's war-wound and consequent inability to be Brett's lover. Freud powerfully called love the overestimation of the object, and Jake hardly overestimates Brett, whom he knows to be addicted to alcohol and to a serial movement from one man to the next. As several critics have noted, Jake's stance towards Brett no longer is that of desire and regret, but is now marked by irony and pity, the classical stances both mocked and exalted by Bill Gorton. It is of some importance in apprehending Brett's character that we see the difference between Jake and Hemingway here, since it would be wrong to affirm that the novel's view of Brett is either ironical or pitying. Perhaps Jake is defending himself against his love for Brett; perhaps his love has modulated largely into compassion. Brett, in any case, holds on to part of her fascination for the reader, at least for the male reader. Her own irony is strong, as she contemplates herself, and her admiring compassion for Romero saves her from victimizing him.

That Brett retains an enigmatic reserve allows her to escape becoming a grand period piece, the Fatal Woman of the Twenties. Jake's excuses for her—the horrors of war encountered during her nursing service; the death of her true love; her marriage to a brutal and stupid aristocrat—do not persuade him, or us, that she is altogether overdetermined, wholly the product of her era. Instead, Jake comes to see that she has chosen the abyss, and his love for her begins to wane. We in turn see the differences between her and Jake: his nostalgia for religion, against her aversion to faith; his aesthetic apprehension of the rituals of death, dignity, and honor in the bullfighter, against her sensual need for Romero. That these differences are to be weighted in Jake's favor is by no means self-evident. Whose novel is it anyway? Take Brett out of it, and vitality would depart. Life, in Brett, has its rancid aspects, but it remains life, rather than death-in-life. Brett cannot be considered a normative heroine; her love for Jake finds its nostalgic elegy in her last remark to him: "we could have had such a damned good time together." His equally famous reply—"Yes. Isn't it pretty to think so?"—manifests a considerable skeptical reserve.

Jake incarnates Hemingway's profound longing for the certitudes and codes of Catholicism; Brett, who refuses certain traditional expectations in regard to women while she reinforces others, is more clearly a prophecy of a world to come. Hemingway's literary fathers were Mark Twain, Joseph Conrad, and more subtly, Walt Whitman. But Lord Byron set more of the pattern for Hemingway's lifestyle as an author, and Lady Brett Ashley is a Byronic personality. As such, she brings together many antithetical qualities, the largest opposition being that between vitalism and the death drive, or the struggle between the blessing of more life and the quest for the abyss. Lurking in Brett's image is the aura of Walter Pater's extraordinary evocation of the Fatal Woman in the portrait of Leonardo's Mona Lisa, "older than the rocks among which she sits." Pater's Lady Lisa has experienced everything, "and all this has been to her but as the sound of lyres and flutes, and lives only in the delicacy with which it has moulded the changing lineaments, and tinged the eyelids and the hands."

The Lady Brett, like the Lady Lisa, asserts her personality against the flux of sensations, and so is exalted as a radiance that dazzles us amidst the flux. For all her rapaciousness, Brett is curiously disinterested and unconcerned, a stance that stems from a refusal to surrender her consciousness to any belief. Despite her disdain for renunciation, she renounces Romero, thus refusing to become the Muse as Destroyer once again, even as she destroyed Robert Cohn. Her inconsistency is an aspect of her freedom, and implicitly she refuses male modes of moral judgment. Whatever her period aura, Brett survives as a major literary character precisely because she represents one element in a woman's essential freedom, even if that liberty is manifested by her voluntary descent into the abyss, or by her use of one man after another as stepping-stones to stay out of the abyss.

—H. B.

CRITICAL EXTRACTS

ERNEST HEMINGWAY

Book I

Chapter I

This is a novel about a lady. Her name is Lady Ashley and when the story begins she is living in Paris and it is Spring. That should be a good setting for a romantic but highly moral story. As every one knows, Paris is a very romantic place. Spring in Paris is a very happy and romantic time. Autumn in Paris, although very beautiful, might give a note of sadness or melancholy that we shall try to keep out of this story.

Lady Ashley was born Elizabeth Brett Murray. Her title came from her second husband. She had divorced one husband for something or other, mutual consent; not until after he had put one of those notices in the papers stating that after this date he would not be responsible for any debt, etc. He was a Scotchman and found Brett much too expensive, especially as she had only married him to get rid of him and to get away from home. At present she had a legal separation from her second husband, who had the title, because he was a dipsomaniac, he having learned it in the North Sea commanding a mine-sweeper, Brett said. When he had gotten to be a proper thoroughgoing dipsomaniac and found that Brett did not love him he tried to kill her, and between times slept on the floor and was never sober and had great spells of crying. Brett always declared that it had been one of the really great mistakes of her life to have married a sailor. She should have known better, she said, but she had sent the one man she had wanted to marry off to Mesopotamia so he would last out the war, and he had died of some very unromantic form of dysentery and she certainly could not marry Jake Barnes, so when she had to marry she had married Lord Robert Ashley, who proceeded to become a dipsomaniac as before stated.

They had a son and Ashley would not divorce, and would not give grounds for divorce, but there was a separation and Brett went off with Mike Campbell to the Continent one afternoon, she having offered to at lunch because Mike was lonely and sick and very companionable, and, as she said, "obviously one of us." They arranged the whole business before the Folkestone-Boulogne train left London at 9:30 that night. Brett was always very proud of that. The speed with which they got passports and raised funds. They came to Paris on their way to the Riviera, and stayed the night in a hotel which had only one room free and that with a double bed. "We'd no idea of anything of that sort," Brett said. "Mike said we should go on and look up another hotel, but I said no, to stop where we were. What's the odds." That was how they happened to be living together.

Mike at that time was ill. It was all he had brought back with him from the two years he had spent in business in Spain, after he had left the army, except the beautifully engraved shares of the company which had absorbed all of the fifteen thousand pounds that had come to him from his father's estate. He was also an undischarged bankrupt, which is quite a serious thing in England, and had various habits that Brett felt sorry for, did not think a man should have, and cured by constant watchfulness and the exercise of her then very strong will.

Mike was a charming companion, one of the most charming. He was nice and he was weak and he had a certain very hard gentleness in him that could not be touched and that never disappeared until the liquor dissolved him entirely. Mike sober was nice, Mike a little drunk was even nicer, Mike quite drunk began to be objectionable, and Mike very drunk was embarrassing.

It was the boredom and the uncertainty of their position that made Brett think as she did. There was nothing of the alcoholic about her. Not, at least, for a long time. They spent their time sleeping as late as possible and then drinking. That is a simple way of stating a very complicated process, and waiting for Mike's weekly allowance, which was always late, and therefore always spent and borrowed into a week or more in advance. There was nothing to do but to drink. The drinking was not done alone in their rooms. It was all at cafés and parties, and each day became a replica of the day before. There were very few differences. You had been to bed late or gone to bed early. You felt good or you felt bad. You felt like eating a little something or you couldn't face the thought of food. It had been a good party the night before or it had been a bore. Michael had behaved abominably or Michael had been a model of admirable behavior. But usually it had been a good party because alcohol, either brandy and soda, or whiskey and soda, had a tendency to make everything much better, and for a time quite all right.

If Michael had behaved well it was probably a good party, and Michael had a strong tendency to behave well. In fact you could always count on him to behave absolutely as he should until the alcoholic process had taken place, which always seemed rather like that old grammar school experiment in which a bone is dissolved in vinegar to prove it has something or other in it. Anyway the vinegar quite changed the bone and made it very unlike itself, and you could bend it back and forth, and if it were a long enough bone and you had used enough vinegar, you could even tie it into a knot.

Brett was very different from Mike about drinking. Brett had a certain grand vitality. She had her looks too. She was not supposed to be beautiful, but in a room with women who were supposed to be beautiful she killed their looks entirely. Men thought she was lovely looking, and women called her striking looking. Painters were always asking her to sit for them and that flattered her, because she herself considered that her looks were not much, and so she spent much of her waking time sitting for portraits, none of which she ever liked. She did not seem to mind how bad the painters were. The worse they were the more it amused her. It was the being asked to sit for her portrait that she liked. One painter was as good as another. Of course the best portrait painters had done her a long time before.

Brett drank much more than Mike liked, but it never dissolved her in any way. She was always clear run, generous, and her lines were always as clear. But when she had been drunk she always spoke of it as having been blind. "Weren't we blind last night, though?" It was short for blind drunk, and the curious part was that she really became, in a way, blind. Drinking, and this does not mean the odd drink, or two or three cocktails before dinner and wine at the meal, but real drinking of that sort that kills off the good drinkers because they are the only ones who can do it, affected Brett in three successive stages. Drinking, say, whiskey and sodas from four o'clock in the afternoon until two o'clock in the morning Brett first lost her power of speech and just sat and listened, then she lost her sight and saw nothing that went on, and finally she ceased to hear. And all the time any one coming into the café would never know she had been drinking. To any one greeting her she would respond automatically, "Hullo, I say I am blind," or something of the sort.

In sleeping and in drinking, playing bridge in the afternoon, usually having her portrait painted by some socially climbing artist who knew the value of a title on a portrait, a party somewhere every night, Brett and Mike passed the time in Paris. They were rather happy. Brett was a very happy person. Then Mike had to go to England, to London to see a lawyer about something connected with the divorce Brett was trying to get, and then to Scotland to visit his people and prove by residence that he was a dutiful son, in order that, among other things, they should not stop his allowance. Brett was left alone in Paris. She had never been very good at being alone.

Chapter II

I did not want to tell this story in the first person but I find that I must. I wanted to stay well outside of the story so that I would not be touched by it in any way, and handle all the people in it with that irony and pity that are so essential to good writing. I even thought I might be amused by all the things that are going to happen to Lady Brett Ashley and Mr. Robert Cohn and Michael Campbell, Esq., and Mr. Jake Barnes. But I made the unfortunate mistake, for a writer, of first having been Mr. Jake Barnes. So it is not going to be splendid and cool and detached after all. "What a pity!" as Brett used to say.

"What a pity!" was a little joke we all had. Brett was having her portrait painted by a very rich American from Philadelphia, who sent his motor-car around each afternoon to bring her from her hotel in Montparnasse up to his Montmartre studio. Along about the third sitting Brett stopped posing for a little while to have tea, and the portrait painter asked her: "And when you get your divorce, Lady Ashley, what will you do then?"

"Marry Mike Campbell," Brett answered.

"And what will your name be then?"

"Mrs. Campbell, of course!"

"What a pity," the portrait-painter said. "What a pity!"

> —ERNEST HEMINGWAY, "The Unpublished Opening of *The Sun Also Rises*"
> [1925], *Antaeus* 33, No. 1 (Spring 1979): 7–10

F. SCOTT FITZGERALD

Anyhow I think parts of *Sun Also* are careless + ineffectual. As I said yesterday (and, as I recollect, in trying to get you to cut the 1st part of 50 Grand) I find in you the same tendency to envelope or (and as it usually turns out) to *embalm* in mere wordiness an anecdote or joke thats casually appealed to you, that I find in myself in trying to preserve a piece of "fine writing." Your first chapter contains about 10 such things and it gives a feeling of condescending *casuallness*. ⟨. . .⟩

Pps. 1+2. Snobbish (not in itself but because the history of English Aristocrats in the war, set down so verbosely so uncritically, so exteriorly and yet so obviously inspired from within, is *shopworn*.) You had the same problem that I had with my Rich Boy, previously debauched by Chambers ect. Either bring more thot to it with the realization that that ground has already raised its wheat + weeds or cut it down to seven sentences. It hasn't even your rythym and the fact that may be "true" is utterly immaterial. ⟨. . .⟩

Pps 64 + 65 with a bit of work should tell all that need be known about *Brett's* past.

> —F. SCOTT FITZGERALD, Letter to Ernest Hemingway (June 1926),
> *Antaeus* 33, No. 1 (Spring 1979): 15–17

ANDRÉ MAUROIS

When I visited Princeton University two years ago, the faculty were discussing a novel which had just been published by Ernest Hemingway. I wanted to know what it was called. *"The Sun Also Rises."*—"Is it good?"—"It's very hard, cynical, and extraordinarily true to life. I don't know whether you would care for it." I bought it. It was very good indeed.

Not on account of the plot, which was practically non-existent. Lady Brett Ashley moves in a set of Montparnasse Americans, drinks, sleeps with men and is bored. She is engaged to a ruined Englishman and is loved by the American newspaper man who tells the story. She goes to San Sebastian with a Jewish boxer and leaves him for a young matador . . . But any plot will do when a novelist knows how to create live human beings and Hemingway's characters are alive. They do not talk about their souls, they do not unravel their feelings. No, they merely order drinks and dinners, swear, have a good time, and yet you know them as well as you do Odette Swann, or Charlus, or Legrandin.

—ANDRÉ MAUROIS, "Ernest Hemingway," *This Quarter* 2, No. I
(July–August–September 1926): 212

ALLEN TATE

The present novel by the author of *In Our Time* supports the recent prophecy that he will be the "big man in American letters." At the time the prophecy was delivered it was meaningless because it was equivocal. Many of the possible inter-pretations now being eliminated, we fear it has turned out to mean something which we shall all regret. Mr. Hemingway has written a book that will be talked about, praised, perhaps imitated; it has already been received in something of that cautiously critical spirit which the followers of Henry James so notoriously maintain toward the master. Mr. Hemingway has produced a successful novel, but not without returning some violence upon the integrity achieved in his first book. He decided for reasons of his own to write a popular novel, or he wrote the only novel which he could write.

To choose the latter conjecture is to clear his intentions, obviously at the cost of impugning his art. One infers moreover that although sentimentality appears explicitly for the first time in his prose, it must have always been there. Its history can be constructed. The method used in *In Our Time* was *pointilliste*, and the sentimentality was submerged. With great skill he reversed the usual and most general formula of prose fiction: instead of selecting the details of physical back-ground and of human behavior for the intensification of a dramatic situation, he employed the minimum of drama for the greatest possible intensification of the observed object. The reference of emphasis for the observed object was therefore not the action; rather, the reference of the action was the object, and the action could be impure or incomplete without risk of detection. It could be mixed and incoherent; it could be brought in when it was advantageous to observation, or left out. The exception, important as such, in Mr. Hemingway's work is the story of Mr. and Mrs. Elliott. Here the definite dramatic conflict inherent in a sexual relation emerged as fantasy, and significantly; presumably he could not handle it otherwise without giving himself away.

In *The Sun Also Rises*, a full-length novel, Mr. Hemingway could not escape such leading situations, and he had besides to approach them with a kind of seriousness. He fails. It is not that Mr. Hemingway is, in the term which he uses in the contempt for the big word, hard-boiled; it is that he is not hard-boiled enough, in the artistic sense. No one can dispute with a writer the significance he derives from his subject-matter; one can only point out that the significance is mixed or incomplete. Brett is a nymphomaniac; Robert Cohn, a most offensive cad; both are puppets. For the emphasis is false; Hemingway doesn't fill out his characters and let them stand for themselves; he isolates one or two chief traits which reduce them to caricature. His perception of the physical object is direct and accurate; his vision of character, singularly oblique. And he actually betrays the interior machinery of his hard-boiled attitude: "It is awfully easy to be hard-boiled about everything in the daytime, but at night it is another thing," says Jake, the sexually impotent, musing on the futile accessibility of Brett. The history of his sentimentality is thus complete.

—ALLEN TATE, "Hard-Boiled," *Nation*, December 15, 1926, pp. 642–44

UNSIGNED

If to report correctly and endlessly the vapid talk and indolent thinking of Montparnasse café idlers is to write a novel, Mr. Hemingway has written a novel. His characters are as shallow as the saucers in which they stack their daily emotions, and instead of interpreting his material—or even challenging it—he has been content merely to make a carbon copy of a not particularly significant surface of life in Paris. "Mike was a bad drunk. Brett was a good drunk. Bill was a good drunk. Cohn was never drunk." "I was quite drunk." "It's funny what a wonderful gentility you get in the bar of a big hotel." There are acres of this, until the novel—aside from a few sprints of humour and now and then a "spill" of incident—begins to assume the rhythm, the monotony, and the absence of colour which one associates with a six-day bicycle race.

—UNSIGNED, Review of *The Sun Also Rises*, *Dial* 82, No. 1 (January 1927): 73

VIRGINIA WOOLF

Recalling *The Sun Also Rises*, certain scenes rise in memory: the bullfight, the character of the Englishman, Harris; here a little landscape which seems to grow behind the people naturally; here a long, lean phrase which goes curling round a situation like the lash of a whip. Now and again this phrase evokes a character brilliantly, more often a scene. Of character, there is little that remains firmly and solidly elucidated. Something indeed seems wrong with the people. If we place them (the comparison is bad) against Tchekov's people, they are flat as cardboard. If we place them (the comparison is better) against Maupassant's people they are crude as a photograph. If we place them (the comparison may be illegitimate) against real people, the people we liken them to are of an unreal type. They are people one may have seen showing off at some café; talking a rapid, high-pitched slang, because slang is the speech of the herd, seemingly much at their ease, and yet if we look at them a little from the shadow not at their ease at all, and, indeed, terribly afraid of being themselves, or they would say things simply in their natural voices. So it would seem that the thing that is faked is character; Mr. Hemingway leans against the flanks of that particular bull after the horns have passed.

—VIRGINIA WOOLF, "An Essay in Criticism" [1927], *Collected Essays,*
ed. Leonard Woolf (New York: Harcourt, Brace & World, 1967),
Volume 2, p. 255

MARK SCHORER

The Sun Also Rises was a representation of the life that Hemingway lived and enjoyed and out of which his values came. The characters in this novel—without belief, without relation to a cultural or national past, without ideological relation to the future—submerge themselves in extravagant sensation and view life as a losing game, a sport like bullfighting which, while it is more nearly tragedy than sport because death is inevitable, is interesting only if it observes strict rules. Hemingway epitomized this not very difficult matter when, in an author's note in *Scribner's Magazine,* he once said, "I've known some very wonderful people who even though they were going directly to the grave . . . managed to put up a very fine performance enroute." This "fine performance" is the sporting attitude, and it is dramatized in the gesture of Lady Ashley when she gives up her lover: "You know I feel rather damned good, Jake . . . it makes one feel rather good deciding not to be a bitch. . . . It's sort of what we have instead of God." Jake has himself observed that morality is what makes you feel good afterwards. Brett feels "rather damned good" because she has behaved according to the tenets of that negative morality, that emphasis on the "performance en route," the *manner* of living, which the group has substituted for belief.

The preoccupation with bullfighting is not accidental; bullfighting is at once the most violent and the most stylized of sports. Its entire excitement depends on the degree to which the matador exposes himself to death *within the rules.* It disregards consequences, regards performance. Both are important. Courage, or unconcern for disaster, is a moral virtue: the best bullfighter works closest to the horns; the best man disregards present and impending catastrophe. Syphilis, the occupational disease of bullfighters, "of all people who lead lives in which a disregard of consequences dominate," is nearly commended. A blundering display of courage, however, is absurd: the matador should "increase the amount of the danger of death"

> *within the rules provided for his protection.* . . . it is to his credit if he does something that he knows how to do in a highly dangerous but still geometrically possible manner. It is to his discredit if he runs danger through ignorance, through disregard of the fundamental rules. . . .

Courage stylized, *style*, then, matters finally, and the experienced spectator looks for this; "what they seek is honesty and true, not tricked, emotion and always classicism and the purity of execution of all the suertes, and . . . they want no sweetening." Since the performance is a matter of the fighter's honor, bullfighting is a *moral* art, and style a *moral* matter.

> So far, about morals, [writes Hemingway] I know only that what is moral is what you feel good after and what is immoral is what you feel bad after and judged by these moral standards . . . the bullfight is very moral to me. . . .

In *The Sun Also Rises*, Romero, who "'fakes" nothing in the fight, who has "the old thing, the holding of his purity of line through the maximum of exposure," is the one character who makes the others feel fine: he is the representation of artistic, hence of moral excellence.

All this carried directly over into Hemingway's concept of prose and into his own prose. The definition of morality and Brett's dramatization of it; the important counterpoint between danger and performance; the concept of art as moral insofar as its style is "honest" or "true" or "pure"—this complex is translated as follows:

> It is much more difficult than poetry. . . . It can be written, *without tricks* and *without cheating. With nothing that will go bad afterwards.* . . . First, there must be talent. . . . Then there must be discipline. . . . Then there must be . . . an *absolute conscience* as unchanging as the standard meter in Paris, to prevent *faking.*

The style which made Hemingway famous—with its ascetic suppression of ornament and figure, its insistence on the objective and the unreflective (for good fighters do not talk), its habit of understatement (or sportsmen boast), the directions and the brevity of its syntactical constructions, its muscularity, the sharpness of its staccato and repetitive effects, "the purity of its line under the maximum of exposure," that is, its continued poise under the weight of event or feeling—this style is an exact transfiguration of Hemingway's moral attitude toward a peculiarly violent and chaotic experience. His style, in effect, is what he had instead of God.

Until God came.

—MARK SCHORER, "The Background of a Style," *Kenyon Review* 3, No. 1 (Winter 1941): 101–3

THEODORE BARDACKE

In Hemingway's first important novel, *The Sun Also Rises*, Brett is the dominating character. She is the embodiment of what the author conceived as the postwar woman. Although not possessive and honorless like Cohn's mistress, Frances, she has been emotionally stunted by a shallow world without spiritual meaning, and has become a woman devoid of womanhood. She has experienced two loveless marriages; the first with a man who died of dysentery during the war, and the second with an officer in the British Navy who returned from the war suffering from shock. Her love life, a kind of war casualty in itself, has decayed into alcoholism and a series of casual sex relations. She is "engaged to marry" Mike who is bankrupt economically and spiritually. The sexual level of their relationship is indicated by the hotel-brothel where they stay in Paris.

Jake, who is genuinely in love with Brett, is kept from her by an impotency that is the result of a war accident rather than any deficiency in his personality. While it mars his life and frustrates his love, the wound establishes Jake as a sympathetic observer of Brett's search for sexual meaning. As a result of her loss of woman-liness and in spite of her promiscuity, Brett has become desexed. She is introduced in the novel with a group of homosexuals and "she was very much with them." This company, her clothes, her mannish felt hat and bobbed hair, all are indications of the loss of her true sexuality. Jake wonders if even her love for him isn't merely a longing for the unattainable. He doubts her very capacity to love as a woman.

However, during the fiesta in Spain when reality is tempered by ritual and celebration and the "fear of consequences" has disappeared, Brett falls in love with the matador Romero. Neither Cohn, who is a shallow sentimentalist, nor Mike understands the importance of Brett's emotional experience. Jake does, though, and is willing to face the anger of his friends, the scorn of the hotel owner, whose respect was hard won, and the possible destruction of the young bullfighter, to arrange Brett's meeting with Romero.

After Brett's union with Romero, Hemingway pictures her as a changed woman. Later, she goes with Jake to church and for the first time tries to pray, but her attempt fails. Just as her praying was unsuccessful because it came too late, Brett finds her relationship with Romero is doomed. She realizes that she is too old, too much the person that the modern world has made her; it is too late to change. Although Romero offers her a relatively pure body, a complete and satisfying relationship of love and sexual fulfillment, and marriage, she cannot accept because it is too late for her to respond completely. This impossible change back to womanliness is symbolized by Romero's wanting her to let her hair grow. Knowing that to remain with her lover would only destroy him, Brett leaves and in so doing preserves the only thing left to her, her self-respect. She becomes heroic in her sacrifice and returns to Mike and his world of shallowness and alcohol because that is, after all, her world too. "He's so damned nice and he's so awful. He's my sort of thing."

—THEODORE BARDACKE, "Hemingway's Women: 1950," Ernest Hemingway: The Man and His Work, ed. John K. M. McCaffery (Cleveland: World Publishing Co., 1950), pp. 342–44

JOHN ATKINS

The most celebrated of all Hemingway's women is Lady Brett Ashley. She is a convenient symbol of the expatriate woman of the 'twenties, with no purpose in her life, and attempting to fill the void with drink and sex. The treatment she has received from the critics is also symbolic of the hasty and superficial approach to his work that has been general over the past two decades and a reminder of the need for re-assessment. Now we have had a chance to assimilate the more sensational aspects of Hemingway's genius it should be possible to probe a little more deeply into the society he portrays and its most typical representatives.

The Brett we know from hearsay, from the impressions of other writers and columnists, is not Hemingway's Brett but a legendary figure that has emerged out of simplification and faulty memory. The critic who is doing his job properly has read his source-books fairly recently, say within the last six months, and his impressions are reasonably fresh and accurate. But the reviewer or literary columnist, who deals with a dozen books a week and frequently refers to others which cling often fortuitously to his memory, may not have read anything by the writer he is discussing (save his latest work) for many years. The anatomy of significance varies widely. A person who reads *For Whom the Bell Tolls* today, especially if for the first time, will have quite a different impression of it from the person who read it when it appeared in 1940 and has not opened it since. What is more, the emphasis which a reader brings to a book from his own bias will be different and can also change in the same person over the years. Hemingway himself has said, 'The memory is never true'. Memory is apt to tell us that Brett is simply a woman who has slept too easily with too many men and lost all normal feeling and self-respect. The legend is as unlike the original as the popular idea of Mr. Micawber, created by people who have never read *David Copperfield* since childhood, is unlike Dickens' Micawber.

Theodore Bardacke, in an essay on 'Hemingway's Women', has given the conventional portrait faithfully. As far as it goes it is a truthful one, but it is still only a profile. The other side of her character is hidden from us.

> She has been emotionally stunted by a shallow world without spiritual meaning, and has become a woman devoid of womanhood. She has experienced two loveless marriages; the first with a man who died of dysentery during the war, and the second with an officer in the British Navy who returned from the war suffering from shock. Her love life, a kind of war casualty in itself, has decayed into alcoholism and a series of casual sex relations. She is 'engaged to marry' Mike who is bankrupt economically and spiritually. The sexual level of their relationship is indicated by the hotel-brothel where they stay in Paris.

I want to make it clear that I am not attacking Bardacke, who is a good critic and was primarily interested in this particular approach of Brett Ashley and her generation. But by itself it suggests that Brett is an utterly hard, insensitive and irredeemable woman. Such a view arises easily by a process of abstraction. All murderers are on the same spiritual level if you divorce them from their circumstances. Bardacke does not suggest why Brett is 'emotionally stunted' by reference to her unfortunate marriages. We must also remember that these marriages took place against a background of aimlessness and destructiveness. It is in fact the truly sensitive person who suffers most in such circumstances. A person of limited sensibility may be untouched but others will either become neurotic or, by an act of will, stubborn against fate. It is impossible to read *Fiesta* bearing this in mind, and miss Brett's honesty, awareness and sincerity. The many insincerities with which a friendly critic could charge her are obviously her little jokes and are accepted as such by her companions. That her emotions were not really stunted, but simply repressed, is clear from the scene with Jake in the taxi, when for a moment she opens the gates and confesses that in this particular situation, when her emotions are dictating to her, she has come up against another kind of barrier. To Jake she is 'a good girl wrecked by frustration'. Henry Seidel Canby calls her 'a good girl who has lost her controls'. The truth is that she has reassembled her controls. There is no doubt of her frustration and we know the events that led to it. But the effect on Brett was a loosening of moral conduct and a tightening of emotional control. This could be called a kind of spiritual surgery. The result is by no means satisfactory and at times is even unpleasant, but there could have been a worse fate for Lady Ashley.

According to Edmund Wilson, one of Hemingway's main characteristics is antagonism to women. He lists a number of instances in which the man behaves brutally or inconsiderately to the woman ('the instinct to get the woman down' is his phrase, which is cunning because we all know such an instinct exists, but not all of us would agree to its use as a universal metaphor of the spiritual truth). Even Jake is avenging his sex on women by being unable to give Brett what she wants. Although Wilson notes that the women in 'Macomber' and 'Kilimanjaro' are 'American bitches of the most soul-destroying sort', he fails to look further. For he is actually on the edge of an important discovery, but withdraws too quickly to make it. In all the examples he gives of this attitude, with one exception, the women are American. The one exception is the peasant's wife in 'An Alpine Idyll', which I have already referred to as an example of the crude, unsensational kind of love which exists among people who live hard, inarticulate lives.

It may be objected that Hemingway, being an American author, naturally finds the objects of his dislike among his fellow-countrymen. But most of his fiction is set outside America and there are many Europeans among his women. And he himself has told us without qualification that American women are the hardest in the world. It is true, he put this thought into the mind of an Englishman but it was an Englishman with whom he appeared to have a great deal of sympathy.

> They are, he thought, the hardest in the world; the hardest, the cruellest, the most predatory and the most attractive and their men have softened or gone to pieces nervously as they have hardened.

And later:

> She is away for twenty minutes and now she is back, simply enamelled in that
> American female cruelty. They are the damnedest women. Really the
> damnedest.

This is presumably Hemingway's contribution to the evidence of the new American
matriarchy, which so delights European males, smarting under the effects of American efficiency and drive.

This is by no means an isolated instance of this attitude. Throughout his work
there runs a strong current of hatred for the American female, expressed through
scorn, denunciation and accusation. It comes to a head in *The Fifth Column*, when
Philip flaunts a Moorish tart in the face of Dorothy, who would like to manage him.
He seems to accuse American women of treating love like a business, where all the
prospectuses are written by female directors and company promoters. The Moorish girl, Anita, says, 'Put the paint in the body, instead of blood. What you get?
American woman'. Here is Philip describing the background of a certain type of
well-to-do American girl.

> They're all the same. Camps, colleges, money in family, no more or less than
> it was, usually less now, men, affairs, abortions, ambitions, and finally marry
> and settle down or don't marry and settle down. They open shops or work
> in shops, some write, others play instruments, some go on the stage, others
> into films. They have something called the Junior League I believe that the
> virgins work at. All for the public good.

A sterile career with neither peaks nor valleys, with ambition the only powerful
stimulus. Philip asks Dorothy, '*Is* it true that the first thing an American woman does
is to try to get the man she's interested in to give up something? You know, boozing
about, or smoking Virginia cigarettes, or wearing gaiters, or hunting, or something
silly?'

Nothing like this and nothing comparable was ever said about English Brett,
Scottish Catherine, Spanish Maria or Italian Renata. The only American woman who
comes off well is Harry Morgan's wife, and she has been to neither college nor
camp nor set up shop nor been in Junior League. It is impossible to feel that
Hemingway regards the moral shortcomings of Lady Ashley as anything like so
destroying as the sterile aggressiveness of the American female. Ultimately the
American woman seeks power over the male—not the power of love with its
willing and fruitful submission but the conquest of personality demanded by the
politician and business man. To compel the men to give something up, to surrender
a portion of his ego, is the sign she seeks for.

The conventional love relationship is almost impossible with such women. Man
is forced to make use of new weapons for his own defence. Where his own
sincerity might be regarded as weakness he must repress it and replace it with less
attractive qualities which, however, will strengthen his position. The only possible
relationship is based on deceit. When you cannot love you pretend to love. Mod-

ern 'love' is in many cases a gigantic sham, a second-best in default of what has been idealised but is no longer possible. Hemingway blames the woman. In her quest for power she has lost her earlier virtues, perhaps even the much prided 'feminine intuition'. It is easier to cheat her than it used to be. In fact, the truth is often lost to her, she responds best to lies because her purposes are based on falsity. The writer in 'Kilimanjaro' found that 'his lies were more successful with women than when he had told them the truth'. And, dying, he made the astounding discovery that he could actually give her more when he lied than when he loved.

Perhaps a man steers more easily through the reefs than a woman. Perhaps the masculine privileges, education, ballot, social freedom, loose language, really are more easily assimilated and managed by men than by women. It is against the spirit of the time to deny these things to women and a modern writer has to accept them even when he notices the maladjustment. It is possible that the feminist victories have resulted in a psychic upheaval which has created a new woman. This is trite in the bare statement but not in its implications. For one of the major implications is that men who have been accustomed to coming to terms with one type of woman may be utterly baffled when faced with another type. There is fairly strong evidence that, despite his early sympathy if not admiration for Lady Brett, Hemingway later renounced this attitude and found the fullest literary satisfaction in the womanly woman. Catherine Barkley is not a 'new' woman. She is sufficiently pre-Shavian to say to Frederick, 'I want what you want. There isn't me any more. Just what you want.' Mrs. Morgan, Maria and Renata are all in the same old-fashioned tradition.

—JOHN ATKINS, "The Women," *The Art of Ernest Hemingway*
(London: Spring Books, 1952), pp. 234–41

CARLOS BAKER

Hemingway's first novel provides an important insight into the special "mythological" methods which he was to employ with increasing assurance and success in the rest of his major writing. It is necessary to distinguish Hemingway's method from such "mythologizing" as that of Joyce in *Ulysses*, or Eliot in *The Waste Land*. For Hemingway early devised and subsequently developed a mythologizing tendency of his own which does not depend on antecedent literatures, learned footnotes, or the recognition of spot passages. *The Sun Also Rises* is a first case in point.

It might be jocularly argued, for example, that there is much more to the portrait of Lady Brett Ashley than meets the non-Homeric eye. It is very pleasant to think of the Pallas Athene, sitting among the statuary in one of her temples like Gertrude Stein among the Picassos in the rue de Fleurus, and murmuring to the Achaeans, homeward bound from the battle of Troy: "You are all a lost generation." As for Brett, Robert Cohn calls her Circe. "He claims she turns men into swine," says Mike Campbell. "Damn good. I wish I were one of these literary chaps."

If Hemingway had been writing about brilliant literary chaps in the manner, say, of Aldous Huxley in *Crome Yellow,* he might have undertaken to develop Cohn's parallel. It would not have been farther-fetched than Joyce's use of the Daedalus legend in *A Portrait of the Artist* or Eliot's kidnapping of Homeric Tiresias to watch over the mean little seductions of *The Waste Land.*

Was not Brett Ashley, on her low-lying island in the Seine, just such a fascinating peril as Circe on Aeaea? Did she not open her doors to all the modern Achaean chaps? When they drank her special potion of French applejack or Spanish wine, did they not become as swine, or in the modern idiom, wolves? Did not Jake Barnes, that wily Odysseus, resist the shameful doom which befell certain of his less wary comrades who became snarling beasts?

There are even parallel passages. Says Jake Barnes, thinking of Brett: "I lay awake thinking and my mind jumping around. . . . Then all of a sudden I started to cry. Then after a while it was better . . . and then I went to sleep." Says Ulysses on Aeaea: "My spirit was broken within me and I wept as I sat on the bed. . . . But when I had my fill of weeping and writhing, I made answer." Or what shall be made of Robert Cohn, quietly and classically asleep on the winecasks in the back room of a Pamplona tavern, wreathed with twisted garlics and dead to the world while Brett and the others carouse in the room beyond? "There was one named Elpenor," says the *Odyssey,* "the youngest of all; not very valiant in war nor sound of understanding, who had laid him down apart from his comrades in the sacred house of Circe, seeking the cool air, for he was heavy with wine. He heard the noise and bustle of his comrades as they moved about."

If he had wished to follow the mythological method of Eliot's *Waste Land* or Joyce's *Ulysses,* Hemingway could obviously have done so. But his own esthetic opinions carried him away from the literary kind of myth-adaptation and over into that deeper area of psychological symbol-building which does not require special literary equipment to be interpreted. One needs only sympathy and a few degrees of heightened emotional awareness. The special virtue of this approach to the problem of literary communication is that it can be grasped by all men and women because they are human beings. None of the best writers are without it. It might even be described as the residuum of "natural knowledge" and belief, visible in every artist after the traditional elements have been siphoned off. This is perhaps roughly what Keats meant by saying that Shakespeare led a life of allegory, his works being the comments on it. Thoreau's phrase for the same thing, as R. L. Cook has pointed out, is "dusky knowledge." Pilar, the Cumaean sybil of *For Whom the Bell Tolls,* moves regularly in this half-subliminal area. She inherits her skill and discernment from Hemingway.

Under the matter-of-factness of the account of the feria of San Fermin a sabidurían symbolism is at work. It does not become formally apparent until the party has assembled to prepare for the festival. Then, in several ways, it develops as a dialectical struggle between paganism and Christian orthodoxy—a natural and brilliant use of the fact that the fiesta is both secular and religious, and that the *riau-riau* dancers unabashedly follow the procession which bears the patron saint through the streets of Pamplona.

The contrast is admirably dramatized through Jake and Brett. Without apology or explanation, Jake Barnes is a religious man. As a professing Catholic, he attends masses at the cathedral before and during fiesta week. On the Saturday before the festival opens, Brett accompanies him. "She said she wanted to hear me go to confession," says Jake, "but I told her that not only was it impossible but it was not as interesting as it sounded, and, besides, it would be in a language she did not know." Jake's remark can be taken doubly. The language Brett does not know is Latin; it is also Spanish; but it is especially the language of the Christian religion. When she goes soon afterwards to have her fortune told at a gypsy camp, Brett presumably hears language that she *can* understand.

Her true symbolic colors are broken out on Sunday afternoon. She is in the streets with Jake watching the religious procession in which the image of San Fermin is translated from one church to another. Ahead of the formal procession and behind it are the *riau-riau* dancers. When Jake and Brett try to enter the chapel they are stopped at the door, ostensibly because she has no hat. But for one sufficiently awake to the ulterior meaning of the incident it strikingly resembles the attempt of a witch to gain entry into a Christian sanctum. Brett's witch-hood is immediately underscored. Back in the street she is encircled by the chanting pagan dancers who prevent her from joining their figure: "They wanted her as an image to dance around." When the song ends, she is rushed to a wineshop and seated on an up-ended wine-cask. The shop is dark and full of men singing,—"hard-voiced singing."

The intent of this episode is quite plain. Brett would not understand the language used in Christian confessional. She is forbidden to follow the religious procession into the chapel. The dancers adopt her as a pagan image. She is perfectly at home on the wine-cask amidst the hard-voiced singing of the non-religious celebrants. Later in fiesta week the point is reemphasized. Jake and Brett enter the San Fermin chapel so that Brett can pray for Romero's success in the final bullfight of the celebration. "After a little," says Jake, "I felt Brett stiffen beside me, and saw she was looking straight ahead." Outside the chapel Brett explains what Jake has already guessed: "I'm damned bad for a religious atmosphere. I've got the wrong type of face."

She has, indeed. Her face belongs in wide-eyed concentration over the Tarot pack of Madame Sosostris, or any equivalent soothsayer in the gypsy camp outside Pamplona. It is perfectly at home in the center of the knot of dancers in the street or in the tavern gloom above the wine-cask. For Brett in her own way is a lamia with a British accent, a Morgan le Fay of Paris and Pamplona, the reigning queen of a paganized wasteland with a wounded fisher-king as her half-cynical squire. She is, rolled into one, the *femme fatale de trente ans damnée.* Yet she is always and conspicuously herself. The other designations are purely arbitrary labels which could be multiplied as long as one's list of enchantresses could be made to last. They are not necessary to the full symbolic meaning which Brett has in her own right and by virtue (if that is the word) of what she is made to do in the book.

Although Hemingway carefully skirts the moralistic, as his artistic beliefs require, the moral drift of the symbolic story is unmistakable. Shortly after *The Sun Also Rises* appeared, he remarked, as he had never overtly done in the book, that "people aren't all as bad as some writers find them or as hollowed out and exhausted emotionally as some of the *Sun* generation." The restriction was conspicuous. He did not say, "the lost generation." He said rather, "some of the *Sun* generation." His indictment, put into dramatic terms, was directed against those who allowed themselves to flounder in an emulsion of ennui and alcohol when there was so much else to be done, whether one was a championship-winning *gueule cassée* like Criqui or an ordinary citizen like Jake, engaged in readjusting himself to peace-time living. In contrast to the "hollow men" who went off the stage with something resembling a whimper, Hemingway presented another set of men who kept their mouths shut and took life as it came.

The emotional exhaustion of "some of the *Sun* generation" is accentuated by the oppositions Hemingway provides. Obviously no accidental intruder in the book is Romero, standing out in youthful dignity and strength against the background of displaced wastrels among whom Jake moves. The same is true of the interlude at Burguete, with Jake and Bill happily disentangled from the wastelanders, as if in wordless echo of Eliot's line: "In the mountains, there you feel free." However fascinating Brett and Cohn and Mike may be as free-wheeling international adventurers, the book's implicit attitude is one of quizzical condemnation towards these and all their kind.

Despite this fact, one finds in the presentation of Brett Ashley an almost Jamesian ambiguity. It is as if the objective view of Brett were intentionally relieved by that kind of chivalry which is never wholly missing from the work of Hemingway. On the straight narrative plane the book appears to offer a study of a war-frustrated love affair between Brett and Jake. Brett's Circean characteristics are only partly responsible for the sympathy with which she is treated, though all enchantresses from Spenser's Acrasia to Coleridge's Geraldine are literally fascinating and Brett is no exception. Whenever Jake takes a long objective view of Lady Ashley, however, he is too honest not to see her for what she objectively is, an alcoholic nymphomaniac. To Cohn's prying questions about her, early in the book, Jake flatly answers: "She's a drunk."

There is, nevertheless, a short history behind her alcoholism and her constant restless shifting from male to male. During the war she was an assistant nurse; her own true love died; she married a psychotic British baronet who maltreated her; and at the time of the book she is waiting for a divorce decree in order to marry the playboy Mike Campbell. Furthermore—and this fact calls forth whatever chivalry one finds—she is in love with Jake, though both of them realize the hopelessness of the situation. She has not, as her fiancé observes, had an absolutely happy life, and Jake is prepared to take this into account when he judges her character. "Don't you know about Irony and Pity?" asks Bill Gorton during a verbal bout at Burguete. Jake knows all about them. They are the combination he uses whenever he thinks about Brett.

One of the ironies in the portrait of Brett is her ability to appreciate quality in the circle of her admirers. After the trip to San Sebastian with Robert Cohn she quickly rejects him. She does not do so sluttishly, merely in order to take up with another man, but rather for what to her is the moral reason that he is unmanly. Towards her fiancé Mike Campbell the attitude is somewhere in the middle ground of amused acceptance. He is Brett's sort, a good drinking companion living on an income nearly sufficient to allow him a perpetual holiday. "He's so damned nice and he's so awful," says Brett. "He's my sort of thing." Even though Brett can be both nice and awful with her special brand of ambiguity, she does save her unambiguous reverence for two men. One is the truly masculine Jake, whose total sexual disability has not destroyed his manhood. The other is Romero, whose sexual ability is obviously a recommendation but is by no means his only claim to admiration. It is finally to Brett's credit, and the measure of her appreciation of quality, that she sends Romero back to the bullring instead of destroying him as she might have done. This is no *belle dame sans merci*. She shows mercy both to her victim and to the remaining shreds of her self-respect.

The Heloisa-Abelard relationship of Brett and Jake is Hemingway's earliest engagement of an ancient formula—the sacrifice of Venus on the altar of Mars. In one way or another, the tragic fact of war or the after-effects of social disruption tend to inhibit and betray the normal course of love, not only in *The Sun Also Rises* but also in *A Farewell to Arms, To Have and Have Not, The Fifth Column, For Whom the Bell Tolls*, and *Across the River and Into the Trees*. Brett, the first of the victims, is a kind of dark Venus. If she had not lost her "true love" in the late war, or if Jake's wound had not permanently destroyed his ability to replace the lost lover, Brett's progressive self-destruction would not have become the inevitable course it now appears to be.

Much of the continuing power of *The Sun Also Rises* comes from its sturdy moral backbone. The portraits of Brett Ashley and Robert Cohn, like that of their antithesis Romero, are fully and memorably drawn. A further and deep-lying cause of the novel's solidity is the subtle operative contrast between vanity and sanity, between paganism and orthodoxy, between the health and humor of Burguete and the sick neuroses of the Montparnassian ne'er-do-wells. Other readers can value the book for the still-fresh representation of "the way it was" in Paris and Pamplona, Bayonne and Burguete, during the now nostalgically remembered middle Twenties. Yet much of the final strength of *The Sun Also Rises* may be attributed to the complicated interplay between the two points of view which it embodies. According to one of them, the novel is a romantic study in sexual and ultimately in spiritual frustration. Beside this more or less orthodox view, however, must be placed the idea that it is a qualitative study of varying degrees of physical and spiritual manhood, projected against a background of ennui and emotional exhaustion which is everywhere implicitly condemned.

—CARLOS BAKER, "Circe and Company," *Hemingway: The Writer as Artist* (Princeton: Princeton University Press, 1952), pp. 87–93

TOM BURNAM

Let us, for the moment, note something peculiar and, I believe, significant in Hemingway's women: Maria and Pilar in *For Whom the Bell Tolls;* Catherine Barkley in *A Farewell to Arms;* Brett Ashley in *The Sun Also Rises;* Margaret (or "Margot") Macomber in the story about her husband's "short happy life"; the wife in "The Snows of Kilimanjaro"; Mrs. Elliott and Mrs. Harry Morgan. Does it not seem obvious that easily—almost too easily—a line can be drawn on one side of which are ranged what can only be called Hemingway's witches, while on the other stand women who are hardly women at all, but simply Hemingway men only slightly, even superficially, altered? And is it not almost always true that those Hemingway women who are not witch-like seem to be punished for it—Maria, raped by the Fascists; Pilar, the sturdy one, who nevertheless all her life has had "this sadness at intervals" and is cruelly hurt by Maria's love for Robert Jordan; Catherine and her death in the agony of still-birth; even the Indian woman who survives a jack-knife Caesarian only to lose her husband, a bloody suicide in the bunk above?

If Hemingway's "good" women seem really to be Hemingway men only slightly changed, it would appear that when Hemingway, in an apparent attempt to create a sympathetic feminine character has (at least in most of his work) endowed her with certain virtues, they are exactly the same virtues with which he has endowed his men: brute courage and individual loyalty, self-sufficiency, even aggressiveness and hostility as in Pilar. I am not suggesting, of course, that these are actually fundamental "masculine" characteristics; to do so would run counter to my whole purpose. I am merely trying to point out that Hemingway has appeared in the past to have only one stock-bin of virtues, and that he has seemed unable to create another set for his women characters. It is not without significance that the slim and boy-like Maria, Hemingway's supreme effort to create a major feminine character who will appeal to the reader's sympathies, is close-cropped, with legs "long and clean from the open cuffs of the trousers," and moves "awkwardly as a colt [or a lad?] moves."

I have said that Hemingway's "good" women are much like his men. Let us now observe how very much one of Hemingway's men, at least, is like a woman—with respect, that is, to all except those culturally-imposed conditions within which, I have implied, Hemingway operates. You will recall that Jake Barnes, the protagonist-narrator of *The Sun Also Rises,* has been wounded in such a way that he is unable to perform the only function which in all human cultures and at all times in human history would identify him as masculine. Yet Jake is nonetheless quite clearly a "man" in Hemingway's terms; it never occurs to us to think of him as anything else. A man indelibly scarred, perhaps (though not destroyed): but still a man. Why? Because he *can* perform those functions which in Hemingway's interpretation of our Anglo-American-European culture identify him as a man. He hikes and fishes and goes to bullfights; he drinks (a masculine virtue in Hemingway: few of his women drink like his men and when they do they seem always to be the Brett Ashleys, never the Marias) and he displays his hostilities and aggressions freely.

In other words, Jake Barnes seems to fulfill every masculine function *except* the only genuinely "primitive" one. Although clearly it is through no fault of his own, yet he need never put his essential manhood to the test. But in terms of the culture in which he lives, he can act the part of a man completely, adequately, and convincingly. Interestingly enough, Jake is also just about the only reasonably happy person in *The Sun Also Rises,* as a careful reading of the book will make plain. His philosophy is not bitter: "Maybe," he says, "if you found out how to live in [the world] you learned from that what it was all about." Nor do I find in Jake's last speech the kind of bitter irony which is so generally assumed. Brett Ashley, we recall, says, "Oh, Jake, we could have had such a damned good time together." As a mounted policeman ahead raises his baton (and you can make of this symbol what you will), Jake answers, "Yes. Isn't it pretty to think so?" If there is irony in this line, it is not directed at Jake's and Brett's present circumstance: it implies, rather, that there is nothing pretty *in imagining anything else.* One can ask only, "Why not?" We shall wish to examine, shortly, some aspects of the search for death by the Hemingway male. For the moment, let us remember that Jake Barnes is one of the very few Hemingway men who do not seem, one way or another and consciously or not, to engage in this death-search.

—TOM BURNAM, "Primitivism and Masculinity in the Work of Ernest Hemingway,"
Modern Fiction Studies I, No. 3 (August 1955): 21–22

DELMORE SCHWARTZ

The desire for sensation is not the sensuality of the dilettante, but a striving for genuine individuality. The sensations of the immediate present have an authenticity which the senses make self-evident. Above all, those sensations which occur in the face of grave physical danger reveal the self's essential reality, since in the face of extreme threat, the self must depend wholly upon its own skill, strength, and courage.

Thus it is literally true that Hemingway's preoccupation with sensation is a preoccupation with genuine selfhood, moral character, and conduct. The holiday provides not only freedom, but good eating, good drinking, good landscapes, and good sexual intercourse under conditions which have the fairness of a game—so that drinking, making love, and most of the pursuits of the holiday become a trial of the self. Any concern with the self and its moral character requires a moral code, and the moral code in Hemingway is unmistakable. The rules of the code require honesty, sincerity, self-control, skill, and above all, personal courage. To be admirable is to play fairly and well; and to be a good loser when one has lost, acknowl-edging the victor and accepting defeat in silence. It is a sportsmanlike morality, which dictates a particular kind of carriage, good manners, and manner of speech: one must speak in clipped tones, condensing the most complex emotion into a few expletives or into the dignity of silence.

Perhaps Cohn, in *The Sun Also Rises,* is the best example of the character who repeatedly violates the Hemingway code. He is rich, gifted, and skillful; he has gone to Princeton, where he excelled in boxing, and he is a novelist and editor. Yet these advantages are unavailing, for he does not play the game according to the rules. He discusses his emotions in great detail, refuses to admit defeat when Brett, the lady with whom he is in love, rejects him, and, when he is hurt, he insists on telling everyone, instead of suffering in silence. Thus he is one of the damned. His damnation shows itself most explicitly when he struggles with Romero, the matador who has won Lady Brett's heart. Unlike several other rejected suitors, Cohn refuses to admit defeat, or the lady's right to choose. Instead he engages the matador in a fist fight, knocks him down again and again, but cannot knock him out since the matador, a true Hemingway hero, takes interminable punishment, silently arising from the floor again and again until Cohn is finally defeated by the matador's fortitude and thus his moral superiority. In a like way, Lady Brett obeys the code and renounces the matador, when, coming to recognize that he fulfills an ideal of conduct as a human being and as a matador, she perceives that she is a threat to his purity: "It isn't the sort of thing one does," she says, adding that she does not want to be "one of these bitches who ruins children ... it makes one feel rather good deciding not to be a bitch. ... It's sort of what we have instead of God."

—DELMORE SCHWARTZ, "The Fiction of Ernest Hemingway," *Perspectives USA* (New York: Intercultural Publications, 1955), pp. 258–59

MALCOLM COWLEY

⟨Hemingway⟩ made another trip to the Irati just before the fiesta of 1925, this time with Hadley, Stewart, and Bill Smith, a friend of his Michigan days. They found that much of the beech forest had been cut down and that construction work on a dam had ruined the fishing. In some ways the fiesta itself was even less successful. The group in Pamplona included, besides the fishermen, Harold Loeb, Patrick Guthrie, who was an English remittance man, and his friend Lady Duff Twysden, who was said to be the heroine of Michael Arlen's immensely popular novel *The Green Hat.* Usually she did wear a floppy-brimmed green felt hat, but she was more widely known for her love affairs and her capacity for holding liquor. Ernest learned that Loeb had lately spent a week with her at Saint-Jean-de-Luz. Everybody drank a great deal at the fiesta and almost everybody quarreled. "Some fiesta," said Loeb, who later described it in his memoirs. Things went better at the bullring, where the principal attraction was Cayetano Ordóñez, also known as Niño de la Palma, who was then in his first season as a matador. After the fiesta, the Hemingways followed Ordóñez to Madrid. There he dedicated one of his bulls to Hadley, killed it to great applause, and presented her with its ear, which she wrapped in a handkerchief and carried back to the hotel. ⟨. . .⟩

The situation in the background of *The Sun Also Rises* is the Great War, in which most of the characters have served and in which some of them have been physically or morally wounded. All the characters except Pedro Romero, the matador, have lost their original code of values. Feeling the loss, they are now trying to live by a simpler code, essentially that of soldiers on furlough, and it is this effort that unites them as a group. "I told you he was one of us," Lady Brett says of Count Mippipopolous after he has unashamedly stripped off his shirt and shown them where an arrow had passed completely through his body. The unashamedness, the wound, and the courage it suggests are all things they have in common. The war has deadened some of their feelings and has left them capable of enjoying only the simplest and strongest pleasures. It has also given them an attitude of resigned acceptance toward all sorts of disasters, including those caused by their own follies. Robert Cohn, however, has never been wounded and has never learned to be resigned; therefore he refuses to let Brett go, fights with his rivals including Romero, and is cast out of the group. Romero is their simple-minded saint. Brett is almost on the point of permanently corrupting him, but she obeys another article of the code and draws back. "You know it makes one feel rather good deciding not to be a bitch," she says (and scores of junior Bretts have echoed). "It's sort of what we have instead of God."

The Sun Also Rises is not, as it is often called, Hemingway's best novel. After all it is his first, and there are signs in it of his struggle to master a new medium. In spite of his deletions from the manuscript, there are still details that do not seem essential, as notably in the street-by-street account of Jake Barnes's wanderings through Paris. There are also a few obvious guideposts for the reader, as when Jake says of Robert Cohn that "he was not so simple" after coming back from New York, "and he was not so nice." Although Cohn's fight with Romero is the physical climax of the action, it is reported at second hand—by Mike Campbell, who has heard the story from Brett, who was the only witness of the fight—instead of being directly presented. More serious than those technical flaws is the sort of timeliness that is always in danger of going stale. Brett was a pathetic brave figure for her time, but the pathos has been cheapened by thousands of imitation Bretts in life and fiction. Bill Gorton's remarks are not so bright now as they once seemed. "You're an expatriate," he tells Jake ironically. "You've lost touch with the soil. You get precious. Fake European standards have ruined you. . . . You hang around cafés." In those days, as I have been reminded by old newspaper clippings, editorial writers with nothing else to say used to deplore and deride the expatriates. Now that the editorials have been forgotten, a reader does not feel as he might have felt in 1926, that Gorton is making exactly the right rejoinder.

Not everything changes. After one has mentioned those wrinkles and scars revealed by age, how much of the novel seems as marvelously fresh as when it first appeared! Count Mippipopolous, his wound, and his champagne; the old couple from Montana on their first trip abroad; the busload of Basque peasants; the whole beautiful episode of the fishing trip in the mountains, in the harsh sunlight, with bright water tumbling over the dam; then by contrast the dark streets of Pamplona crowded with *riau-riau* dancers, who formed a circle round Brett as if she were a revered witch—as indeed she was, and as Jake in a way was the impotent Fisher King ruling over a sterile land—in all this there is nothing that has gone bad and not a word to be changed after so many years. It is all carved in stone, bigger and truer than life, and it is the work of a man who, having ended his busy term of apprenticeship, was already a master at twenty-six.

—MALCOLM COWLEY, "Hemingway in Paris," *A Second Flowering: Works and Days
    of the Lost Generation* (London: Andre Deutsch, 1956), pp. 69, 71–73

W. M. FROHOCK

In the light of the discipline, the emotional pattern of the book as a whole becomes important; and we had better reconstruct it, since the passing of time is obscuring it more and more, at least to the new reader. The whole job of reading this book has changed from what it was when it came out. The Lost Generation has achieved the dignity—and unreality—of a historical concept. It is increasingly hard to remember that the American expatriates of the middle twenties were serious artists and not spoiled brats; it may be too much to expect that a group which fled America because it did not feel emotionally secure and at home there should seem anything other than trivial to another generation which, after a different kind of war, is compellingly impressed by the insecurity of mere *physical* life anywhere on the planet.

Certainly Hemingway's despair, like that of Eliot in *The Waste Land,* is the kind which can be contemplated with leisure and some ease; it is despair without terror. As a matter of fact, the years of the great depression blunted its point; too many people discovered that it is even more important to eat regularly than to feel quite in place among one's contemporaries. And consequently it is easy to miss the essential datum, that the emotional mood of the first part of *The Sun Also Rises* is a ceaseless, dull ache. The reader is supposed to know that Jake's physical disability is in large part a symbol for the general feeling of frustration and pointlessness of life, that if Jake were physically qualified to possess Brett it would make very little difference, that Brett's nymphomania is really unimportant because if she ever managed to overcome it she would be accomplishing the eradication of a symptom without doing anything for the sickness of the soul. I should think that it might be impossible for anyone opening the book now to find anything much, other than irrelevant digression, in the pages about the self-made Greek Count whose fantastic wine-parties, of course, used to have so much to do with the reader's getting the mood of the whole first part—since Jake so palpably feels that while such things are not a very profitable occupation they are certainly as profitable as anything else.

Yet only if we understand the essential emotional mood of the first part of the book can we appreciate the careful balance between the emotions and the writing—otherwise there is no reasonable explanation for Hemingway's writing so completely under wraps. We risk seeing much more of the snaffle and the bit than we do of the bloody horse. Either we feel the appropriateness of the constant toning down of the whole Paris episode or it will seem like a somewhat staged preparation for the Spanish part, designed to make the latter look brilliant by contrast. We have to know that we get a scant and referential treatment of the Paris scene because Jake is so used to it, and it is so much a part of his dull ache that he does not really see it. We get some of the free-associative spoofing that Hemingway loves to do, about taxidermy and the possibility of stuffed dogs as gifts, but this, as compared with the lovely examples of the same stuff in the Burguete episode, is carefully restrained. The characters do not yet appear as particularly interesting people; we know that Cohn is an importunate romantic oaf, that Mike Campbell is a drunken chronic bankrupt, that Brett is a drunk with a tendency toward promiscuity—and even of her we get something short of a full picture until the Paris episode is over and we discover that she has been sleeping with Cohn, for whom she cares absolutely nothing. Of them all we know just enough so that nothing they do later in the story will catch us by surprise.

Hemingway's whole method in this first part is pretty well summed up in his description of Brett as she is riding with Jake in a taxi. It is night. Illumination is provided by an occasional shop window and by the flares of workmen who are repairing trolley tracks. All that you actually get of Brett (and here again Hemingway is sticking to his purpose of giving you what the character actually sees, not what he should see) is the whiteness of her face and the long line of her neck—even though these people are alone and they are as much in love as their personal disabilities will permit. Substitute in this instance the idea of emotion for light and you have Hemingway's guiding motive throughout the first part: he sees and says only what the abomination-of-desolation mood permits. Obviously, if the emotional climate should be lost on the reader, the whole point would also be lost.

—W. M. FROHOCK, "Ernest Hemingway: The River and the Hawk," *The Novel of Violence in America* (Dallas: Southern Methodist University Press, 1957), pp. 170–72

LESLIE A. FIEDLER

The British bitch is for Hemingway only a demi-bitch, ⟨. . .⟩ as the English are only, as it were, demi-Americans. Catherine is delivered from her doom by death; Brett Ashley in *The Sun Also Rises* (1926) is permitted, once at least, the gesture of herself rejecting her mythical role. But it is quite a feat at that, and Brett cannot leave off congratulating herself: "You know it makes one feel rather good deciding not to be a bitch." Yet Brett never becomes a woman really; she is mythicized rather than redeemed. And if she is the most satisfactory female character in all of Hemingway, this is because for once she is presented not as an animal or as a nightmare but quite audaciously as a goddess, the bitch-goddess with a boyish bob (Hemingway is rather fond of women who seem as much boy as girl), the Lilith of the '20's. No man embraces her without being in some sense castrated, except for Jake Barnes who is unmanned to begin with; no man approaches her without *wanting* to be castrated, except for Romero, who thinks naïvely that she is—or can easily become—a woman. Indeed, when Brett leaves that nineteen-year-old bullfighter, one suspects that, though she avows it is because she will not be "one of these bitches who ruins children," she is really running away because she thinks he might *make* her a woman. Certainly, Romero's insistence that she let her hair grow out has something to do with it: "He wanted me to grow my hair out. Me, with long hair. I'd look so like hell. . . . He said it would make me more womanly. I'd look a fright."

To yield up her cropped head would be to yield up her emancipation from female servitude, to become feminine rather than phallic; and this Brett cannot do. She thinks of herself as a flapper, though the word perhaps would not have occurred to her, as a member of the "Lost Generation"; but the Spaniards know her immediately as a terrible goddess, the avatar of an ancient archetype. She tries in vain to enter into the circle of Christian communion, but is always turned aside at the door; she changes her mind, she has forgotten her hat—the apparent reason never matters; she belongs to a world alien and prior to that of the Christian churches in which Jake finds a kind of peace. In Pamplona, Brett is surrounded by a group of *riau-riau* dancers, who desert a religious procession to follow her, set her up as a rival to Saint Fermin: "Some dancers formed a circle around Brett and started to dance. They wore big wreaths of white garlic around their necks. . . . They were all chanting. Brett wanted to dance but they did not want her to. They wanted her as an image to dance around." Incapable of love except as a moment in bed, Brett can bestow on her worshipers nothing more than the brief joy of a drunken ecstasy—followed by suffering and deprivation and regret. In the end, not only are her physical lovers unmanned and degraded, but even Jake, who is her priest and is protected by his terrible wound, is humiliated. For her service is a betrayal not only of his Catholic faith but of his pure passion for bullfighting and trout-fishing; and the priest of the bitch-goddess is, on the purely human level, a pimp.

—LESLIE A. FIEDLER, "Good Good Girls and Good Bad Boys: Clarissa as a Juvenile," *Love and Death in the American Novel* (New York: Criterion Books, 1960; rev. ed. New York: Stein & Day, 1966), pp. 319–20

ARTHUR MIZENER

Occasionally, as in Hemingway's two best novels, *The Sun Also Rises* and *A Farewell to Arms,* the over-arching emotion evoked in him by the total occasion is so intense that it dominates and controls his immediate responses to the separate episodes which make up the whole, and then the local feelings of each episode are united into a single, final effect. *The Sun Also Rises* is an example of coherence achieved in this way. We know that after Hemingway had spent a week-end with Fitzgerald going over what he presumably thought a completed test of the novel, he went back to Paris and cut a long passage which preceded the present brilliant opening; clearly the novel was not written to a careful plan, yet its only serious defects are failures of local insight like Brett's painfully embarrassing formulation of one of Hemingway's deepest feelings, when she says that the way she feels because she has decided 'not to be a bitch' is 'sort of what we have instead of God'. The design of the novel, however, is very beautiful.

In the very first paragraph we learn that 'in (Cohn's) last year at Princeton he read too much and took to wearing spectacles'. In Hemingway that is, of course, a very bad sign, and presently it turns out that Cohn is a great admirer of W. H. Hudson's *The Purple Land*—'a very sinister book if read too late in life. It recounts the splendid amorous adventures of a perfect English gentleman in an intensely romantic land, the scenery of which is very well described. . . . Cohn, I believe, took every word of [it] as literally as though it had been an R. G. Dun report.' Out of this apparently casual opening there emerges the whole action of the book.

Under the sinister influence of *The Purple Land,* Cohn persuades Brett to go off with him for a week-end. It is a casual experience for her, but Cohn, living as he imagines like 'the perfect English gentleman' in romantic circumstances, takes it all very seriously and attempts to play the part of a Tennysonian Launcelot to the Guinevere he insists Brett is, despite everything she does to dissuade him: to the amused despair of honest characters in the book, he calls Brett Circe. 'He claims she turns men into swine,' Mike Campbell says: 'Damn good. I wish I were one of those literary chaps.' Over against Cohn, Hemingway sets Jake. Jake and Brett are in love, but this love will never come to anything because Jake has been castrated by a shell fragment. Their honour—its exercise is a daily necessity—is to confront their situation without behaving badly. 'Why don't you get married, you two?' says the count. 'We want to lead our own lives,' says Jake, parodying the superficial code of their age, and Brett, the disoriented girl who is marrying Mike Campbell in sheer desperation, adds: 'We have our careers.'

—ARTHUR MIZENER, "The Two Hemingways," *The Great Experiment in American Literature,* ed. Carl Bode (New York: Praeger, 1961), pp. 139–40

CLEANTH BROOKS

The virtues that Hemingway celebrates are narrower than those celebrated by political liberalism. They are much narrower than those affirmed by Christianity. There should be no illusion about this. But the virtues Hemingway celebrates are ultimately necessary to Christianity, and, as we have seen, they look toward Christianity. For they have everything to do with man's dignity as a free spirit—they're "spiritual" even though the irony is that the creature who yearns after them is in Hemingway's view a dying animal in a purely mechanistic universe.

It is almost as if Hemingway, driven back out of theism, dispossessed of his heritage, insists upon stubbornly defending whatever he has felt could still be held. It is a kind of rear-guard action that he fights. The point comes out clearly enough in his very first novel, *The Sun Also Rises*. As the book ends, Brett is talking to her friend Jake. Jake and Brett should be married to each other. They understand each other. There is a real bond between them. But fate has played one of its ugly tricks. Jake has been emasculated by a wound received in the war. No marriage between them is possible. Yet Brett relies upon Jake, and now, as the novel ends, she has wired him to come to Madrid to be with her. She has just left the young Spanish bullfighter to whom she has been tremendously attracted and whom she has proceeded to seduce. She has, however, almost immediately given him up because she has realized that she will ruin him and because she has told herself that "I'm not going to be one of these bitches that ruins children."

Brett confides to Jake something of the feelings that possess her at having made this gesture of denial. She tells Jake: "You know it makes one feel rather good deciding not to be a bitch," and when Jake says, "Yes," she goes on to say, "It's sort of what we have instead of God." Jake observes dryly that "Some people have God. Quite a lot." But neither he nor Brett has God, nor do most of the characters with whom Hemingway concerns himself. And perhaps this very honesty, this lack of sentimentality, this refusal to mix up categories, is the thing which makes Hemingway most useful to the reader who does have a religious commitment. Even men and women who do not have God must try to make up for him in some sense, quixotic as that gesture will seem and, in ultimate terms at least, desperate as that gesture must be. The Christian will feel that it is ultimately desperate in that man can never find anything that will prove a substitute for God. But the Christian will do well to recognize his God though hidden by the incognito which He sometimes assumes. Jake's courage is such an incognito and manifests the divine reality, though of course not fully and not in specifically religious terms.

Hemingway is perfectly right to confine himself to his secular terms. Artistic integrity, fidelity to his vision of reality, honesty in portraying the reactions of the Jakes and Bretts of our world—all conduce to this proper limitation. The Christian reader will therefore be very imperceptive if he fails to see how honestly and sensitively Hemingway has portrayed a situation that exists; he will show an unconscionable smugness if he fails to appreciate the gallantry of actions taken in full consciousness that there is no God to approve or sanction them. He will even hesitate to say "There but for the grace of God go I." For it might be presumptuous of him to assume that, deprived of grace, he could go at all along the road that Hemingway's heroes are forced to take.

—CLEANTH BROOKS, "Ernest Hemingway: Man on His Moral Uppers,"
The Hidden God: Studies in Hemingway, Faulkner, Yeats, Eliot, and Warren
(New Haven: Yale University Press, 1963), pp. 20–21

PHILIP YOUNG AND CHARLES W. MANN

Readers of Fitzgerald's letter who can neither remember the period in which it was written or qualify as serious students of the Twenties may need a little help with it—particularly toward the end where the names, not all of them famous, come thick and fast. At the start there should be no special trouble. "Bunny" is of course the Princeton name for Edmund Wilson (1895–   ) the critic, who "wrote a novel" later on. Maxwell Perkins (1884–1947) was Fitzgerald's editor at Scribner's, and Hemingway's; he never wrote a novel. Neither did Katherine Tighe, who was a childhood friend of Fitzgerald's in St. Paul, Minnesota. O. Henry (William Sydney Porter, 1862–1910), mentioned a few lines later, was a writer of short stories, whose "surprise endings" Hemingway's stories did much to outmode.

As for trying to get Hemingway to "cut the first part of 50 Grand," it should be remembered that Fitzgerald succeeded. Its author regretted the cut a good deal later on, as he seems never to have regretted junking the first part of *The Sun Also Rises.* But he did drop three opening pages of typescript from the draft of "Fifty Grand" that his friend read. (A photograph of the original first page appears in the trade edition of *The Hemingway Manuscripts: An Inventory,* 1969; all three pages are reproduced in the limited edition. Why Hemingway struck so much more than the very brief anecdote Fitzgerald—mistakenly?—though stale is not clear.) Nor is the anecdote in the novel that Fitzgerald found "flat as hell without naming Ford" really all that flat, but since it appeared toward the end of the first chapter-and-a-half it disappeared when that did. Hemingway never forgot either anecdote, however, and this one was related at much greater length as "Ford Madox Ford and the Devil's Disciple" in one of the funniest parts of *A Moveable Feast.* ⟨...⟩

Of the women whose names Fitzgerald invokes, three are characters from fiction, two were characters in fact, and one—whom he suspected of having "dramatized herself in terms of" fiction—was both. The last is Lady Twysden, Duff—the real-life Lady Ashley, Brett—of whom Fitzgerald was not an admirer. In June, 1926, he wrote Perkins that—"perhaps because I don't like the original"—he didn't like Brett in the novel; in *A Moveable Feast* he calls her "that girl with the phoney title who was so rude...." Rude or not, the title was genuine—acquired by marriage. And the lady who held it was such stuff as legends are made on. Bertram D. Sarason, editor of *The Connecticut Review,* and Edward Fisher, a novelist who knew her, have helped to straighten out her actual story. She was born Mary Duff Stirling Smurthwaite in Yorkshire in 1892. According to her she was married for not quite two days in 1917 to an "older man" (apparently named Byron), before eloping with his best man, Sir Roger Thomas Twysden, who is said always to have been either drunk or "away." (There was a son, however; born 1918, died 1946, no issue.) In 1926, shortly after the action of the novel, she and Sir Roger were divorced. She did not marry Pat Guthrie, the suitor called Mike Campbell in the Hemingway version, but a painter from Texas named Clinton King, who was promptly disinherited. A painter herself, she and her husband headed an art school in New City, New York, in 1934; the writer Jerome Bahr, for whom Hemingway once wrote a preface, remembers going out drinking with her in New York. The story Hemingway told the credulous A. E. Hotchner about her funeral in Taxco with her ex-lovers as pallbearers (who dropped the casket, which split in two) was pure apocrypha. Apparently tubercular, she died Mary Duff Stirling Smurthwaite Byron Twysden King in St. Vincent's Hospital, Sante Fé, New Mexico, on June 27, 1938, and was cremated.

In theorizing that Duff dramatized herself in terms of Arlen's dramatization, Fitzgerald has in mind Iris March, promiscuous heroine of Arlen's *The Green Hat,* 1924, a very best-selling novel about some "lost generation" British. Fitzgerald was a thoughtful student of such matters; in *A Moveable Feast* Hemingway wrote that once "He gave me a sort of oral Ph.D. thesis" on Arlen's work. And it is true that Iris and Duff/Brett had some things in common. Iris affects "bravely" a green felt hat; Brett's is a "man's felt hat," and when Duff came to see Edward Fisher in his Paris apartment ("very graceful," and a "musical laugh") the hat was green. More striking, Arlen's narrator remarks that Iris was "'the first Englishwoman I ever saw with 'shingled' hair. This was in 1922." Hemingway's narrator says Brett's hair "was brushed back like a boy's. She started all that." The critic and literary historian Malcolm Cowley (1898–   ) also remembers Duff's "floppy-brimmed" felt hat as green, and he reports that she "was believed to be the heroine of . . . *The Green Hat.*" If so, then Duff did not dramatize herself in terms of Arlen's dramatization so much as play—or be—herself.

> —PHILIP YOUNG AND CHARLES W. MANN, "Fitzgerald's *Sun Also Rises:*
> Notes and Comment," *Fitzgerald/Hemingway Annual 1970,* pp. 1–4

DOLORES BARRACANO SCHMIDT

It is somewhat surprising to find that the man-eating female in American literature is not the ambitious career woman competing in a man's world, not the unwomanly intellectual whose mind outweighs her heart, nor the unsexed non-woman, fearful and envious of penis-power. Instead she is always wife and, quite often, mother; she does not work outside the home, except, perhaps, as a volunteer, more sociable than social in impulse; she is educated, but not intellectual; well-informed, but not cultivated; her house is usually clean, orderly, well-run, though she is not a house-wife in the sense of one devoted to domesticity. Here, perhaps, is both equation and solution: the woman who is neither a career woman nor a hausfrau *equals* the woman without clear-cut identity *equals* the confused, dissatisfied wife *equals* the Great American Bitch. The praying-mantis, around which, according to Simone de Beauvoir, has crystallized the myth of devouring femininity, shows her cruelty especially in captivity; but under natural conditions, when she is free in the midst of abundant food, she rarely dines on the male.

When one considers the period during which this figure becomes established in our literature, the picture comes into clearer focus. The two decades from 1900–1920 represent a new high in effort and achievement for American feminism: women were fighting for equality. The final battle for the ballot was fought by the growing numbers of college-trained women and won in 1920, the year, according to Betty Friedan, which was the turning-point in woman's identity in America. The most dramatic alteration in the image of the American woman came right after World War I, and the flapper of the '20s, remains the symbol of the emancipated woman. She was a joyous symbol: single, free, worldly, independent, confident—and thoroughly unlike the girl who had married dear old Dad.

The old saw, "Imagine the courage it took to be the first man to cook and eat a lobster," might well be applied here, for the writers coming of age during this period—Hemingway, Lewis, Fitzgerald, Anderson—, the writers who created the Great American Bitch archetype (or did they merely record social history?), were the courageous men who first wooed and won and attempted to set up happy homes with the new, emancipated American woman. Somehow the emphasis on the woman question had failed to acknowledge that there might be a man question, too. If woman had new rights and powers, had men lost old ones? If femininity no longer consisted of cooking and sewing and tending the babies, what did it consist of? Or did it cease to exist? What about masculinity? It is surely no coincidence that the themes of sexual identity, of homosexuality, of proving one's manhood in sexual terms, of impotent and unfulfilled lives dominate the literature of the twenties in America.

Consider *The Sun Also Rises,* that sad novel of the twenties—written in the twenties about the twenties by a writer then in his twenties—a novel in which sexual activity abounds but sexual fulfillment is totally absent. Brett with her "hair brushed back like a boy's," a jersey sweater and tweed skirt, her man's felt hat, her freedom to travel, drink, and talk like one of the chaps, is, nonetheless, "damned attractive," an extremely desirable woman, whose ability to dominate every man she meets dooms her to a life of unfulfillment. This represents, however, a man's view of female fulfillment, explicitly sexual in nature and based solely on the subordination-domination pattern.

A great many of the people in Hemingway's world are sexually incomplete, vaguely dissatisfied with their roles in the brave new post–World War I world. In "Cat in the Rain," the young American wife complains:

> "I get so tired of it," she said. "I get so tired of looking like a boy."
> George shifted his position on the bed. He hadn't looked away from her since she started to speak.
> "You look pretty darn nice," he said.
> "I want to pull my hair back tight and smooth and make a big knot at the back that I can feel," she said. "I want to have a kitty to sit on my lap and purr when I stroke her."

"Yeah?" George said from the bed.

"And I want to eat at a table with my own silver and I want candles. And I want it to be spring and I want to brush my hair out in front of a mirror and I want a kitty and I want some new clothes."

"Oh, shut up, and get something to read," George said.

The perfect squelch! If she is an educated, emancipated woman, she should develop her mind and curb her emotions, choose the intellect over the senses, prefer ideas to things. Her husband views her as his "'equal," that is, one not free to develop her own tastes and attitudes as a fellow human being, but one competent and worthy of sharing his.

What, then, of that new, free spirit—the flapper? At what point does that charming hoyden turn into the Great American Bitch?—a question, incidentally, which represents the theme of practically all of F. Scott Fitzgerald's work. Notice how subtly, how insidiously, that glorious new freedom is being defined by men: an independent woman will never find true happiness, and "Shut up and get something to read." Unmated, she is incomplete; once mated, she has neither the freedom of self-determination nor the possibility of returning to the traditional roles of woman, wife, mother. Political equality at least as represented by the ballot had been won, but social equality within the institution of marriage was still far from a reality. The revision of marriage to accommodate equals turned the woman problem into a man problem. Lewis's Cass Timberlane, who believed that "If the world of the twentieth century . . . cannot succeed in . . . married love, then it has committed suicide," remarks on the impulsiveness of his young wife:

> Like all these girls, she feels—and how can you blame her—that she must have her own life. Besides that, I'm no longer the family priest to her or a guide or a refuge; I'm just A Husband.

> —DOLORES BARRACANO SCHMIDT, "The Great American Bitch,"
> *College English* 32, No. 8 (May 1971): 901–3

J. M. LINEBARGER

Ernest Hemingway often quietly arranges symbols to reinforce the meanings within his fiction. The several hats in *The Sun Also Rises* form such a pattern; they become symbols of masculinity that, when they are worn by Brett Ashley, illustrate her unladylike desire to dominate men.

The first mention of a hat in the novel occurs when Jake Barnes asks the prostitute, Georgette, to remove hers while they are at a dancing club: " 'Take off your hat,' " he suggests, indicating, whether he knows it or not, his distaste for women who dominate their men. Immediately afterwards, Lady Brett enters the club with a group of homosexuals. She is not described as wearing a hat, but must have one on, for when she and Jake leave the club in a taxi he notes, "Brett's hat was off." Since Brett loves Jake, she apparently does not attempt to dominate him, at least not when they are alone together. But as they alight from the cab at the Café Select, Brett puts her hat back on. Jake describes the hat here for the first time as a "man's felt hat."

Brett's hat as a symbol of assumed masculinity again occurs after Michael Campbell's arrival in Paris. At the Select, Mike says " 'You *are* a lovely lady, Brett. Where did you get that hat?' " Brett replies that a "chap" bought it for her and asks, " 'Don't you like it?' " Mike's response is " 'It's a dreadful hat. Do get a new hat.' " On the same page, the tipsy Mike repeats his request: " 'I say, Brett, do get a new hat.' " Since Brett dominates Mike, she does not answer him but "pull[s] the felt hat down far over one eye and smile[s] out from under it."

Lady Brett has replaced the felt hat by the time Jake first sees her, Michael, and Cohn in Pamplona: "Brett was wearing a Basque beret. So was Mike. Robert Cohn was bareheaded . . ." Since Cohn can never assume the role of a Hemingway male, he does not get to wear hats or any other head covering during the novel.

On the opening day of the fiesta, Brett does not have a hat on. She is stopped from entering a chapel "because she had no hat." Without a hat, she becomes a symbol of femininity to the festival dancers who surround her: "They were all chanting. Brett wanted to dance but they did not want her to. They wanted her as an image to dance around."

Lady Brett relinquishes her feminine role again, however, when she decides that she wants to make a conquest of Pedro Romero, the young bullfighter. Brett asks him,

> "What are bull-fighters like?"
> He laughed and tipped his hat down over his eyes. . . .
> "I would like a hat like that," Brett said.
> "Good. I'll get you one."
> "Right. See that you do."
> "I will. I'll get you one to-night."

Romero's gesture of tipping the hat over his eyes is itself a symbol of masculine dominance, just as it was for Brett when she did not answer Mike's earlier request to " 'get a new hat.' " When Romero enters the bull ring after his night with Brett and the beating by Cohn, he still wears "his tricornered hat . . . low down over his eyes," and his purpose is not only to hide his battered face, but also I think to indicate that he has retained his masculinity along with his hat. That suggested meaning is reinforced on the next page of the novel, when Romero and two other matadors bow before the President's box, "holding their hats on," an appropriate symbolic gesture for the kind of men Hemingway presents as paragons of masculinity. Incidentally, Lady Brett never succeeds in getting either Romero's hat or one like it; the novel ends without hats being mentioned further.

—J. M. LINEBARGER, "Symbolic Hats in *The Sun Also Rises*,"
Fitzgerald/Hemingway Annual 1972, pp. 323–24

ROBERT BRAINARD PEARSALL

Of the five particular people to whom he behaved most treacherously, two were his literary supporters Sherwood Anderson and Gertrude Stein, two were his Left Bank friends Lady Duff Twysden and Harold Loeb, and the fifth his wife Hadley. The overt attacks on Anderson and Gertrude Stein still lay a little in the future. They germinated at the time, however, through the general remarks of the New York critics concerning the two main sources of his prose style. It was always anathema to Hemingway to be told that he had borrowed anything from anyone else, or been helped in any other way; and he refused to let Anderson and Gertrude Stein be credited even with friendship. Lady Twysden and Harold Loeb were so far as possible slaughtered in *The Sun Also Rises,* the novel he now began to write. In the same book a number of other old friends and colleagues were held up to scorn or dislike, always on personal grounds, never on literary. He had begun to criticise Hadley and to prefer the company of other women, and would demand a divorce from her at the end of the period. By the time he finished his book in 1925, he had all but demolished the agreeable circle into which he had moved so modestly and charmingly in 1922.

The attack on Lady Duff Twysden and Harold Loeb, called Lady Brett Ashley and Robert Cohn in the book, developed from ordinary sexual jealousy, to which was added tourist-versus-tourist contempt for fellow expatriates, plus clubhouse jingoism and antisemitism. Loeb was an American, a Jew from a good New York family. He had attended Yale University, had the usual mixed experiences of what are now called "Ivy Jews," and developed good literary tastes and a limited talent as a writer. For a time he controlled the avant-garde magazine *Broom.* He had been an infantry sergeant during the war, a fact Hemingway jealously suppressed when he reviewed Cohn's history in the novel. In character he was simple-minded, disingenuous, and easy to hurt, wearing his heart as it were on his sleeve. Women liked and trusted him, and he liked and trusted women. In the novel Hemingway makes him only the "tennis friend" of Jake Barnes, the protagonist, but Hemingway and Loeb were all-around friends, confidential and mutually agreeable. Among the things they shared was a taste for Lady Twysden.

Lady Duff Twysden was a pretty woman of thirty-two, slender and soft-spoken, who was acting out the part of black sheep and lost lady. Her title was real, and she had enjoyed a career as debutante and officer's wife in London society. As a black sheep in Paris she drank heavily, ran out of money at inconvenient times, and spread her tenderness out over too many men. She enjoyed making maxims. Hemingway on one occasion jotted down some of her semi-philosophical sayings. One was "It is like living with fourteen men so no one will know there is someone you love." Another fine saying was, "You must make fantastic statements to cover things." One he liked especially, though it is softer and wetter than these, was "You can't hurt people. It's what we have in place of God." This statement, the most pretentious of the lot, was given to Lady Brett Ashley on the next-to-last page of

The Sun Also Rises. In addition to being something of a philosopher, Lady Twysden was *à la mode*, fashionably tarnished, with that Mayfair accent and manner which Hemingway doted on but had not till then encountered in an available woman. Like his other women Agnes von Kurowsky and Hadley Richardson, she was six or seven years older than he, and ahead of him in experience and general culture. As a popular Jezebel in town, and a pleasantly warmhearted one also, she had a considerable following. This included a Scottish black sheep named Pat Guthrie and a casual chorus of homosexuals and fantastics. Guthrie was her steady companion. Loeb earned Hemingway's vengeful hatred by being her companion for one week at a hotel in San Sebastian.

Hemingway was never Lady Twysden's companion. She slept with others, she rejected him. The fury in the book is the fury of a hurt and angry man.

—ROBERT BRAINARD PEARSALL, *The Life and Writings of Ernest Hemingway* (Amsterdam: Rodopi, 1973), pp. 72–74

SUNITA JAIN

There exists an inevitable though subtle similarity between Brett Ashley, heroine of Hemingway's first novel, *The Sun Also Rises,* and Catherine Barkley, heroine of his second novel, *A Farewell to Arms.* Certain noticeable surface differences between them have made the critics ignore this aspect. Most of the critics have accepted Brett Ashley in her obvious role of a 'bitch', and Catherine in her burgeoning pose of a 'goddess'. To Carlos Baker, for example, Brett and Catherine are 'norm-women'. Brett is an epitome of the 'deadly' female while Catherine is the incarnation of all that is womanly. "Brett's neurosis," says Baker, "drives her from bar to bar, from man to man . . . as if she were a half-woman half in love with damnation. Catherine Barkley, on the other hand is all woman . . . she is a completing agent for the hero and is in turn completed by her association with him. But Brett . . . is an agent of depletion. . . ." However, as one reads *A Farewell to Arms,* one has a steady but irresistible feeling that Catherine Barkley is Brett Ashley in another country, in another role, reminding us portentously what a woman can be.

In fact the two heroines are not two types of female as Baker has pointed out: one "selfish, corrupt, and predatory . . . 'bad' for the men with whom she is involved", and the other 'temperamentally monogamous' without the other's "geographical restlessness", rather they are two conscious portrayals by Hemingway of the woman of a certain timber. The basic similarity between the two and their surface differences together point up the theme of both the novels: man helpless, 'trapped biologically', living, in one case, a death in life, and, in the second, cheated of life when most alive.

Our first glimpse of Brett Ashley is at the crowded bar, hair close-cropped, wearing a slipover jersey sweater and drunk: a perfect still shot of a cool clean ice cube unmelted at the bottom of a drained glass. We watch the futile melting as a little later she dances with a group of homosexuals; and when she is not able to stand the nearness of her lover, Jake Barnes, who has been rendered impotent due to a war wound, Brett leaves with Count Mippipopolous to spend the rest of the evening. She disappears a few days later with Robert Cohn, the man who whines about his love for her and follows her around like a sick steer; Brett actually detests Cohn. Engaged to marry Mike Campbell, whom she does not love, Brett brazenly seduces the nineteen-year-old bull fighter, Romero, and has a passionate affair with him. But the man in Romero wakes the woman in Brett and she decides to give Romero up because the affairs would have ruined the boy. She says she won't "be one of these bitches that ruins children" and feels good about it. Contrasted to this portrait of Brett is Catherine Barkley's delineation in *A Farewell to Arms*. Catherine is happily afloat—she has found love and life in love in Frederic Henry's arms. Nevertheless, it is not difficult to see that Catherine's fulfillment in and constancy to Frederic is not necessarily because of her being monogamous temperamentally just as Brett's bitchiness is not due to any overriding animalistic compulsion.

Enamoured of Catherine's soft self-surrender, one tends to overlook the crystal-like hardness which keeps her straight about Frederic; that Catherine is hard and clear-eyed is evident from the initial love scene in the novel. Not yet sure of Frederic Henry's love, not even hoping for it, Catherine makes him say that he loves her and closes her own eyes to make believe that it is her boy-lover who has kissed her. This need to drive out her remorse and waste virginity willfully, which originally she had saved for her lover's return from the war, would have made Catherine fly into the arms of one soldier after another—not due to wantonness, of course, but due to sheer desperation—had Frederic not actually returned her love. Determined not to let it remain a game of chess, she salvages Henry's love. And as he falls in love, Catherine has no need to be 'crazy and Scottish'. She can let go of herself and just live each moment like an eternity, for she had learned that death is the end of life and there is nothing after death. The wooden stick which she received from her boy-lover's parents after his death is a reminder of the finality of death to her; and chastity which mattered so much earlier means nothing to her now: "He could have had anything he wanted if I had known. I would have married him or anything. I know all about it now." There is only a reflex resistance in her to the first kiss by Frederic when Catherine slaps him. Within a few moments after that she hopes he will be good to her as they were "going to have a strange life."

Catherine's complete merger in Frederic is possible not because they wanted "love making without end in a scarcely real country to which neither owed life or allegiance," but because of her resolute understanding of the relationship of life and death and her equation of life with love. Everything that Catherine does or says speaks of "a certain obsessive watchfulness and mindfulness;" and if Hemingway's novels come down "to one character haunted by danger, reviving each time he could recover his balance by handling each detail in his path with the gravest self-importance" as Alfred Kazin suggests, then that one character in *A Farewell to Arms* is Catherine Barkley. In this context what Catherine says about having no 'religion' acquires larger significance; her statement that she has no religion is not just a sequel statement to what she had said earlier to Frederic, "You're my religion." The two statements together are not a declaration of insipient love that an un-complex girl has felt for her lover, rather they testify to the tremendous effort Catherine has made to love not just Frederic but the life force itself. The shy, chaste, prude Catherine of early scenes with Frederic was actually all the time selecting her mate. Rinaldi noticed that she preferred Frederic to him. She does not hesitate to reach out for what she wants. Catherine has little qualm when she gives herself to Frederic in the hospital. She asks for no promises and makes no vows, Frederic returns her love and that is enough. She does not even get upset about her pregnancy. Her friend Ferguson is shocked at this wicked shamelessness on Cather-ine's part, but Ferguson does not understand that when human frailty is pitched against the forces of annihilation, every Catherine Barkley becomes a Brett Ashley, instinctively putting aside conventions of the civilised world in an effort to perse-vere, and last.

Brett Ashley makes that effort in *The Sun Also Rises,* but her cross is heavier to bear. After losing her boy friend (he died of dysentery in the war), she too falls in love like Catherine. But Brett's new lover, Jake Barnes, is physically handicapped and unable to return her love. In the meantime Lord Ashley, whom Brett married, made her sleep on bare floor at night and kept a loaded pistol under his pillow. Thus, unable to dissolve herself like Catherine is able to, yet made of essentially the same metal, raked by the same lust for life, Brett disintegrates steadily, but she is not an ordinary pale-passioned woman who indiscriminately goes to bed and is "incapable of love except as a moment in bed." In fact, she has as much kindness and pity as Catherine has. Had Jake been normal, had there been no torture when near him, no denial each time of the consummate passion for each other, Brett Ashley would have kept her hair long and just loved like Catherine, but she must go away from Jake, for when he touches her she simply turns to jelly, and her nearness gives Jake terrible headaches. The physical suffering on both sides— suffering that has to be stoically borne—sends this warm, beautiful woman whirling in circles of meaningless affairs indulged in because of pity (for others) and often because of self-pity, since further suffering is inevitable for a woman who is hope-lessly in love yet allows other men to have her. Brett went off with Cohn because she felt sorry for him, but this pity for Cohn wrecks her even more and she has to wash away Cohn by flirting with Romero. But unexpected return of love by Romero, who is a man complete in every way, makes Brett blossom into all the goodness and selflessness of a Catherine Barkley. She sends Romero away even though she needed him.

It was, then, a design of purpose rather than any bankruptcy of imagination that made Hemingway create these two women so terribly similar in every way; their difference in behaviour due to individual circumstances is exploited to convey an image of life so compulsively chaotic: all human effort and will to impose order and meaning are ultimately abortive. Thus, Brett's restlessness avails not and Catherine's peace avails not. Both are beautiful and brave, but beauty and courage avail not. Brett found not life as she desperately tried to dispel death, and death folded its claws around Catherine when she was most alive.

—SUNITA JAIN, "Of Women and Bitches: A Defence of Two Hemingway Heroines,"
Journal of the School of Languages 12, No. 2 (Winter 1975–76): 132–35

JEROME MECKIER

⟨Aldous Huxley's⟩ *Antic Hay* (1923) and *The Sun Also Rises* both end with hero and heroine, who are unable to satisfy one another, riding rather aimlessly in a taxi. As Gumbril, Jr. and Myra Viveash crisscross London in search of companions to relieve their boredom, this conveyance becomes the perfect symbol for the pointlessness of modern life, an in-transit existence between a vanished world order and new patterns which have yet to emerge. In fact, *Antic Hay* is packed with images of purposeless motion. The taxi Brett and Jake take in Hemingway's final chapter is probably meant to remind the reader of Huxley's novel. No reliable still-point materializes for lovers in either novel. Like *Antic Hay* and *Those Barren Leaves*, which fail to produce a single convincingly successful marriage or love affair, *The Sun Also Rises* is sceptical about love. In a variety of ways all three novels use the inability or refusal of their characters to love, whether to love at all or to do so rewardingly, as the major sign of a generation's frustrated idealism and general disillusionment. ⟨. . .⟩

Novels of the twenties, especially *The Sun Also Rises,* also follow Huxley's lead whenever they use a *femme fatale* to personify the modern world's destructive allure, its Circe-like propensity to attract the young Romantic idealist so that it can enchant him and then fail to satisfy. In Huxley, however, the satire works both ways. Unlike Hemingway, who sympathizes completely with Frederic Henry and Jake Barnes, Huxley ridicules the egotism of his youthful protagonists. He treats them as severely as Hemingway handles his cruelest version of them in Robert Cohn. Huxley's young men are satirized because they expect the world to conform to the designs they generate within their own minds. They demand that life substantiate the ideals they have culled from the best literature of the preceding hundred years, especially the poetry of Wordsworth, Shelley, Keats, and Tennyson. There is ultimately little difference in Huxley's novels between these younger men and their seemingly more eccentric, more Peacockian elders, who create private worlds for themselves where they can keep their theories of life intact. These younger men, though nurtured on Romantic poetry rather than Pavlov, are just as conditioned and therefore limited as the brave new worldians. Intellectual though he is, overly cerebral to many, Huxley consistently lambastes his characters for their naive, rationalist assumption that mind controls matter. This is the silliest illusion of all, a sort of ultra-Romanticism, and it is perennial. The aberration was exalted by the Romantics but Huxley demonstrates that it has been shared by other eras and writers as well. Thus he has the Elizabethan founder of Crome, Sir Ferdinando, build his privies in the topmost room of the house. This enables him to sustain his theory of human nature by feeling noble and close to heaven even while emptying his bowels. And Sir Hercules the Dwarf, his eighteenth-century descendant, builds a dwarf-sized world at Crome to protect his ego in a milieu rudely tailored to his limitations. Like the Romantics, Huxley implies, Elizabethans, eighteenth-century Rationalists, twentieth-century Behaviorists, and mankind in general are always quite willing to distort the world until it flatters their interpretations. The belief that man's reason can half perceive and half create because it is easily as versatile as the material world always provokes Huxley's derisive laughter. As Denis Stone laments, "In the world of ideas everything was clear; in life all was obscure, embroiled." In Huxley's opinion, this counterpoint of mind against matter is largely responsible for man's persistent unhappiness. Throughout his work Huxley discredits the glorious overviews of poet and scientist alike. But at the same time, the disillusioned idealist within him, the deprived Romantic, despises the world of matter for its fundamental ugliness beneath the deceptive veneer, for being so uncooperative and malign, so intricate, intriguingly chaotic, and yet thoroughly alien to man's explanations and designs. To humble the idealist's ego and also to express its author's personal dissatisfaction with the nature of things, Huxley's early poetry marshals a veritable regiment of women who stand for the undependable enticements of love and the futility of all love affairs with the modern world. The list includes "She" in "The Walk," the girl in "The Defeat of Youth," and perhaps even the heroine of "Leda," with whom Jove enjoys an all-too-brief union. Frequently without any excess of malice, these women are simply the unreliable vessels into which Huxley's male protagonists pour their own untenable idealistic notions of how love, beauty, and the world of matter ought to perform. More often, these symbolic women prove heartlessly indifferent. In the early novels they become increasingly more ruthless: the flighty Anne Wimbush of *Crome Yellow* leads to the death-in-life figure of Myra Viveash in *Antic Hay,* the insipid, mindlessly vulgar Barbara Wates of *Those Barren Leaves,* the master sadist, Lucy Tantamount in *Point Counter Point,* and Lenina the parodic Juliet from *Brave New World.* Huxley's recurrent negative myth, the collision of idealistic males and vapid or heartless females to signify reality's refusal to correspond to the presumptuous designs of the mind, is a sad revelation of life's inability to imitate art. It proves that dualism and dichotomy are the essence of life. This negative myth assails the positive one on which the Modern Age, that is, the period since Descartes, has built its grandest hopes; the belief that man can know and manage the world by the unaided efforts of his reason.

Hemingway, and later Fitzgerald and Waugh, do not take over Huxley's somewhat anti-feminist myth literally, nor do they seem to have understood its full scope. It is philosophical and metaphysical as well as social. But all three borrow from it liberally, albeit with variations, in fashioning comparable defeats for their major protagonists. And it is Huxley's myth that so much of Lawrence strenuously combats and actually tries to reverse. Cohn accurately calls Brett a Circe. The similarity of their roles and the resemblance in their names suggest that Myra Vive*ash*, who makes the males in *Antic Hay* dance with unsatisfied desire, is the prototype for Brett Ashley. Both sirens inspire love in others without ever truly satisfying them or themselves. Although Brett is a nymphomaniac and Myra so emotionally exhausted, so incapable of serious involvement, that she seems liable to expire at any moment, the two are different extremes of the same malady, two burnt-out cases in the modern waste land. They are both victims of the war and become in turn impressive symbols of the discrepancies between romance and reality, promise and fulfillment, which the war so painfully pointed out. The parallel extends even further because Myra's despair can be traced to the battlefield death of Tony Lamb, sacrificially named, the only man she apparently ever loved: and Brett's frustrations are heightened, though not caused entirely, by Jake's war wound. Moreover, Jake claims that Brett married Ashley during the war after "Her own true love had just kicked off with the dysentery."

Incurably listless though she appears, Myra was a fertile enough creation to inspire a line of disaster-producing *femme fatales* that includes Lady Brett, Daisy Buchanan, Brenda Last, Margot Beste-Chetwynde, and Virginia Crouchback-Blackhouse-Troy. When a bomb falls on Uncle Peregrine's London flat toward the end of World War Two and destroys Virginia, Waugh's Everard Spruce, the asinine editor of *Survival*, functions for once as a perceptive critic. He eulogizes Virginia as "the last of twenty years' succession of heroines," the last of those "ghosts of romance who walked between the wars." To have known Virginia, he concludes, is to understand Michael Arlen and Scott Fitzgerald. Spruce reads from *Antic Hay* a paragraph which describes with appreciation the alluring magic of Myra simply crossing a street, and then he expounds on it:

> . . . the passage I read, believe it or not, is Aldous Huxley 1922. Mrs. Viveash. Hemingway coarsened the image with his Bret, but the type persisted—in books and in life. Virginia was the last of them—with expiring voices—a whole generation younger. We shall never see anyone like her again in literature or in life and I'm very glad to have known her.

Although Spruce fixes the date of Huxley's novel a year too early and spells Brett with only one *t*, he traces Virginia's genesis correctly, provides her a fitting epitaph, and corroborates my argument. The phrase "ghosts of romance" is particularly apt. But Huxley's males are not as glad to court Myra or Hemingway's to know Brett as Spruce is to have met Virginia. Myra, Brett, Daisy, Brenda, and Margot, along with Lucy Tantamount, form a sextet that seems responsible for ninety percent of the emotional carnage in novels of the twenties.

Huxley's original impetus was probably no more than a determination to parody Petrarch's veneration for Laura, Dante's vision of Beatrice, and all the more recent repetitions of such scenes in Keats' *Endymion*, Shelley's *Epipsychidion*, and the famous epiphany of the wading girl which climaxes Stephen Dedalus' search for identity and vocation in chapter four of *Portrait of the Artist as a Young Man*.

However, he quickly invested his parodies of these false, unrealistic, romantic sequences with the status of a negative myth which was peculiarly suited to express the young modern's disappointment with a meaningless world of counterpoints and insurmountable contraries. Huxley's negative myth of defeated youths in a Circle-like world caught on because it summarized the feelings of his generation. Hence it reappeared in a variety of forms in the novels of his contemporaries, principally Hemingway, Fitzgerald, and Waugh.

If Hemingway and Huxley were the primary apostles of the lost generation, the writers who brought its condition most accurately into print, they were definitely not strict contemporaries. Vital differences aside, Hemingway sometimes follows from Huxley by a kind of apostolic succession, and important elements in Fitzgerald and Waugh are also the outcome of this transmission. Though these two writers disagree radically about the uses of literature and the nature of good style. Huxley's early work illuminates Hemingway's and *vice versa.* Indeed, Huxley, Hemingway, Fitzgerald, and Waugh, not to mention the effect *The Waste Land* had on *Antic Hay, The Great Gatsby* and *A Handful of Dust,* supply a fascinating series of complex trans-Atlantic interactions, the Huxleyan impact on Hemingway by no means the least interesting. Studies of the twenties which ignore the Anglo-American interplay do so at their peril. Hemingway may have leafed through Huxley and Lawrence *after* producing his own daily allotment of words, but he remembered what he had read when next he sat down to write. Miss Stein's reservations to the contrary, reading those books from Sylvia Beach's or purchased along the quais paid off handsomely.

—JEROME MECKIER, "Hemingway Reads Huxley: An Occasion for Some Observations on the Twenties and the Apostolate of the Lost Generation," *Fitzgerald/Hemingway Annual 1976,* pp. 173, 180–84

LEON F. SELTZER

Circumstantially, probably the best evidence of Count Mippipopolous' sexual impairment is in his proposing to Brett that she accompany him to the resort town Biarritz for the sum of ten thousand dollars. Such an extravagant offer can be seen as extended in recompense for his inability to offer her physical satisfaction. Certainly the novel contains not the slightest suggestion that the Count aspires to make Brett his mistress—and if he did, his offering of such a monetary reward would be in strict transgression of the social/moral code to which, as "one of them," he is firmly bound. It might, incidentally, be noted that at one point Jake reflects on his own relationship with Brett as violating the "exchange of values" ethic by which he too wishes to live. He thinks unhappily of her friendship and love for him as "something for nothing," which "only delayed the presentation of the bill," since "the bill always came" (148). And he knows of course that he cannot settle his debt by offering himself to her physically (given their situation it is utterly inappropriate for him to offer a monetary reward). This may in fact be the primary explanation for his complying with Brett's request that he take her to Romero—obviously his sexual substitute—even though such compliance, as critics have sometimes remarked, involves humiliating compromises to his integrity and self-respect. His strongly felt obligation to "pay all his bills" may be viewed as leaving him with very little choice in the matter.

About Brett one might observe that she will neither take money for sexual favors nor accept it in replacement for such favors. She does not confer her favors on Robert Cohn at San Sebastian for a price, and when she ends her brief affair with Romero she tells him outright (despite her being completely without funds) that she couldn't think of accepting a gift of money from him. Depicted in the novel as insecure and sexually frustrated—and needing therefore to control men through sex—it is only logical that she should decline Count Mippipopolous' magnanimous offer. For even though she is very fond of the Count, his offer seriously threatens her sexual supremacy: he quite literally proposes to buy Brett's companionship—and to "pay for" in this novel carries certain indisputable rights of control. Since Brett cannot in this instance use her body to "contract" some degree of control herself, to accept the Count's offer would be to relinquish the essentially dominant, even masculine, role she has achieved in her desperately "liberated" relations to men. When she refuses to grow her hair long for Romero (i.e., to become more feminine for him), she evidences still further her fear of accepting the more traditional subordinate role in male-female relationships.

Returning to the Count, we might initially be inclined to think that his own truncated relationship with Brett implies his submission to the kind of subordinate or quiescent role that Brett has rejected. An inspection of his life style, however, actually suggests a hearty engagement with life missing from every other character in the narrative but Romero. For Hemingway demonstrates that the Count has moved beyond the sometimes psychologically crippling restraints that finally both Jake and Brett feel compelled to impose on themselves and has contrived to realize himself in and through his value system as has no one else in the novel. Unquestionably he is the only character described as completely content, and he therefore deserves much more attention than he has yet received as an example—if not necessarily a practically achievable goal—of how someone might overcome the "deadly" initiation of war and evolve, existentially, a framework of values impregnable to the daily onslaughts of reality.

Inasmuch as Count Mippipopolous is a sort of successful Jake Barnes, it is instructive to view him, technically, as Jake's double. Both Robert Cohn and Pedro Romero have sometimes been seen as alter-egos for Jake, but the Count—both in his impotence and in his *transcendence* of this impotence—needs also to be understood as Jake's double if the novel's richly complex thematic design is to be fully appreciated. Only by such considerations can we complete the intricate pattern of possibilities toward love and loving delineated in the novel through the author's handling not only of Jake and Brett, but also of Cohn, Campbell, and Romero. With all the male characters the love object, needless to say, is Brett, who emerges figuratively, both as the novel's bitch goddess and *femme fatale*. Brett is pictured as harmless only to the Count, who while susceptible to her (Brett herself complacently announces to Jake: "He's mad about me"), never becomes "captivated by" (i.e., emotionally dependent upon) her. Brett's refusal to join him in his travels does not appear to disturb him in the least: in fact his reaction is to graciously invite her—and Jake also, whom he ironically assumes to be her lover—to join him in a sumptuous dinner. When the three of them spend the evening together, apparently a very pleasurable one until Brett is seized by depression and becomes anxious to leave, the Count good-humoredly assents, even offering his chauffeured car to the love-frustrated couple as he stays contentedly behind at the club. As the two depart, Jake takes a final glance back and is immediately greeted by the sight of three girls at the Count's table.

All this suggests indirectly that the Count's relations with women are satisfying because he has, practically, overcome his impotence by subduing the understandable masculine need to assert himself sexually with them. Unlike Jake, who admits that he is "blind, unforgivingly jealous" of Cohn for his affair with Brett; Cohn, who futilely follows Brett around and then just as futilely fights for her hand; Mike, who dejectedly drinks himself into a stupor when Brett deserts him to run off with Romero; and even Romero, who wants Brett to become "more womanly" for him so that he can marry her, the Count can accept Brett entirely for what she is and relish her company without experiencing the slightest need to possess her. He finds her charming, whether she is drunk or sober, and when (careless in all things) she speaks insultingly to him in front of Jake, calling him an ass and accusing him of being dead and without values, his extraordinary composure is left undisturbed. His prodigious detachment is the measure of his resistance to psychological pain; and the novel abundantly illustrates how almost all of Jake's problems result from his failure to detach himself sufficiently from the inescapable provocations of life.

—LEON F. SELTZER, "The Opportunity of Impotence: Count Mippipopolous in *The Sun Also Rises," Renascence* 31, No. 1 (Autumn 1978): 7–9

FREDERIC JOSEPH SVOBODA

Early in the novel, around page 55, Brett and Jake sit together on Jake's bed. It is evening; Brett has just sent her escort, Count Mippipopolous, out for champagne so that she and Jake can talk.

Hemingway expended considerable effort on revising this scene, particularly on the section in which Jake and Brett most directly discuss their love for each other. In the published version, the essence of the conversation is contained in this exchange between the two, with Brett maintaining her distance as a defense against the pain inherent in the impossibility of the whole relationship, given Jake's wound:

> "Isn't it rotten? There isn't any use my telling you I love you."
> "You know I love you." [says Jake]
> "Let's not talk. Talking's all bilge. I'm going away from you, and then Michael's coming back."

Words are inadequate to the situation, and Brett's rejection of them at once serves to characterize her, to define the situation, and to introduce a thematic distrust of verbal communication which is later most clearly shown as the aficionados of the corrida must *touch* Jake before they are willing to believe him as fellow aficionado. For Jake and Brett, of course, touching is impossible, and words are inadequate to express the lovers' feelings; but in earlier versions, words were even less adequate, neither meaningful nor seemly. The lovers became maudlin—words ran away with and overwhelmed the exchange. The notebook first draft version of the conversation was much longer:

> "Isn[']t it rotten.[?] You know I feel rather quiet and ~~good~~ cool today too. It's good to talk it out now when we're quiet. *[There]* I *[i]sn't any use my telling you I love you.*"
> *"You know I love you."*
> "I love you and I'll love you always ~~and~~. I never told any man that."
> "I love you and I'll love you always."
> "It's terrible loving when you've loved so many times that you know what it is."
> "I don't know. I've never loved a lot of people."
> "Yes you have."
> "Not the same way."
> "Oh I*[L]et[']s not talk. Talking's all bilge. I'm going away from you [,] and then* ~~Mike's~~ *Michael's coming back.*" [Italics indicate the elements that Hemingway eventually chose to include in the published work; square brackets indicate changes that he made.]

The eventual reduction from 109 words, constituting 9 units of dialogue, to 34 words, constituting 4 units, heightens the desperation of the situation as well as the ironic commentary upon the different meanings of the word *love*. In this first-draft version the tension of the situation is obscured by a torrent of words; indeed, Brett's statement on talking it out "now when we're quiet" operates in opposition to the thematic distrust of words and in opposition to Brett's essential wary toughness. And here the repetition of "I love you" carries no weight. It merely seems trite—it is not the sort of repetition that Gertrude Stein termed *insistence*, the haunting periodic repetition of a word or phrase that so often marks Hemingway's best work.

By the time of the typescript second draft, Hemingway had cut the scene somewhat, yet he was still having some problems. Indeed, this section is notable as being the one scene that had been worked over in some detail in the typist's copy of the novel. A sense of fatality is introduced in this typed version. Instead of "I love you and I'll love you always," Jake says, "I love you and *I suppose I'll have to love you* always" (my italics). Brett then replies, "It's *a terrible business* loving when you've loved so many times that you know what it is" (my italics). In that resort to a conventional idiom, Hemingway moved toward a more reserved Brett, a Brett who was more like the coolly controlled woman we see through so much of the published novel. But Jake was presented more petulantly in this draft; Hemingway underlined the iron of his "Not the same way" by adding a self-pitying second statement: "Never had a chance."

But even these revisions did not satisfy him; on the typescript copy Hemingway crossed out the two lines that eventually appeared in print and added other material that underlined the ironic fatality of the lovers' predicament. The amended typescript (starting the quote a line or two earlier than above) reads this way:

> "It wouldn't be any good. I'll go if you like. But I couldn't live quietly in the country. Not with my own true love." *If I'd ever had one—*"
>
> "I know."
>
> ~~"Isn't it rotten? Isn't any use my telling you I love you."~~
> ~~"You know I love you."~~
>
> "I love you and I'll love you always. I never told any man that."
>
> "I love you and I suppose I'll have to love you always." *I felt like some question and answer game. I didn't love anybody. I only wanted Brett.*
>
> "It's a terrible business loving when you've loved so many times that you know what it is."
>
> "I don't know.*," I said,* "I've never loved a lot of people."
>
> "Yes you have."
>
> "Not the same way. Never had a chance."
>
> "Let's not talk. . . ."
>
> [Hemingway's handwritten additions to the typescript are in italics; his deletions are lined through.]

Eventually, in the draft from which the novel was set, Hemingway restored the two deleted sections of dialogue and pared away the rest. In the final version of the exchange, the pain *and* Jake and Brett's love are clearly presented; in this amended typescript version, Hemingway seems to have corrected the maudlin quality of the first-draft version by casting considerable doubt on the quality of the relationship between the two.

In the typescript draft above, Brett's "If I'd ever had [a true love]—" suggests that she has never had a completely fulfilling relationship with a man, but it also suggests that Jake does not really love her. Such an implication is far different from the impression Hemingway eventually decided to convey, that Jake was emotionally Brett's true love though physically he could never be her lover. And while Jake's "I didn't love anybody. I only wanted Brett" suggests his intense feeling and confusion of emotion at being close to Brett, it again undercuts the sense that he is her "true love." Instead, in the typescript version, Jake seems much more like the Frederic Henry we see early in *A Farewell to Arms*, playing the word games that will let him take advantage of the need of a Catherine Barkley whom he does not yet love. (But here again, in Jake's mention of the "question and answer game," notice a return to the distrust of words that Hemingway eventually embodied in the scene's terse final version.)

All the conflicting elements of this typescript version of the scene—and similarly inappropriate elements in the notebook first draft—work against the effect that Hemingway finally decided upon. In this first private meeting between the lovers, he must establish clearly that Jake and Brett emotionally *are* lovers—he must strike a clear note that will resonate through the novel—and so he finally decides upon a restraint in the use of language which echoes and reinforces our perception of the inescapable restraints that fate has placed on the relationship between Brett and Jake.

—FREDERIC JOSEPH SVOBODA, "The Most Difficult Job of Revision,' "
Hemingway and The Sun Also Rises: *The Crafting of a Style*
(Lawrence: University Press of Kansas, 1983), pp. 45–50

JOYCE CAROL OATES

The Sun Also Rises, written in Paris and published when Hemingway was twenty-seven years old, immediately established his reputation as one of the most brilliant and original writers of his generation; he was lauded as an unsentimental, if not pitiless, interpreter of post–World War I society. The novel's idle, self-absorbed characters are American and English expatriates in Paris in the early 1920s, veterans in one way or another of the war: the newspaperman narrator Jake Barnes was wounded on the Italian front and is sexually impotent ("No," Jake says self-mockingly, "I just had an accident"); the woman he loves, Lady Brett Ashley, is estranged from an English baronet who became mentally deranged during his service in the Royal Navy, and is something of a nymphomaniac alcoholic ("I've always done just what I wanted," Brett says helplessly to Jake; "I do feel such a bitch"). The Novel's title, perfectly chosen, taken from the first chapter of Ecclesiastes ("One generation passeth away, and another generation cometh; but the earth abideth for ever. The sun also ariseth, and the sun goeth down, and hasten to his place where he arose"), strikes exactly the right chord of ennui and resignation and succeeds in lifting Hemingway's story of drifting, alienated, rather superficial men and women to a mythopoetic level. And the novel's other epigraph, long since famous, is Gertrude Stein's: "You are all a lost generation." (In fact, as Hemingway discloses in *A Moveable Feast,* Stein herself appropriated the remark from the manager of a Parisian gas station.)

Reading Hemingway's first novel today, one is likely to be struck by its "mod-

ern" sound: the effectless, meiotic prose, the confrontations that purposefully es-
chew emotion, the circular and even desultory movement of its narrative. The
generation of the 1920s was perhaps no more lost than many another postwar
generation, but the self-consciousness of being lost, being special, "damned," casually committed to self-destruction (Jake and his friends are virtually all alcoholics or
on their way to becoming so) sounds a new note in prose fiction. Jake's impotence
is of course not accidental. Being estranged from conventional society (that is, one's
family back home) and religion (for Jake, Catholicism: a "grand" religion) establishes
the primary bond between the novel's characters. Brett says defensively at the
novel's end, after she has made a surely minimal gesture of doing good, "It makes
one feel rather good deciding not to be a bitch. . . . It's sort of what we have instead
of God."

As for morality—Jake wonders if it isn't simply what goads a man to feel
self-disgust after he has done something shameful.

It seems not to be generally recognized that Hemingway's classic novel owes
a good deal to F. Scott Fitzgerald's *The Great Gatsby,* which Hemingway read in
1925, after having made Fitzgerald's acquaintance, and admired greatly. Each novel
is narrated by a disaffected young man who observes but does not participate
centrally in the action; each novel traces the quixotic love of an outsider for a
beautiful if infantile woman; each is an excoriation from within of the "lost generation" and the "fiesta concept of life" (Hemingway's phrase)—the aristocratic rich
"who give each day the quality of a festival and who, when they have passed and
taken the nourishment they need, leave everything dead." Fitzgerald's Daisy is
unhappily married to the wealthy Tom Buchanan, whom Gatsby bravely challenges
for her love; Hemingway's Brett intends to marry the drunkard wealthy-bankrupt
Mike Campbell, whom the hapless Robert Cohn fights with his fists. (Cohn knocks
the inebriated Campbell down but loses Brett, at least temporarily, to a nineteen-
year-old bullfighter.) In each novel men and women set themselves the task of
being entertained, absorbed, diverted, not by work (though Jake Barnes is a newspaperman of a literary sort) but primarily by drinking and talking. Hemingway's
people in particular are obsessed with various forms of sport—golfing, tennis,
swimming, hiking, trout fishing, attending boxing matches and bullfights. And drinking. Only in Malcolm Lowry's *Under the Volcano* are drinks so rigorously cata-
logued, described: whiskey, brandy, champagne, wines of various kinds, absinthe,
liqueurs. Long passages are devoted to the correct use of the wine bag in the
Spanish Basque region: the drinker should hold the bag at arm's length, then
squeeze it so that a long stream of wine "hisses" into the back of the mouth. After
a long drunken sequence Jake thinks, "Under the wine I lost the disgusted feeling
and was happy. It seemed they were all such nice people."

As a story, *The Sun Also Rises* depends primarily upon the reader's acceptance of Jake Barnes as an intelligent and reliable observer; and of Brett in the role
of a thirty-four-year-old Circe awash in alcohol and cheery despair. Though based,
like many of Hemingway's characters, on a real person (Lady Duff Twysden, a

"legend" in Montparnasse during the time Hemingway and his first wife, Hadley, lived there), Brett is sketchily portrayed: she is "nice," "damned nice," "lovely," "of a very good family," "built with curves like the hull of a racing yacht," but the reader has difficulty envisioning her; Hemingway gives her so little to say that we cannot come to know her as a person. (Whereas Duff Twysden was evidently an artist of some talent and seems to have been an unusually vivacious and intelligent woman.) Another problematic character is the Jew Robert Cohn, who evokes everyone's scorn by "behaving badly"—he follows Brett around and intrudes where he isn't wanted. Cohn is so much the scapegoat for the others' cruelty ("That kike!" "Isn't he awful!" "Was I rude enough to him?" "He doesn't add much to the gaiety," "He has a wonderful quality of bringing out the worst in anybody") that most readers will end up feeling sympathy for him. The fact that Cohn cannot drink as heavily as the others, that the bullfight sickens him (especially the disemboweling of the picador's horse), that in this noisy macho milieu he finally breaks down and cries— these things seem altogether to his credit; he emerges as the novel's most distinctly drawn character. One waits in vain, however, for Jake Barnes to rise to Nick Carraway's judgment of Jay Gatsby: "You're worth the whole damn bunch put together."

The Sun Also Rises is a novel of manners and a homoerotic (though not homosexual) romance, merely in outline a "love story" of unconsummated passion. Like most of Hemingway's books, fiction and nonfiction, it celebrates the myste-rious bonds of masculine friendship, sometimes ritualized and sometimes sponta-neous; women are viewed with suspicion and an exaggerated awe that turns with mythic ease to contempt. Jake is happiest when he and his friend Bill are away from the company of women altogether and fishing alone in the Rio de la Fabrica valley in Spain. There they achieve a degree of intimacy impossible elsewhere. ("Listen," says Bill. "You're a hell of a good guy, and I'm fonder of you than anybody on earth. I couldn't tell you that in New York. It'd mean I was a faggot.") Of equal importance with male friendship is the worship of the matador, the master of the bull, the only person (in Hemingway's judgment) to really live his life to the full. *Afición* means passion, and an aficionado is one who feels intense passion for the bullfight. Says Jake, "Somehow it was taken for granted that an American could not have *afición*. He might simulate it or confuse it with excitement, but he could not really have it. When they saw that I had *afición*, and there was no password, no set questions that could bring it out, rather it was a sort of oral spiritual examination . . . there was this same embarrassed putting the hand on the shoulder, or a 'Buen hombre.' But nearly always there was the actual touching." Only at certain rigorously defined moments are men allowed to touch one another, just as, in the ritual of the bullfight (bloody and barbarous to those of us who are not aficionados) the tormented bull and the matador "become one" (in Hemingway's repeated phrase) at the moment of the kill. These are quite clearly sacred rites in Hemingway's private cosmology.

If many men are disturbed by Hemingway's code of ethics—as, surely, many women are disturbed by it—it is because Hemingway's exaggerated sense of maleness really excludes most men. The less than exemplary bullfighter is jeered in the ring, even if he has been gored; poor Robert Cohn, whose flaw seems to have been to have felt too deeply and too openly, is ridiculed, broken, and finally banished from the clique.

If it seems to us highly unjust that Hemingway's men and women derive their sense of themselves by excluding others and by establishing codes of behavior that enforce these exclusions, it should be recalled that Hemingway prided himself on his ability to write of things as they are, not as they might, or should, be. One can object that he does not rise above his prejudices; he celebrates *afición* where he finds it, in the postwar malaise of the 1920s and in his own enigmatic heart.

—JOYCE CAROL OATES, "The Hemingway Mystique" [1984], *(Woman) Writer: Occasions and Opportunities* (New York: E. P. Dutton, 1988), pp. 304–9

NINA SCHWARTZ

Brett is of course the perfect love object precisely because she affords so many opportunities for rivalry and its consequent evocation of desire. Collecting lovers, finding pleasure in the growing ranks of her sexual conquests, Brett can nevertheless be counted upon to return to Jake, depending upon him to define her own otherwise sordid promiscuity as the result of her tragic desire for the only man she could never have. Brett's romantic history suggests that her desire has always depended upon a master/slave dynamic: she married her husband after "her own true love" had died, thus effectively mastering her desire. Michael, her present fiancé, is someone she "nursed," as he mentions in the context of her "looking after" the wounded Romero: "But she loves looking after people. That's how we came to go off together. She was looking after me." Similarly, her relationship with Jake began when she served as a nurse in the English hospital where Jake was sent after his injury. All her lovers, though, are too easily mastered, too easily made dependent upon her. Like the dead man, only Jake, her current "own true love," remains an appropriate object of desire since he allows the maintenance of their dialectic: she must continue to want him because he can never be possessed, and his love for her legitimizes their economic relation.

Jake actually says as much when he "explains" to Brett how he feels about their affair:

> '. . . what happened to me is supposed to be funny. I never think about it.'
> 'Oh, no. I'll lay you don't.'
> 'Well, let's shut up about it. . . .
> 'It's funny,' I said. 'It's very funny. And it's a lot of fun, too, to be in love.'
> 'Do you think so?' her eyes looked flat again.
> 'I don't mean fun that way. In a way it's an enjoyable feeling.'

It's fun to be in love when one will never have to risk the degeneration of the love relation, when one will never be forced to experience the lapse of desire in its "fulfillment." One thus feels one's love object to be a compulsion, the fated and necessary complement to one's being, rather than a manufactured and mediated occasion for the experience of desire.

The success of the relation depends precisely upon its capacity to withstand the threat of satisfaction. It thus perpetuates the delusion that the two are victims of a fate beyond their control. But the control they exert is nevertheless apparent:

> She was sitting up now. My arm was around her and she was leaning back against me, and we were quite calm. She was looking into my eyes with that way she had of looking that made you wonder whether she really saw out of her own eyes. They would look on and on after every one else's eyes in the world would have stopped looking.

From whose eyes could Brett look out at Jake so dependably if not from his own, her vision here determined by Jake's power to author her as one who desires. She can be counted upon to continue looking on "after every one else's eyes in the world would have stopped looking" because she is the stable mirror of his own image. After all, looking into Brett's eyes to see what she sees, Jake would of course see only his own reflection: he masters her by effecting her castration in imitation of his own.

Jake's fury at the homosexuals who accompany Brett to a nightclub becomes clearer when we recognize the power his castration confers on him. That rage is not resentment over the homosexual's willing abnegation of the conventional male sexuality Jake has been forced to sacrifice. Rather, it results from the serious threat the homosexual might pose to Jake's privileged relation to Brett. The homosexual is the only other male figure who might be able, like Jake, to evoke in Brett a desire that he would refuse to fulfill; indeed, the homosexual lover might even be preferable to Jake, who does not refuse to satisfy Brett's desire but is physically unable to do so. If anyone might displace Jake and his authority over Brett, it would be the homosexual man, so his response is fury over the "superior" composure of the gays.

What Jake requires in the way of an effective mediator to his own desire is someone who can temporarily replace him by becoming Brett's lover. Such a displacement is necessary because the temporary gratification of Brett's sexual desire will simply convince her that the true object of her desire is unpossessed. Brett's lover's sexual potency is thus requisite to ensure his impotence and Jake's continued mastery of her. He maintains his mastery by choosing the figures who will supplant him. Even as he announces his wish that the two of them could live quietly together, Jake's manipulation of Brett is clear:

> 'Couldn't we live together, Brett? Couldn't we just live together?'

'I don't think so. I'd just *tromper* you with everybody. You couldn't stand it.'

'I stand it now.'

'That would be different. It's my fault, Jake. It's the way I'm made.'

'Couldn't we go off in the country for a while?'

'It wouldn't be any good. I'll go if you like. But I couldn't live quietly in the country. Not with my own true love.'

'I know.'

'Isn't it rotten? There isn't any use my telling you I love you.'

'You know I love you.'

'Let's not talk. Talking's all bilge. I'm going away from you, and then Michael's coming back.'

Brett's apparent willingness to give Jake up, for both their sakes, simultaneously ensures the preservation of their bond: her companion at San Sebastian will be Cohn, whom she has met through Jake and who is thus associated with her forbidden love. Cohn's displacement of Jake will only remind Brett of what she is denied and will thus guarantee her eventual return to her author.

Jake is even more clearly to be seen authoring Brett's desire for Romero. What might appear to be her "natural" fascination with the handsome boy who performs his dangerous task so gracefully is in fact a product of Jake's maneuvering. Like Pandarus's describing Troilus's exploits as if he were a character in the romance, provoking Criseyde to ask confusedly "Who yaf me drinke?" Jake composes Romero's romantic persona. The matador is already clearly associated with Jake: the trip to Pamplona is Jake's yearly pilgrimage to his "holy land," and he is marked by Montoya as one who possesses the ineffable *afición*. If Brett falls in love with Romero, it is at least partially in imitation of Jake's own passion for the boy. However, Jake carefully encourages Brett's interest:

> Brett sat between Mike and me at the barrera.... Romero was the whole show. I do not think Brett saw any other bull-fighter.... I sat beside Brett and explained to Brett what it was all about.... I had her watch how Romero took the bull away from a fallen horse with his cape, and how he held him with the cape and turned him, smoothly and suavely, never wasting the bull.... She saw why she liked Romero's cape-work and why she did not like the others.

Brett can see no other bull-fighter because Jake will not allow her to. The parallels between Jake's mastery of Brett's vision and the matador's mastery of the bull reveal the particular strategy by which Jake transfers Brett's desire toward Romero: he makes her see the matador as the seductive master of the beast's desire.

The parallels suggest an even more curious link between the bull-fight and the affair with Brett, however. Jake's representation of the bull-fight depends upon and perpetuates the same mode of interpretation that underlies his representation of castration. Jake transcends his impotence, that is, only by repressing its textuality;

now, he "naturalizes" the bull-fight. Brett instinctively recognizes the superiority of Romero's cape-work, Jake says, while he merely explains the technical skills involved in manifesting that superiority. The artifice of the cape-work, as absolute as the artifice of Jake's mastery of Brett, is denied when Jake identifies the ritual's conventions as mere tokens of the greater truths they hide. Depending upon both Brett and the reader to remain committed to the ideal of the hidden truth, Jake can thus represent the bull-fight as the formal and legitimizing account of his own struggles with castration.

—NINA SCHWARTZ, "Lovers' Discourse in *The Sun Also Rises:*
A Cock and Bull Story," *Criticism* 26, No. 1 (Winter 1984): 57–60

CAROL H. SMITH

Lady Brett Ashley in *The Sun Also Rises* is another heroine who has been wounded by love and war and yet compulsively seeks to reestablish the special world of lovers. She is one of Hemingway's bad women, a Circe who turns men into swine, but even as she invades and violates the masculine world of the matador she offers to Jake and Romero and Robert Cohn alike the supreme allurement of a beautiful woman aroused to insatiable passion. Hemingway makes clear that she cannot help herself; she, like the men she tantalizes, is sick with unrequited love. She is a threat to men because she forces them to recognize the primitiveness of their desire and the fragility of male bonding when threatened by lust, sexual need, or competition for a woman.

Lady Brett has generally been considered to differ fundamentally from Hemingway's more positive portraits of women. Carlos Baker says, for example, that though Brett and Catherine share nationality and have both lost lovers in the Great War, "here the resemblances stop":

> Brett's neurosis drives her from bar to bar, from man to man, from city to city. None of it is any good: her polygamy, with or without benefit of justices of the peace, leads only to more of the same, as one drink leads to another in the endless round. Brett is not "good" for the men she knows. Romero wants her to let her hair grow out, to become more feminine, to marry and live with him. The basic abnormality at work in Brett opposes such feminization.

It is true that her hair is bobbed, that she likes to wear male dress and to drink like the men she emulates, but beneath her pose Lady Brett bears a striking resemblance to Hemingway's other heroines. That she is sick with love is evident early in the novel when she and Jake escape from their drunken friends at the Bal Musette. Once in the cab, Brett gives up her pretense of brittle gaiety and confesses her misery and her desire for Jake.

> Brett was leaning back in the corner, her eyes closed. I got in and sat beside her. The cab started with a jerk.

"Oh, darling, I've been so miserable," Brett said.

They both struggle with the desire to be with each other and the realization that they can never be lovers. Their relationship is a study in approach-avoidance. When Brett appears drunk at Jake's flat, and when she seeks him out for help and comfort, she is following the approach arc of his vicious circle. When she goes off with other men, she hopes to find in the drug of sex a way to forget the future and the past. The Paris section of the novel is filled with negative portraits of women, the prostitute with bad teeth, rich and superficial women, and women like Frances, "bitches" who seek marriage when they have lost their looks and who destroy the freedom of men like Cohn who are cowed by them. In this company Brett appears more honest than the rest; her "abnormality" is actually a brave attempt to conceal her pain and to find substitute comforts for true love. The difference between Brett and Hemingway's good women lies not in her desperate need for love nor in her willingness to follow wherever love leads but in the degree of sexual anxiety she arouses. Dangerous as she is, like all of Hemingway's women, she is defined by love. Although she is unreliable and a drunk, she is the mirror image of Hemingway's good girls. She is a good woman the world has broken. Even so, she and Jake Barnes remain a pair: it is he she calls upon when she is in trouble and he responds by coming to her rescue. Neither Brett nor Jake can fully live the stoical code that Count Mippipopolous endorses when he says, "You see, Mr. Barnes, it is because I have lived very much that now I can enjoy everything so well" (p. 60). Being in love does not allow them the luxury of gaining the cool perspective that time and distance could provide. They attempt to fake that perspective as best they can and to keep the pain to themselves.

Brett's attempts to conceal her pain by remaining drunk or by "going off with someone" are relatively successful in the social chaos of expatriate life in Paris. In the traditional world of Spain, however, they are disruptive. Brett's dishonor is that her need for the emotional fix of an affair spills over into the public arena. Although she finally acknowledges the code of honor by sending Romero away, even Jake is stunned by the dangerousness of loving women. His famous response to her comment that they could have had "such a damned good time together" ("Yes, . . . Isn't it pretty to think so?") seems to suggest his self-disgust and his wish for disengagement.

—CAROL H. SMITH, "Women and the Loss of Eden," *Ernest Hemingway: The Writer in Context,* ed. James Nagel (Madison: University of Wisconsin Press, 1984), pp. 132–34

ADELINE R. TINTNER

There is also an interesting relationship between James's *The Ambassadors* and *The Sun Also Rises.* It is well known from Toklas's correspondence that Gertrude Stein admired the last novels of James. Hemingway must have heard those late novels, of which *The Ambassadors* is the first, praised by her, by Ford Madox Ford, and by Hadley. Be that as it may, the correspondences are very striking. In fact, Hemingway's is the only novel about Americans in Paris after James's that is also considered a masterpiece.

The opening of *The Sun Also Rises* is so close to the opening of *The Ambassadors* that it is hard to believe that Hemingway had not read it. Robert Cohn's life, summarized in the early pages of the book, is close to Strether's. Both now have been taken up by forceful women who own journals that both men edit. At the beginning of each novel that particular relationship is approaching its end as the men start really "living." Robert's speech to Jake about wanting to live is a striking condensation of Strether's speech to Little Bilham at Gloriani's party in *The Ambassadors*:

> "Listen, Jake," he leaned forward on the bar. "Don't you ever get the feeling that all your life is going by and you're not taking advantage of it? Do you realize you've lived nearly half the time you have to live already?"

Strether says: "Live all you can; it's a mistake not to. It doesn't so much matter what you do in particular, so long as you have your life. If you haven't had that what *have* you had? . . . One lives in fine as one can." Yet Strether himself refuses life and love in Paris because of a kind of emotional impotence. It is possible that Hemingway entertained the notion that Strether cannot respond to the advances of Maria Gostrey or Marie de Vionnet because of a "horrid" hurt, a real as well as spiritual impotence. This is where Robert Cohn ceases to be the only character based on Strether, for now Jake takes over the James model of the impotent writer.

As in *The Ambassadors*, all the characters in *The Sun Also Rises* are expatriates. The only important foreigner in both novels is the *femme fatale*, in one Lady Brett and in the other the Countess de Vionnet, and desperation is a characteristic of both. Marie de Vionnet says, "the only certainty is that I shall be the loser in the end." Nor is she the only loser in the book. Maria Gostrey, who loves Strether, also loses, but it is Strether who is the prime example of the "winner take nothing" motif of all Hemingway's work. At the end of *The Ambassadors* Strether rejects Miss Gostrey's proffered love: "But all the same I must go. . . . To be right. . . . That, you see, is my only logic. Not, out of the whole affair, to have got anything for myself."

When Brett goes off with the "bullfighter chap," Jake's reaction to it is like Strether's reaction to his discovery that Marie and Chad are actually lovers. Brett summons Jake, just as, after her exposure as the mistress of Chad, Marie summons Strether. Both women want to be seen through the separation from their lovers by the hero. Although their methods of enslavement vary, they tangle erotically with all the characters and have a blocked sexual relation with the impotent heroes, Strether and Barnes.

The piece that Glenway Wescott wrote for the *Hound and Horn* issue on James in 1934 is interesting in this connection for it sheds light on the attitudes of

Hemingway's group toward James's late novels. According to Wescott, they seem "to have originated in . . . excitement about some bold, sad, and scabrous problem, some overt perversity or real bad behaviour. . . . In regard to the motherly heroine, the match-making Circe, James's allusive handling raises a moral issue: if he had not somewhat expurgated his conception of her conduct as he went along, would she not have seemed simply villainous?" This point of view, which seems today too hard on Marie, may offer an understanding of the kinship between Brett and Marie, both of whom play havoc with expatriate and castrated heroes. Lady Brett is actually called Circe in the novel.

—ADELINE R. TINTNER, "Ernest and Henry: Hemingway's Lover's Quarrel with James," *Ernest Hemingway: The Writer in Context,* ed. James Nagel (Madison: University of Wisconsin Press, 1984), pp. 171–72

MIMI REISEL GLADSTEIN

Lady Brett Ashley is perhaps one of Hemingway's most attractive destructive women. Her androgynous appearance heightens rather than detracts from her sex appeal. Though she wears her hair like a man's, her figure is described as having "curves like the hull of a racing yacht," and as Jake Barnes notes, she accentuates those curves by wearing a wool jersey. She does not want to adopt a traditionally feminine hairdo and remarks cryptically to Jake that one of the things wrong with her relationship with Pedro Romero was that he wanted her to grow her hair long. "He wanted me to grow my hair out. Me, with long hair. I'd look so like hell." Not only does Brett wear her hair in a boyish bob, but she also dresses in mannish clothing. She wears a "man's felt hat" and "a slipover jersey sweater and a tweed skirt." Her bisexual image is also suggested by her first appearance in the novel. She walks into the scene with a group of her homosexual friends. Jake describes them first. They too are wearing jerseys. "With them was Brett. She looked very lovely and she was very much with them." The suggestion here is that she is very much part of this group, who are men and yet, in Jake's description, mince and gesture in parodies of femininity, masculine and feminine at the same time. Another of Brett's characteristics which acts to blur sexual distinctions is her habit of calling herself "chap." She calls men chaps—"Hello, you chaps"—and then she calls herself the same in ordering a drink—"I say, give a chap a brandy and soda."

The men in her life serve her in much the same manner as religious prostitutes served Aphrodite. First they worship at her shrine; then they prostitute themselves. Jake expresses his adoration of Brett early in the story, telling her he loves her, begging her to live with him. Afterwards, he acts the pimp for her when he sets her up with Pedro Romero. Robert Cohn calls him just that. What is worse, he corrupts his *afición;* that is to say, he prostitutes his passion in order to serve hers. The price is high. At one time he had been acknowledged as one who possessed true *afición:* "When they saw that I had afición, and there was no password, no set questions that could bring it out, rather it was a sort of oral spiritual examination . . . At once he [they] forgave me all my friends." Jake's clout with Montoya, the high priest of the bull cult, has been strong. When Jake prostitutes his *afición* by introducing Pedro Romero to the kind of woman who will, in the eyes of the *aficionados,* ruin him, Montoya will not even nod at Jake. When Jake leaves the hotel, Montoya does not come near him.

But Jake is not the only supplicant for the goddess's favor; more than one of her acolytes prostitutes himself for her. Robert Cohn, in the tradition of giving oneself to a stranger, offers himself to Brett, who is little more than a stranger to him. Once their weekend at San Sebastian is over, she rejects his attempts to give their relationship any special significance. His slavish devotion to her and doglike worship destroy his pride, earn him the animosity of the group, and leave him nothing. In his own words, "I've been through such hell, Jake. Now everything's gone. Everything." The final memento he has to carry away from his encounter with Brett is a sock in the face from Pedro Romero.

Mike Campbell is another of the men who is reduced by his association with Brett while she is affected minimally. Not much can be said for Mike's character to begin with, but it is not enhanced by his association with Brett. At the end of the book he has been "cuckolded" in a sense and left alone and penniless. In fact, he is put in the position of a kept man as Brett puts up most of the money that he gives Montoya to pay their bill in Pamplona. Mike's complete degradation is shown in his final scene with Bill Gorton and Jake Barnes when he commits the unpardonable sin of gambling without money to back his bet. He has spent the last bit of money he has buying drinks and giving extravagant tips to the bartender. His complete lack of character is explored by Bill Gorton as he establishes the fact that Mike not only did not have the money to gamble with, but that he has taken all of Brett's money and still intends to sponge off yet another acquaintance when they drop him off.

Brett's role as a goddess to be worshipped is underscored in the scene with the *riau-riau* dancers. "Brett wanted to dance but they did not want her to. They wanted her as an image to dance around." Robert Cohn articulates her fatal attraction for men. " 'He calls her Circe,' Mike said. 'He claims she turns men into swine.' " Figuratively she does just that. She calls Mike a swine for the way he treats Robert Cohn, responding to Jake's defense of Mike by saying, "Yes. But he didn't need to be a swine." Cohn's behavior is also swinish, as he follows Brett around, sniveling and squealing.

But Brett is not pure bitch-goddess. Certain aspects of her positive mothering qualities are also stressed. She had been a nurse during the war. She and Jake met in a hospital. She "nurses" Romero after his fistfight with Cohn. Mike Campbell comments about her mothering qualities, "She loves looking after people. That's how we came to go off together. She was looking after me." Her mothering role is underscored as she tries to maintain harmony in the group, placating the rivalrous siblings. She chides Mike when he is ugly to Cohn. Her effect on the men is analogous to the effect a strong mother has on her sons. Those who do not exert their independence and kill the domination of the Terrible Mother remain tied to her, thereby abdicating their manhood. Those who are strong, like Romero, who maintain their independence and their principles, are set free. Brett's choice to set Romero free is significant here. She chooses to leave him because she knows she is not good for him. In her depiction of her choice she stresses the difference in their ages. "I'm thirty-four, you know. I'm not going to be one of these bitches that ruins children."

But analyzing Brett in terms of bitch-goddess or Terrible Mother does not do justice to her. On one level, she does function in that capacity, but Hemingway has done much more with her character. In his original version of *The Sun Also Rises* Brett is more the heroine than she appears in the book as published. She is a complex woman who has suffered much and endured. Her indestructible qualities are revealed as we become aware of her past. Jake tells Cohn that she had married Lord Ashley during the war. "Her own true love had just kicked off with the dysentery." The marriage to Ashley is disastrous. According to Mike Campbell,

> Ashley, chap she got the title from, was a sailor, you know. Ninth baronet. When he came home he wouldn't sleep in a bed. Always made Brett sleep on the floor. Finally, when he got really bad, he used to tell her he'd kill her. Always slept with a loaded service revolver. Brett used to take the shells out when he'd gone to sleep. She hasn't had an absolutely happy life, Brett. Damned shame, too. She enjoys things so.

Besides these two devastating personal relationships, her love affair with Jake is a source of continuing frustration because of his inability to consummate the relationship sexually.

Her personal attractiveness and desirability are not affected by her lifestyle. The men want her regardless of her behavior. Though their self-images are dealt blows by their encounters with Brett, she remains with her illusions intact, her desirability unquestioned, and her worshippers still devoted. After he has pimped for her, corrupted his *afición,* been beat up by Cohn, disillusioned with Mike, Jake still comes the moment she beckons him. He goes to Madrid to bail her out of the hotel where she has sent Pedro Romero away though he had wanted to marry her. She claims that she would have lived with Romero if she hadn't seen that it was bad for him. Though Jake is left with next to nothing, Brett comes away from her relationship with Romero with a sense of satisfaction. Romero had loved her, wanting to marry her to prevent her from ever leaving him, but she has decided for his own good not to stay with him. "I'm not going to be that way. I feel rather good, you know. I feel rather set up." Brett is able to rationalize to herself; Jake is not. He tries to escape in drink. "Don't get drunk, Jake," she said. "You don't have to." Jake answers, "How do you know?" But even getting drunk does not help Jake. In the final scene Brett still retains the unshakable illusion that all of her problems would not have been if only she and Jake could have been married. Her "life lie" is safely entrenched. One has the sense that she will go forward to her next affair or marriage armed with the satisfaction of having decided not to be a bitch and the rationalization that all would have been well if only she could have married Jake. She is undaunted. Jake, however, is not so lucky. He does not even have the illusion of the lost chance with her to sustain him anymore. His final remark in the novel clearly indicates that. When Brett says to him, "Oh, Jake, we could have had such a damned good time together," his yes is qualified with "Isn't it pretty to think so?" The word "pretty" for a man like Jake says it all. Pretty is a woman's word. The notion that all would have been good, if only . . . , is an attractive one, a pretty notion, but it is not sound, not substantial.

—MIMI REISEL GLADSTEIN, "Hemingway," The Indestructible Woman in
Faulkner, Hemingway, and Steinbeck (Ann Arbor:
UMI Research Press, 1986), pp. 59–62

PETER GRIFFIN

In Ernest's fictional world, there were only two "real" people: himself and the woman he loved. Everyone else was shaped, modified, distorted. Everyone else played a role, or rather had one created for them. Ernest claimed that, as an artist, he did not think, he noticed—that he was objective, clinical in his observation. But everything Ernest wrote was autobiography in colossal cipher. In *The Sun Also Rises*, Ernest is most himself in Jake Barnes, the reporter with a war wound that, according to his decoration, had cost him, "more than life itself." Barnes had lost his penis in combat, but he still had his testicles. He was the quintessential twentieth-century man—alive, sensate, but without the capacity to act. Although Ernest had not been sexually mutilated in the war, he'd been rendered impotent in Pamplona. In love with Duff, passionately desirous of her, Ernest was repelled by what he saw as her vulgarities with Loeb. Yes, she was a dope addict, and needed money for her habit, money Ernest could not hope to supply. But she had acquiesced to all Loeb was, had played the romantic whore for him.

For the heroine of his novel, Ernest would use Duff. He would call her Brett Ashley, and make her a "Lady." She would have Duff's appearance and attitude, her habits and vices. There would be no mention of Duff's drug addiction—just the suggestion of a vague ennui and the mysterious need to bathe.

Ironically, Duff, in the novel, is herself an addiction—for the men she seduces. Robert Cohn calls her Circe because, he felt, she turned men into swine. Jake Barnes is "hard-boiled" with everyone, even himself, when he fights his own weakness for self-pity. But, as Robert Cohn says, Jake will play the pimp for Lady Brett. When Brett drops the bullfighter, and is alone and broke in Madrid, Jake wires he'll take the Sud Express that very night. Then he reflects: "Send a girl off with one man. Introduce her to another to go off with him. Now go and bring her back. And sign the wire with love. That was it all right. I went to lunch."

But Lady Brett Ashley is not all Duff. After reading *The Sun Also Rises*, Duff told Ernest he had "got" her pretty well, except that she hadn't "slept with the bloody bullfighter." And she hadn't. Lady Brett in *The Sun Also Rises* sleeps with the handsome young matador, Pedro Romero, because Ernest suspected Hadley wanted to make love, and perhaps had, with Cayetano Ordóñez.

⟨. . .⟩ To Ernest, a man could make love with only his body. A woman made love heart and soul. Therefore, Hadley must never be unfaithful to Ernest. In deed or even in desire. If she were, she would break their bond of innocence. Hadley, in her attempt to "fight fire with fire," to make Ernest as jealous of her desire for Ordóñez as she had been of his for Duff, had, Ernest felt, broken the bond. In the novel, Brett allows Jake to use, when needed, a cherished illusion of Ernest's youth—he is her "one and only love." It is an illusion Jake denies at the end, but only temporarily. Jake Barnes and Lady Brett, the reader understands, will go on and on. But Ernest and Hadley would not.

—PETER GRIFFIN, "No Swan So Fine," *Less Than a Treason: Hemingway in Paris*
(New York: Oxford University Press, 1990), pp. 113–15

MICHAEL REYNOLDS

Before leaving Valencia, ⟨Hemingway⟩ got all the characters but Niño set up: Duff ⟨Brett⟩, Cohn, Jake, Bill Gorton, Mike Campbell. He also got a couple of the Quarterites fixed to his page like rare specimens. He changed Ford and Stella Bowen into the bumbling Braddocks who could not recognize a whore when they met one. First, he let Jake pick up a *poule* for supper conversation and then take her to one of Ford's *bal musette* parties where he introduced her as Georgette Leblanc. It was Jake's joke. Georgette Leblanc was a singer and the loving friend for whom Margaret Anderson had left Jane Heap. Even better, no one at the *dancing* got the joke, only the reader.

Then Duff arrived in the company of homosexuals, which did not surprise Hemingway's Left Bank readers who recognized the *bal musette* in rue de la Montagne Sainte Geneviève as a homosexual bar. Hemingway had cut out most of Jake's remarks about the "fairies" who flitted about the Quarter in swarms, but this part would stand up. Taking in the white hands and wavy hair of Brett's entourage, the policeman at the door smiled at Jake: there was no need to say anything. And "with them was Duff." Inside, the two men immediately spotted Georgette.

"I do declare. There is an actual harlot. I'm going to dance with her, Lett. You watch me."

The tall dark one called Lett said: "Now don't you be rash."

That was enough: readers in the Quarter would recognize Arthur Lett-Haines, lover of Cedric Morris the painter, and Ernest's neighbors on Notre-Dame-des-Champs. Jake arrived by taxi with a whore; Duff by taxi with homosexuals. Duff and Jake departed together by taxi, leaving the white-handed young man with wavy hair dancing with the *poule*.

—MICHAEL REYNOLDS, "Summer of the Sun," *Hemingway: The Paris Years*
(Oxford: Basil Blackwell, 1989), pp. 310–11

DENIS BRIAN

GEORGE SELDES: Duff Twysden used to boast that she was the bitch "Lady Brett" in the *The Sun Also Rises.*

HAROLD LOEB: Duff tried to pretend she didn't much mind his picture of her, but I heard from others that she minded a bit. She was quite something. Hemingway made her into a tramp. I don't think she was at all. He made her promiscuous, a drunkard, all of which I can't support. She was elegant in a way.

DENIS BRIAN: By not being promiscuous do you mean she wouldn't sleep with a man unless she liked him?

HAROLD LOEB: I suppose. I can't prove it. ⟨. . .⟩

GEORGE SELDES: I can certainly understand Harold Loeb and Hemingway being fascinated by Duff Twysden. I met her in Paris when I was working for the *Chicago Tribune,* and living in a two-dollar-a-day room at the Hotel Liberia. No telephone. The concierge yelled up there's a call for me. There were two women there. One was the Countess Modici, who had been a friend of Vincent Sheean, a newspaperman, in Rome. She said, "This is Duff Twysden." And Duff said, "How would you like to join us and Captain Paterson at a nightclub?" Countess Modici had a great love affair with a man with whom she tried to cross the English channel in a rowboat—it's a great story. Duff was fascinating, and I thought I was honored to be invited to her party. As the evening drew on and the third expensive bottle of champagne was drunk, the two women had to go to the ladies' room. That didn't surprise me. Then Captain Paterson said he had to go to the men's room. And I sat there. This is an old holdup game. I always thought I was a tough newspaperman, but this had never happened to me before. A half hour went by and the waiter handed me a bill for something like fifty dollars for all the champagne, most of which had been drunk before I arrived. I never saw any of them again. And that's how I got stuck by Duff Twysden. That's my Lady Brett story. She was the kind of gal almost everybody falls for, like a Ziegfeld girl. They're picked for their universal attraction to men.

DENIS BRIAN: Duff Twysden eventually married artist Clinton King and died in Texas of tuberculosis when she was forty-five. Hemingway told [A. E.] Hotchner that Duff's pallbearers had all been her lovers, one of whom slipped on the church steps, dropping the casket which split open. A likely story! She was cremated.

—DENIS BRIAN, "The Sun Also Burns," *The True Gen: An Intimate Portrait of Ernest Hemingway by Those Who Knew Him* (New York: Grove Press, 1988), pp. 58, 60–61

CRITICAL ESSAYS

Robert W. Lewis

TRISTAN OR JACOB?

My Love is of a birth as rare
As 'tis for object strange and high:
It was begotten by despair
Upon Impossibility.
                    —Andrew Marvell, "The Definition of Love"

Love in her Sunny Eyes does basking play;
    Love walks the pleasant Mazes of her Hair;
Love does on both her Lips for ever stray;
And *sows* and *reaps* a thousand *kisses* there.
In all her outward parts *Love's* always seen;
    But, oh, He never went within.
                    —Abraham Cowley, "The Change"

*T*he *Sun Also Rises* was Hemingway's first serious venture into the craft of the novel, and in some ways the 1926 novel may be his best. The style is wonderfully controlled; there is no self-consciousness, no self-imitation; the characters are well-conceived and executed; and there is the feeling if not the certainty of multiple levels of meaning to the story. In short, the novel is an esthetic success.

As a reflection of its times it is also valuable, providing as it does a detailed historical picture of the expatriates and the self-styled lost generation that Hemingway referred to in his epigraph from Gertrude Stein. (In fact, one of his sensitive readers felt compelled to defend himself from a too-exact identification of himself with the Robert Cohn of the novel.)[1]

But in terms of Hemingway's present canon and the themes of love in his work as a whole, the interest of the novel is more than esthetic or historical. In *The Sun*

From *Hemingway on Love* (Austin: University of Texas Press, 1965), pp. 19–35.

Also Rises, the dominant themes that run through all of Hemingway's novels begin to emerge. The emphases of the different themes will vary as will the images which he will use to convey them, but basically the subject of Hemingway's novels has been chosen in this first novel, and that subject is love. If it were not for gradually changing attitudes toward that subject, the canon might truly be as monotonous as Hemingway's deprecators say it is, but with each novel some changes are evident, though the themes are familiar from *The Sun Also Rises* on.

Most simply, the love themes can be divided into three: eros, agape, and romantic love. (Supplementary classifications such as loneliness and love of nature can be seen as variations found from novel to novel in greater or lesser degree.) Using the threefold division in viewing *The Sun Also Rises,* one can see that it is not so much a novel about eros as it is about romantic love. Sex is surely of paramount interest to the characters, but to Hemingway, eros in this novel is secondary. It is as if Hemingway was carefully testing three views of love, and in this first novel romantic love is examined and rejected. Eros will subsequently receive a similar scrutiny, but in *The Sun Also Rises* it is as yet in the background, as is agape, the third and ultimately accepted form of love.

Further, the method of this first novel is much more heavily ironical than that of the work of the middle and later Hemingway. Thus one can see Hemingway destroying romantic illusions much more easily than one can see the construction of positive ideals. In terms of the later Hemingway as well as in terms of the second, more hopeful, epigraph from Ecclesiastes, it is possible to read into *The Sun Also Rises* foreshadowing of the rebirth of love; but mainly the impression of the novel is negative. Loss rather than eternal return and renewal is clearly more strongly felt, in spite of the title and the Biblical epigraph. The irony seems a natural shield for this loss as well as for the novelist's and the hero's sensitivity, self-pity, and lack of a constructive, positive faith to fill the void. To keep from blubbering when a Brett presses against one's sexless body and moans, "Oh, Jake . . . we could have had such a damned good time together," one must hide behind the thin hard shield of irony and say, as Jake does, "Isn't it pretty to think so?"[2]

Jake *is* in desperate straits, but Hemingway reminds us, through Bill Gorton, that irony and pity are, after all, a little cheap: "Don't you know about Irony and Pity? . . . They're mad about it in New York. It's just like the Fratellinis [a team of circus acrobats] used to be" (114).

For all his worldly wisdom, his being an *aficionado,* his wide experience and skills, and his interesting friends, Jake Barnes strikes one as almost deserving of being indicted by Bill's jocular observations:

> "You're an expatriate. You've lost touch with the soil. You get precious. Fake European standards have ruined you. You drink yourself to death. You become obsessed by sex. You spend all your time talking, not working. You are an expatriate, see? You hang around cafes."
>
> "It sounds like a swell life," I said. "When do I work?"

"You don't work. One group claims women support you. Another group claims you're impotent." (115)

In his essay, "The Death of Love in *The Sun Also Rises*," Mark Spilka explains that Jake as well as Cohn is a romantic, but that Jake's romanticism is a partially hidden weakness while Cohn's is public. Jake, Spilka continues, stands as an unhappy medium between the extremes of the Romantic Hero Cohn and the Code Hero Romero, the young bullfighter. The assumption is, of course, that romantic love is dead and that Cohn's clinging to it and Jake's failure to break away from an old reverence for and delight in it are stupid, silly weaknesses with no place in the "real" world.[3]

It would seem more accurate to say that *The Sun Also Rises* is not so much about the death of love as it is about its sickness, a sickness unto death, but by no means a fatal illness. As has been demonstrated by Denis de Rougemont in *Love in the Western World*, romantic love is still very much alive. More pertinently, in Hemingway's novel the chief proponent of it, Cohn, is complemented by Jake and Brett, whose frustrated love is much more like the traditional love of a Tristan and Iseult than is the idealistic love of Cohn for Brett. Furthermore Spilka fails to point out the survival and strength of agape or brotherly love among the characters. It is a love that is overshadowed by the clearly central romantic love, that is true, but its presence is definite, and in perspective it assumes importance and foreshadows its emergence in the later Hemingway.

The central theme of romantic love is expressed most clearly in the character of Robert Cohn, a well-to-do expatriate and a would-be professional writer. Robert Stephens calls him Hemingway's Don Quixote, but it would be more accurate to call him Hemingway's first Tristan, for he is much more obsessed with love than Don Quixote ever was, and much less concerned with idealism in spheres beyond love's compass. Hemingway explicitly compares Cohn to a medieval chivalric knight when he describes him in the Pamplona brawl with Mike Campbell as "proudly and firmly waiting for the assault, ready to do battle for his lady love" (178). Cohn's view of Brett as a golden-haired angel is of course ridiculous, as Jake and the others see it, but Cohn's whole life with women has been molded on principles different from those of the other expatriates. And Cohn, Jake knows, is very stubborn; he will not surrender his ideals simply because others laugh at him and harbor other, equally misguided, ideals—or anti-ideals.

Lest one think that Cohn is not the pivotal character, if not the central one, Hemingway devotes the first two chapters of this economical novel to a history of Cohn's past and recent life. Like some subsequent Hemingway heroes, from Francis Macomber to Colonel Cantwell, Cohn had been married to a bitch. Presently, he has a mistress, Frances Clyne, to whom Jake satirically refers as Cohn's "lady," and she is another bitch. As Jake views it, Cohn has acquired her, as he did his wife, not because of love but because of convenience and style; as Frances says, "Robert's always wanted to have a mistress"—the idea of a mistress is what appealed to Cohn (51).

I am sure he had never been in love in his life.

He had married on the rebound from the rotten time he had in college, and Frances took him on the rebound from his discovery that he had not been everything to his first wife. He was not in love yet but he realized that he was an attractive quantity to women, and that the fact of a woman caring for him and wanting to live with him was not simply a divine miracle. This changed him so that he was not so pleasant to have around. (8–9)

Further, Cohn has, like Don Quixote, learned his way of life from books, specifically W. H. Hudson's *The Purple Land.*

It recounts splendid imaginary amorous adventures of a perfect English gentleman in an intensely romantic land, the scenery of which is very well described. For a man to take it at thirty-four as a guide-book to what life holds is about as safe as it would be for a man of the same age to enter Wall Street direct from a French convent, equipped with a complete set of the more practical Alger books. Cohn, I believe, took every word of "The Purple Land" as literally as though it had been an R. G. Dun report. (9)

It is not unexpected that he would marry the wrong woman and have no forewarning that she might leave him, or that he would acquire Frances, with whom he has so little in common, or that he would fall in love "at first sight" with Brett—like Iseult someone else's woman, and like Quixote's servant girl misunderstood, not seen for the base thing she really is. Love for Cohn, as for all Tristans, is a sickness. It affects the mind and the body. It dominates and one becomes a slave to it. One is in love with love. As in the words of a popular song of the late thirties, "This can't be love because I feel so well." So Jake knows Cohn is in love when the latter's tennis game goes "all to pieces" (45). He must suffer, and the more he suffers, the happier (theoretically) he will be.

Even his break with Frances is needlessly prolonged and painful, almost as if Cohn enjoyed his mistress' acrimony: " 'We have dreadful scenes, and he cries and begs me to be reasonable, but he says he just can't do it [marry Frances]' " (47).

Frances in her turn fails to see the contradiction of her desire to marry Cohn. Now that she sees her prey slipping away, she realizes their two-and-a-half-year courtship has been a waste to her; when Jake defends Cohn to her, she replies that he doesn't know the real selfishness of Cohn, and then she caustically insults Cohn to his face in Jake's presence. In practical terms, her futile pursuit of security and wealth has been a waste of time, and her labeling of Cohn as selfish and cruel is not simply sour grapes. But how such realistic views, that could be reconciled to marriage, contrast with the ideal of wedded bliss! Frances perceives Cohn's real reason for not marrying his mistress: "if he marries me . . . that would be the end of all the romance" (51). And since Frances, aging a bit, her figure and face fading, sees little future as an Iseult, she is not afraid of touching on the truth of Cohn's actions.

In Book II, Cohn's Tristanizing can have free play. He has had his little fling with Brett (a *real* English lady), and now that the preliminary amour is over, he can get down to serious suffering, which is the joy of romantic love. Where Tristan had only King Mark as a rival, Cohn luxuriates in having as rivals for Brett's love Mike, her fiancé; Pedro Romero, her current lover; Jake, her handicapped but constant lover; and assorted peripheral admirers such as Bill Gorton and the ghost of her first true love, dead of dysentery in the War. Just as he endured having Frances berate him in front of Jake, so Cohn endures great abuse from his so-called friends at the Pamplona fiesta. Brett's lovers have various claims on her, but Cohn's claim is honored by the tradition with which he is imbued: he will play his role knowingly and well, accepting ridicule (141–142), but at the same time asserting the superiority earned by his suffering (162). He has no armed battles to fight, no guarded boudoirs to broach, but he is faithful to the principle of love. Mike brutally insults him:

> His face had the sallow, yellow look it got when he was insulted, but somehow he seemed to be enjoying it. The childish, drunken heroics of it. It was his affair with a lady of title. (178)

Finally even Brett is rude to him and drives him off. His best friend, Jake, has come to hate him, and specifically they hate him because he suffers (182).

When Cohn is finally driven to do real combat for his lady love, he then discovers the ineffectuality of his role. Having been a middleweight boxing champion in college, Cohn has no trouble winning separate pugilistic jousts with Jake, Mike, and Pedro Romero, who has displaced Cohn in Brett's affections, Cohn thinks. But the courageous Romero, though beaten badly, refuses to yield graciously. He promises to kill Cohn, and Brett refuses to leave with the Pyrrhic victor. No one plays it as it is in the movies or in W. H. Hudson's *The Purple Land.* The script has been rewritten, and no one told Cohn that his role was thrown out.

> That damn Cohn. He should have hit somebody the first time he was insulted, and then gone away. He was so sure that Brett loved him. He was going to stay, and true love would conquer all. (199)

Jake makes fun of Cohn's chivalric suffering, but his and Brett's notions of love are just as insidious, perhaps more so because of their hypocrisy and their concealment of their notions behind a tough facade. Jake clearly views Cohn as a misguided romantic, and by dating the whore Georgette he denies to Brett that *he* is getting romantic: he is bored, not romantic (23). But Brett and Jake follow the pattern of Tristan and Iseult with little variation. Theirs is a hopeless love, the course of which is filled with the obstacles of love: rivals aplenty, Jake's maiming wound, and Jake's mixed allegiances. Tristan's problems were similar. One could even imagine Georgette as a type of Iseult of the White Hand, the first Iseult's (Brett's) rival.

But the chief parallel is not in action or characters but in the common theme of suffering for love, of being possessed by love and made its slave, of having no love except outside the bonds of marriage, and of the spiritualization of love or its severance from man's animal nature. Cohn's sufferings are academic; he goes literally by the book, and that is, no doubt, why he is scorned. Brett and Jake are really sick with love. And thus the essential comedy of the whole story—of any romantic love story—in which the lovers claim a special role and ask for a special sympathy because they are really crazy (only *they* are entitled, they would seem to plead, to belittle the scapegoat Cohn who plays at insanity but really isn't mad, as they are). Once after extended classroom discussion of this novel, a prettily smiling coed asked, "If Jake and Brett are really in love, why don't they get married?" More worldly students grinned and guffawed, but the coed had, inadvertently, no doubt, asked a very intelligent question on the mythic level.

The success and continued acclaim of the novel is remarkable in that Hemingway has created such a convincing version of an old theme that is usually read as an attack on the old Tristan and Iseult story—the death of love in *The Sun Also Rises*—but this story is of a sick love, a hypochondriac love, of lovers who enjoy poor health, poor love, sick love. But the love never dies.

At Brett and Jake's first meeting in the novel, the lovers escape from their friends at a dance to be alone. The action and tone are greatly restrained, but there is no mistaking the source of Brett's pleading cry: "Oh, darling, I've been so miserable" (24). There is more than frustrated eros in the scenes in which Brett and Jake are alone. After all, Brett has slept with just about whoever pleased her. Jake's wound is presumably not an emasculation but the loss of his penis, and thus he has no accompanying loss or diminution of sexual desire.[4] Tristan's wound was only symbolically castrative, and he voluntarily abstained from intercourse with Iseult even when there were no obstacles to his pleasure. But Jake can never have intercourse with Brett; his predicament is a little laughable, as Jake himself points out (26). And to the ancient Greeks who regarded romantic love as a sickness and a calamity, his wound would be funny, but it is not funny to the romanticist who lives for love.

Brett is compelled by her love for Jake; she has no freedom. She kisses him and then she breaks away from him because she "can't stand it." She turns "all to jelly" when he touches her, and she has a look in her eyes as if she were possessed. Apparently they have tried to find some method of mutual physical relief that was a "hell" that ended in failure, but when Jake suggests that they "keep away from each other," Brett insists, " 'But darling, I have to see you. It isn't all that [sex] you know.' "

" 'No, but it always gets to be.' "

Then they discuss Jake's wound:

> "It's funny," I said. "It's very funny. And it's a lot of fun, too, to be in love."
> "Do you think so?" her eyes looked flat again.

"I don't mean fun that way. In a way it's an enjoyable feeling."
"No," she said. "I think it's hell on earth."
"It's good to see each other."
"No. I don't think it is."
"Don't you want to?"
"I have to." (26–27)

Brett is compelled to torture herself and to enjoy her torment. Before rejoining their friends she asks Jake for just one more kiss.

When he retires that night, he looks at his body in the mirror, thinks some more of his problem, thinks that Brett "only wanted what she couldn't have," cries, finally falls asleep, and is shortly awakened, at four-thirty, by the drunken Brett's arrival with Count Mippipopolous. She simply must torture herself about Jake, that unattainable commodity, even if it means being rude and thoughtless, that is, lacking respect for her love object—in effect, having passion, lacking agape. And Jake, though knowing Brett for what she is, is still touched by her presence (30–34).

In short, though Jake perceives the folly of their relationship more sharply than Brett does, he nonetheless submits to the tyranny of romantic love. Telling Cohn about Brett, Jake with conscious irony says that during the war Brett's "own true love . . . kicked off with the dysentery" (39). The idealistic Cohn won't believe Brett would subsequently marry anyone she didn't love, but Jake, accepting the terms of the adulterous Tristan-Iseult love, says that Brett has already married twice without love.

Later that same day it is Brett's turn to use the phrase "true love," and she of course applies it to Jake during one of their frequent scenes of misery. They avow their love for one another, and they think what a "bad time" they have because of their consummate inconsummable love. With her love vow on her lips and un-known to Jake, Brett is planning her trip to San Sebastian where she will have a brief fling with Robert Cohn, Jake's friend, before her fiancé (whom she later admits she hasn't thought of in a week) returns from Britain! Jake wants to try living together with Brett, but, says Brett, it is better for Jake and better for her that they live apart (55).

Jake hates Cohn and is jealous of him when he learns of his tryst with Brett (she herself casually tells Jake of the affair). A King Mark like Mike Campbell is one thing, but Iseult shouldn't "take up social service," as Jake sarcastically says (84). Yet Jake still "loves" her, and his passion again returns to submerge his irony and bitterness. On his fishing trip with Bill Gorton, he reads a romantic novel by A. E. W. Mason, and once more Jake ironically uses the phrase "true love" (120). He realizes the comic stupidity of the "wonderful" story in which a man falls into a glacier and his bride waits twenty-four years "for his body to come out on the moraine," but still he voluntarily chooses to read the story. He begins to protest too much. Like many another denigrator, Jake accompanies his irony with a large amount of pity, in this case, self-pity. Both Jake and Brett have to let others know how they suffer; so Jake tells Bill about his love for Brett, and Brett tells Mike about her affairs, and tells Jake about her new-found passion for Pedro Romero. At the same time, she has to know if *Jake* still loves her (183), for he is still the only person she has (no doubt because he is the only person she has not "had" and never can have). She apparently justifies her promiscuity and torture of Jake, her true love, on the grounds of her unique role; she is the fair lady and, tortured by love herself, her role is to torture, to be, as Cohn calls her, a Circe.

Only after Jake acts as her pimp with Romero does he finally begin to emerge from his passive role, and it is Cohn who has to label Jake for what he is (190). Of course, in resorting to violence, Cohn also plays the fool, but after his Quixotic fights with Jake, Mike, and Romero, Jake's attitudes seem to clear. The progress of the book is toward a frenzied, idiotic climax of action and "romance" at the end of the fiesta. Afterwards there is calmness, cleanliness, catharsis—at least for Jake. His love for Brett has undergone a subtle change. From unreasoning passion it has gone through a period of bitter awareness to an ending which describes a relationship of responsibility and care. Passion is submerged if not subdued.

That is, there is the growing presence of agape in the course of the novel, and it is finally extended to include the two great lovers themselves; the lovers are at last ready to love. In Book I, the epitome of love was Count Mippipopolous, a phony Greek count who is "one of us," (32), as Brett says, because he has taste, manners, the right values, and above all, past sufferings (60). The Count is "always in love" (61), for love too has a place in his system of values. The Count is a charming host, but in spite of his frankness Brett and Jake never become intimate with him. He remains an eccentric.

In Book II, the focus of this other possibility of love is Bill Gorton, Jake's writer friend who goes fishing with him before the fiesta. Gorton is significantly different from the expatriates in that he has remained at home and he works. He is productive as are none of the others except Jake himself. Perhaps the symbol of this difference is the sport of fishing—the fish themselves representing a kind of fertility. Bill and Jake meet a materialistic tourist and a border guard (a representative of authority) who do not care for fishing. Cohn is not keen for it either, and Brett and Mike don't arrive in time to join Bill and Jake as scheduled. Without the parasitic, unloving others, Bill and Jake have a splendid, carefree trip. Their mutual affection is complemented by their easy friendship with the pastoral Basques with whom they ride in a bus into the green, undefiled mountains where the fast, cold trout stream runs. They also meet the pleasant Wilson-Harris, another fisherman, another disciple of the sexless brotherhood of man, who is greatly touched by Bill and Jake's friendliness. The trouble is that the Burguete interlude is just that—an idyllic escape into an unreal world of simple military or boyhood relationships. One must go back to work, and one must go back to a more complicated, sexual society where women rather than fish contest with the lovers.

Back at Pamplona, then, Jake assumes a new social role that can be seen as a maturing of the uncomplicated, male love of fellow fishermen. At the fiesta the parallels between Jake and the sexless steers that herd the fertile bulls have been prepared for by the earlier establishment of parallels between Jake and Ecclesiastes, literally the Preacher of "steer" of the Old Testament.

Because of the title of the novel and its second epigraph, one may assume that Hemingway read the book of Ecclesiastes. Like the Hebrew writer living in another Waste Land, Hemingway too was skeptical and pessimistic, and his hero Jake Barnes had the same doubts and the same sharp awareness of transiency and death.[5] Learning and wisdom are futile, for God's ways are mysterious, the Preacher says (Eccles. 7:16, 8:17, 11:5, 12:12). "Time and chance happeneth to . . . all" (Eccles. 9:11). In the midst of prosperity and life is the seed of desolation and death (Eccles. 12:1–7). There are, however, some positive values to cling to: food and drink are good (Eccles. 2:3, 2:24–26, 5:18–20, 8:15, 9:7, 10:19); companionship and fellowship are good—"two are better than one" (Eccles. 4:9–12); a wise man has heart, but a fool does not (Eccles. 10:2); a good name is desirable—one should live by the "code" (Eccles. 7:1); this means, in part, helping others (Eccles. 11:1–2); in spite of impermanence and futility, life is sweet (Eccles. 9:4–6). The direct parallels are extended and consistent.

Like the author of Ecclesiastes, Jake Barnes is alienated from his faith, Catholicism, which he clings to but cannot sincerely practice. Pragmatically, it does not work, but it seems to offer to fill the void in his spirit, and he wants it to work. In Jake, Hemingway is moving from the even more complete lack of faith of Frederic Henry in *A Farewell To Arms* to the more complete acceptance of Robert Jordan (with a Biblical allusion in his last name) in *For Whom the Bell Tolls* and of the Catholic fisherman Santiago in *The Old Man and the Sea*. The reader is reminded that "Jake" is "a hell of a biblical name" (22), and if one should add up the total of all Hemingway heroes, one could see Jake Barnes as the first stage of the composite hero's parallel of Jacob's life, which ran the cycle of sin and fraud in youth, much suffering and then repentance in maturity, and final exaltation of God's ways in his old age.

Another possible parallel occurs in Book II where the setting shifts to San Sebastian. It is there that Brett goes for her fling with Cohn and later for a pre-honeymoon with Mike. It is also the place where Jake goes after the Pamplona fiesta (Book III). Saint Sebastian and Jake have significant ironic similarities: the saint was martyred during a Roman saturnalia—Jake goes through agony because of his impotence and Brett's great sexuality; after being stoned and shot through with arrows (equivalent to Jake's suffering), Sebastian was nursed back to health by a devout woman—Brett has not only destructive but recuperative powers upon Jake, Cohn, and Mike. Of taking Cohn to San Sebastian, she says it was "good for him" (83), and Jake says she was probably good for Pedro Romero too (241). She literally does nurse Romero back to health, just as she had nursed Jake when she first met him in a hospital during the war (38); "She loves looking after people," Mike says (203). Furthermore, in sacred art Sebastian is usually depicted as a young soldier, which Jake once was. In these parallels, even if the details are extravagant,

the general image of martyrdom is clear enough, and Brett's complexity is emphasized.

Jake is one even mildly religious character in the central group of characters.
He is, however, only "technically" Catholic, he explains (124). Like the Preacher
of Ecclesiastes, he is skeptical and yet devout; he does not believe, but he wants
to believe. He goes through the motions of his faith hoping that somehow it will
succeed in giving him an anchor in his disintegrating worldly milieu. Jake is world-
weary as the Preacher is: "All things have I seen in the days of my vanity" (Eccles.
7:15), but, also like the Preacher, Jake does not completely abandon his god.
Thus Jake, though bitterly, considers the Church's counsel regarding sex—"don't
think of it"—and is always noting and visiting churches. Notre Dame in Paris was
"squatting against the night sky" (77), a personification picturing Mary in a bestial
pose. On his trip to Spain, another Catholic country, he "took a look at the
cathedral" in Bayonne, France (90). He notes churches in Spain, and Pamplona is
a city of churches with a "great brown cathedral, and the broken skyline of the
other churches" (93–94). A monastery dominates Burguete where Jake and Bill
go fishing; it is up in the mountains, like Kilimanjaro "cold" and "high" (108). Jake
notes a steel engraving of Nuestra Señora de Roncesvalles in his Burguete room
(109), and later Bill, "good old Wilson-Harris," and he visit the monastery. Bill and
Harris admit they are "not much on those sort of places," but Jake says nothing
(128).

In Pamplona Jake goes to church remarkably often for a skeptic. He first
thought the facade of the cathedral ugly, but he later liked it, and it is "dim and dark"
and peaceful inside. Jake prays there in a rather naive manner, but at least he prays
and thinks about praying, regretting that he is "such a rotten Catholic" but holding
out some hope of being a better one in the future (96–97). After returning to
Pamplona, Jake casually mentions going to church "a couple of times, once with
Brett" (150). Jake implies that he still confesses himself, for Brett wants to witness
his confession. Jake says she could not and adds, significantly, that "it would be in a
language she did not know" (151). Both literally—it would be in Spanish—and
figuratively the Brett who then goes to the pagan rite of having her fortune told
cannot understand his faith. Even in the excitement of the festival, Jake continues to
go to church; he goes to mass the first day of the fiesta, noting that the saturnalian
"San Fermin is also a religious festival" that begins with a big religious procession
which Jake apparently followed (153, 155). Once more he goes to church with
Brett, and once more the pagan fertility bitch-goddess is rejected: she has no hat,
no symbol of deference. But outside in the bright sunlight she realizes her role as
the dancing Spaniards form a gay circle of homage around her: "They wanted her
as an image to dance around" (155). The church remains as a backdrop for the
frenzied action. Jake walks as far as the church, once by himself and once with Brett
(156, 182). A third time he and Brett go to church "Where the show started on
Sunday" (208). Brett tries to pray for Romero, but she stiffens and becomes
"damned nervous. . . . I'm damned bad for a religious atmosphere," she says (208).

Jake jokes about praying, but he also says praying works for him and he is "pretty religious" (209). Later Jake tells Brett that "some people have God" (245).

Jake also apparently likes to bathe, to purify or rebaptize himself. Brett too rushes off to bathe several times: "Must clean myself. . . . Must bathe," she says after returning from her vacation with Cohn (74), and after a night in a hotel (that looks like a brothel) with her fiancé Mike, she also "must bathe" (83). Twice during the wild fiesta she also has to bathe (144, 159). The other romantic, Cohn, also tries to wash away his dirt after his brief affair with Brett (81, 96, 97). But it is Jake who makes almost a ritual, like baptism, out of bathing. After the disappointing, fight-marred end of the partly pagan fiesta, Jake returns to the fertile sea for purification. Hemingway describes at length two swims: the water is green, dark, and cold (235); it is also buoyant—"It felt as though you could never sink" (237). After the renewal of the sea, Jake is ready to answer the call of help from those without even his tentative faith, once more to play the role of sexless priest and steer for his friends, his "parish," his "herd."

In addition to these more or less direct allusions to Ecclesiastes in particular and Judeo-Christian attitudes in general—especially to agape—Jake's relation to bullfighting is also fraught with religious overtones, as is bullfighting itself. As with the story of Saint Sebastian, the Roman, or pagan, and Christian elements overlap. Bullfighting was a favorite sport in imperial Rome, and Pedro Romero's last name hints at a Roman root even if there is no etymological connection. The *espadas* pass through a trying novitiate just as priests do before they may perform publicly. The pomp and brilliance of costume and decoration in the *plaza de toros* parallels the richness of dress and the colorful setting of the Catholic Church. In the *corrida de toros* itself there are the trinities of the triple mule team, of the *espadas*, of the *suertes* or divisions of the fight, and of the bulls, each fighter usually getting three in one afternoon. The *suertes* divide into lancing, planting the darts, and killing, with parallels to the Crucifixion that Hemingway would specifically refer to in the later novels *Across the River and into the Trees* and *The Old Man and the Sea*.

Pedro Romero stays in a room whose two beds are "separated by a monastic partition" (163), and, as with a priest, his retinue believes that women will corrupt the young bullfighter. Montoya, Jake's *aficionado* friend, observes that "He shouldn't mix in that stuff" (172). The very word *afición*—"aficion means passion" (131)—recalls the similarity of love imagery in the language of the Catholic Church since the Middle Ages. Those who are *aficionados* have a secret fellowship that is discovered by "a sort of oral spiritual examination" concluded by a laying on of hands: "nearly always there was the actual touching. It seemed as though they wanted to touch you to make it certain" (132). If you had *afición*, like faith, anything could be forgiven you, as Montoya initially forgives Jake his friends who lack it. It seems significant that of Jake's friends it is the Jewish Cohn who is the least interested in the *corrida;* he is even afraid he might be bored (162). Like the revered blood of Christ and the symbolic Communion wine, the blood of the bullfights disturbs only the uninitiated; Brett learns from Jake how to watch and then comments, "Funny. . . . How one doesn't mind the blood" (211). Also remindful of the Passion is the sense of tragedy that the *aficionados* derive from the fights: "People went . . . to be given tragic sensations" (214).

Hemingway once circumvented the question of parallels between the bullfight and the characters, but he does have Jake make a comparison between one bull and a boxer, which Cohn once was (139), and the parallels are instructive.[6] Jake's relation to his friends is paralleled by the steers' role in the *corridas*. The sexless steers—"like old maids"—quiet the bulls in the corrals and keep them from fighting. Sometimes the steers are gored by the bulls. "Can't the steers do anything?" Bill asks. "No," Jake answers. "Must be swell being a steer," Bill later adds (133). At the corral Brett observes that the steers don't look happy, but the bull is "beautiful." The bulls, like Jake's sexually active friends, "are only dangerous when they're alone, or only two or three of them together" (140). Bill makes the analogy clear when he says, "Don't you ever detach me from the herd," and Cohn says, "It's no life being a steer" (141). In the end, Jake's role as a steer is once more demonstrated when he rescues Brett. Jake recalls that he was the one who introduced the bitch-goddess to one bull, Cohn, and later to another bull, Romero. Then he must go fetch her back to the custody of still another bull, Mike (239). The Catholic priest is also celibate, also has a role of explaining ritual to the uninitiated, of confirming and blessing (laying on of hands), and of protecting his flock—his "herd," if you will.

Ecclesiastes once more provides the text and enlightening parallels that Hemingway must have been aware of. Men are like beasts: "they themselves are beasts. For that which befalleth the sons of men befalleth beasts . . ." (Eccles. 3:18–19). The Biblical Preacher, like Jake, believes it is good to study death, which is the real subject of the bullfight. Further, the Preacher sees that the battle is not to the strong—the bulls—as the race is not to the swift, nor riches to men of understanding (Eccles. 9:11). Thus a good man—a good preacher, a good steer—must help others: "Cast thy bread upon the waters; for thou shalt find it after many days," as Jake does, and a good man must be content in God's wisdom (Eccles. 11:1). All may be vanity, but yet man does not know the ways of God: ". . . thou knowest not what is the way of the spirit . . ." (Eccles. 11:5). Though he may not be a bull, a live steer is better than a dead bull, just as "a living dog is better than a dead lion," another beast symbolic of eros (Eccles. 9:4). Even more startling is the suggestion in Ecclesiastes that a man (Jake) is lucky to be sexless, for woman is a trap: "And I find more bitter than death the woman, whose heart is snares and nets, and her hands as bands: whoso pleaseth God shall escape from her; but the sinner shall be taken by her" (Eccles. 7:26). Jake may be unhappy, but he is not tormented by Brett in the way Mike, Cohn, and Romero are; they know they are able to possess Brett. To Cohn, at least, Brett is quite appropriately a Circe, a goddess who turns men into swine (144).

Like the Preacher of Ecclesiastes and Jake's namesake, the Biblical Jacob, Jake Barnes is passing through a period of doubt and vexation in which superficial values and actions are seen for what they are, even though they may be sanctioned by the

Church, like the action of the pilgrims who monopolize the dining car on Jake and Bill's train. Neither Jake nor Hemingway nor the Preacher seem quite sure of what is enduring and valuable, but like Jacob they are learning and perhaps will discover a fuller faith as they grow older. The essence of this faith is perhaps imaged in Jake's description of how Romero fought a good bull especially for his loved one, Brett:

> Pedro Romero had the greatness. He loved bull-fighting, and I think he loved the bulls, and I think he loved Brett. Everything of which he could control the locality he did in front of her all that afternoon. Never once did he look up. He made it stronger that way, and did it for himself, too, as well as for her. Because he did not look up to ask if it pleased he did it all for himself inside, and it strengthened him, and yet he did it for her, too. But he did not do it for her at any loss to himself. He gained by it all through the afternoon. (216)

This doing for another without individual loss is a sign of agape which the simple uncorrupted Romero possesses. Knowing her own self-centeredness and perhaps perceiving this somewhat paradoxical performance as Jake does, Brett can also make a paradoxical sacrifice. In the quiet but climactic Book III, she knows that her selfishness and her bitchery would eventually hurt Romero, as Montoya predicted, and so she selflessly drives him away (241–243).

Jake also seems to have come to a greater knowledge of his condition than at any other time. It is true that the concluding note of the novel is still one of irony and pity, but he does not give way to maudlin tears or resort to bitter invective over Brett's cruelty in using him as a pimp and then a rescuer when she is down and out in Madrid. We are not much, they say by their actions, but we are all that we have. Like the polite bartender of the last chapter, they must exercise some devotion to each other by simple acts of kindness. Such is the skeptical but not nihilistic conclusion of Hemingway's first novel.

NOTES

[1] See Harold Loeb, The Way It Was (New York: Criterion Books, 1959).
[2] Ernest Hemingway, The Sun Also Rises (New York: Charles Scribner's Sons, 1926), p. 247. Subsequent references in this chapter to this novel will be in the text itself.
[3] Mark Spilka, "The Death of Love in The Sun Also Rises," Twelve Original Essays on Great American Novels, Charles Shapiro, ed. (Detroit: Wayne State University Press, 1958), pp. 238–256. See, however, the view of Cohn as the real hero of the novel as expressed by Arthur L. Scott, "In Defense of Robert Cohn," College English, 18 (March 1957), 309–314. Robert O. Stephens argues in a similar vein that Cohn's idealism is not entirely foolish or outdated: "Hemingway's Don Quixote in Pamplona," College English, 23 (December 1961), 216–218.
[4] See George Plimpton, "Ernest Hemingway," Paris Review, 18 (Spring 1958), 61–82. Reprinted in Writers at Work, second series (New York: Viking Press, 1963), p. 230.
[5] Ecclesiastes 3:1, 7:1–4, 8:8. Subsequent references to Ecclesiastes will be in the text itself.
[6] See Plimpton's interview (note 4 above), p. 230.

Jackson J. Benson

ROLES AND THE MASCULINE WRITER

Like Fielding, who launched his novel-writing career in protest against the blatant falsity and emotionalism of the first sentimental novels, Hemingway launched his own career in protest against the emotional excesses and rampant self-pity of his own time, first in a parody of emotionalism in *The Torrents of Spring* and then in a satire of self-pity in *The Sun Also Rises.* Unlike Fielding's, however, Hemingway's attack was not directed at specific works (aside from the parody of *Dark Laughter* in *Torrents of Spring*) as much as it was at emotionalism in general and the entire "romance" attitude toward life which had moved from literature to pervade the entire cultural value structure. Love between man and woman is one of the themes that recurs in every one of Hemingway's major novels except the last one and is explored very specifically in a number of his short stories; it will become obvious as we examine these works in some detail that Hemingway was vitally concerned with re-establishing what he felt were the proper roles of man and woman in their relationship to each other. The courtly love–feminine tradition demanded that the love object be removed; Hemingway insists on close physical contact as a prerequisite to love. The feminine tradition insisted that love be based on a "spiritualization" of the relationship, and on the emotions of yearning or desire (which must remain unfulfilled); Hemingway depicts love as being founded on sexual intercourse and requiring that satisfaction be given and gained. The feminine tradition rejects pleasure for the "joy" of suffering; Hemingway embraces pleasure as the substance of love (which, although based on physical satisfaction, is given and received on many different levels). Furthermore, the feminine tradition in literature (in conjunction with those other cultural forces we term *feminism*) tends to confuse the roles of one sex with the other, so that the man is the weaker sex and the woman the stronger, the woman the leader and the man the dependent. Hemingway views

From *Hemingway . . . The Writer's Art of Self-Defense* (Minneapolis: University of Minnesota Press, 1969), pp. 28–42.

the roles of man and woman as given, deriving from biology, and the masculine tradition as more ancient and general than the feminine tradition.[1]

In connection with this Hemingway counterattack, we might note that the two favorite stereotypes of sentimental literature have been the "martyr-victim" and the "all-wise mother"—women studiously avoided in Hemingway's fiction. Instead of the "martyr-victim," Hemingway offers the girl who frankly enjoys sex and who is genuinely able to give of herself, ungrudgingly, without a sense of sacrifice. The "all-wise mother" becomes the "all-around bitch," the aggressive, unwomanly female.[2]

Hemingway's emphasis on the masculine point of view is easily the most characteristic aspect of his writing, and although it is only one among many elements in his work used to channel emotion into non-sentimental directions, it serves to unify them all. Firmly within the masculine tradition are the self-reliant hero, the heroic encounter within conventionally masculine settings, the lusty and direct encounters with life rather than intellectualizations of experience, the dramatizations of the circumstances leading to emotion rather than the discussion of emotion, the continual satirization of pretense and illusion, and the emphasis on virile and direct language.[3]

This approach may embody a superficial view of life, but we may cry "Bravo!" instead of "For shame!" as we wade through a history of fiction weighted down with drawing rooms, assignations, and hand-wringings. But it may not even be true that simplicity and directness necessarily involve simplemindedness.

A good place to start looking to see whether simplicity is equivalent to simple-mindedness is Hemingway's first major novel, *The Sun Also Rises,* wherein he launches his sharpest attack against the modern confusions of male and female roles and his most sustained satire of sentimental illusion. It is true that there are many obvious things about the book. One of them is that it is the story of a male who becomes a man even though his male equipment does not work, and a female who never becomes a woman even though she is blessed with the best equipment available. But there must be some things about the novel that are not quite so obvious, for although this book has been one of the most frequently glossed American novels, I do not think that anyone has yet really touched on the spirit of the novel as Hemingway surely intended it. This is probably because so few people have given Hemingway credit for having any sense. If the reader is of the opinion that Hemingway never stood back from his experiences to make judgments about them, but only reacted to and recorded his experiences like a stimulated literate amoeba, the reader is bound to feel, as many do, that this novel is primarily of historical interest—a "journal of the lost generation"—and that the hero is merely some kind of projection of the author's ego.

So it is that most critics have viewed the novel as a contrast between an in-group (those who behave well) and an outsider (he who does not behave well) in a time of moral and spiritual chaos that requires the individual to define his own values. Jake, the narrator (usually closely identified with Hemingway's own point of

view) is thought of, despite a lapse or two, as being admirable in his stoic acceptance of his sexual disability and its consequent emotional frustrations. He, along
with his friend, Bill Gorton, his love interest, Lady Brett, her fiancé, Mike Campbell,
and a minor character, the Count, make up the in-group that more or less adheres
to what has come to be known as the Hemingway "code." At opposite poles on the
behavior scale outside the group, but connected to it, are Romero the bullfighter,
an almost perfect personification of the "code," and Robert Cohn, an almost
perfect personification of the "code" violated.

Further, the novel has been often seen as a kind of modern "sexual tragedy"
that symbolizes a general breakdown of social order and cultural values (T. S. Eliot's
The Waste Land is a frequently cited parallel). This is closer to the spirit of satire
in the novel. I would differ only in declining to see the characters in the novel as sad;
they are certainly confused and they are certainly sad about themselves, but to us
they should appear to be rather foolish.

There is no doubt that they have their sexual problems. Jake, like the Fisher
King, is sexually impotent; Brett assumes a male role in appearance, dress, and
manner, and at the same time behaves like a nymphomaniac (confusing?); Mike
Campbell, the fiancé, is ignored while Brett, in love with Jake, without any attempt
at secrecy (she even shows Cohn's letters to Mike), has affairs with Robert Cohn
and then Romero. Mike, in the meantime, continually makes lascivious remarks to
and about Brett in public, but remains impotently falling-down drunk. Robert Cohn
lives with a woman, Frances, who dominates and maintains him like a mother. Bill
Gorton is a bachelor who plays the field, and the Count is a bachelor who is "always
in love." Other added touches of sexual chaos are the presence of the homosexuals
with Brett upon her initial appearance in the novel, and the joke engagement of Jake
early in the novel to a prostitute with bad teeth who is later taken up by the
homosexuals (and is almost danced to exhaustion as one homosexual follows
another in a parody of the courtship ritual).[4] Finally, there is the super-irony of the
confrontation of Jake, the impotent, and Brett, the nymphomaniac.

There is, of course, a general validity in these collective views of the novel's
themes and structure, but as I have indicated, there is in my mind a crucial question
concerning the assumed relation of the author to his characters in this novel. It is
generally thought, with few dissenters, that the author's sympathy is with the
"insiders"—that is, he is actually predicating a code through them that he endorses
(and continues and modifies in the fiction that follows The Sun Also Rises).[5] This
question of an author's "distance" is one that critics have often run afoul of, particularly in dealing with contemporary authors whose physical presence so frequently complicates our thinking about their work. It has particularly complicated
our thinking about Hemingway's work, making The Sun Also Rises and For Whom
the Bell Tolls social or historical documents that they were never intended to be,
and probably making Across the River and into the Trees a worse novel than it is
and The Old Man and the Sea a better one than it is. A warning about the distance
Hemingway may have from his material in The Sun Also Rises might be taken by

noting the numerous satirical sketches he wrote as a journalist and the fact that his first published novel, *The Torrents of Spring,* was a blunt satirical parody. Charles A. Fenton make it clear in his book *The Apprenticeship of Ernest Hemingway* that from high school sketches all the way through his later parody of Anderson in his first novel, Hemingway's most typical mode of expression was *satire*—a fact to which no one, except Fenton himself, seems to have given any importance.[6] Some hint might also be taken from the title of the novel, a sardonic blast at those who take themselves too seriously (see pp. 42–43).

If, as I think, Hemingway does not back the in-group and its behavior, the whole focus of the novel and its structure changes. Jake becomes less admirable (as the most admirable member of the group), and Cohn less a villain for his violations of the group's sensibilities. Major and minor characters alike (with the possible exception of Romero, who assumes a special status that I shall discuss later) become possible objects for satirical scrutiny rather than subjective projections of various Hemingway attitudes.

We might best look at the book as Hemingway's own version of the "Book of the Grotesque," for, like Anderson, Hemingway treats his characters with a mixture of sympathy and ironic detachment. There is no "norm" established in the novel except by implication; essentially, a rainbow pattern of abnormality is shifted back and forth to evoke a number of ironic contrasts, one with another. Most of these contrasts can be seen as anti-sentimental in nature. Rather than a sad and desperate "sexual tragedy," this is really a sexual comedy,[7] wherein all the possible deviations from the sentimental pattern of love are depicted alongside the traditional, sentimental patterns themselves (with a few ragged edges, it must be admitted). And all is presented as realistically as possible, with perhaps the same rebellious spirit that led Sinclair Lewis to depict the absurdities and ironic contrasts of a different scene.

In *The Sun Also Rises* we have the extreme irony of a man, Jake Barnes, who gains his wholeness by renouncing the sentimentality that has really crippled him more than his physical wound—the sentimental self-deception that leads him to propose that Brett and he "just live together" to help ease his anguish for her. We also have a man, Robert Cohn, who is led to make a strutting fool of himself by engaging in the classically defined ritual of sentimental courtship (even continually pomading and combing his hair) with a girl who is trying her best not to look like a girl and who has gone beyond that kind of sentiment to a more immediately rewarding state of continual self-pity and self-justified indulgence.

Cohn thinks Brett is "awfully straight"! Even to the layman, her initial appearance and entrance must suggest more descriptive terms from abnormal psychology than any one person really deserves: *narcissism, masochism, sadism,* and *transvestism* are enough for a good beginning. Poor Cohn is either killed or cured by his adherence to the gospel of romance; the novel does not specify which. But there is no doubt that he is a humorous character and not a villain.

There is, of course, a certain element of sadness in the comedy of Cohn's slapstick blunders (knocking everybody down and then trying to shake hands is really Chaplin-esque), his posing ("I'm just worried I'll be bored" when going to the bullfight), and the absurd contrast of his peacock preening and his doormat ability to be continually stepped on. But as with the circus clown or the Chaplin character, the sadness of Cohn's predicaments should not spoil the fun. After all, like Rollo in the Katzenjammer Kids, "He only brings it on himself."

As I say, aside from the absolutely convincing quality of the characterization, the only reason I can think of for the inability of so many readers to see the comedy here is the tendency to take Jake, Brett, and company much more seriously than the author does. The same type of character as Cohn has been comic ever since Chaucer and Elizabethan comedy—his name is really Sir Ernest Wishwash Love-folly. Even Lady Brett, with her mixture of lust and self-pity, has a distant relative in Fielding's Lady Booby.

Why should we take any of these characters and their so-called "code" seri-ously? Just because they do? That should make it even more humorous. Self-pity is satirized so heavily at times it brings the novel to the edge of farce. Mike, Jake, Brett, and Cohn absolutely wallow in it. The really funny thing is that the "code" forbids the expression of emotion.[8] Jake lies down on the bed and weeps because the dark is different from the daytime. You may be sympathetic if you like, but the name of this particular black pit is still self-pity. Mike is continually drunk; wallowing in and enjoying his bankruptcy and his "lost" status, he sulks and snaps at the first target of opportunity. The fact that he really does nothing at all but drink or sleep it off makes it seem odd that so many readers have become snappish along with him and would like Cohn "to go away, like a good fellow." In the meantime, feeling particu-larly low, Brett is informing her loved-but-cannot-have one, Jake, that to make herself feel better (to hell with Jake, or Mike, or Cohn, or anybody) she has just *got* to have Romero. Nothing short of this new toy will do the trick of temporarily raising her spirits. So she makes Jake pimp for her (which is sad and acidly humorous—Jake is more like Cohn than many readers are willing to believe) and take her back to destroy the one symbol of clean honesty that Jake at the moment has. (She is completely unaware of Jake's emotional involvement with Romero, as she is completely ignorant of, or chooses to ignore, everyone else's emotions throughout the novel.) The "code" comes to resemble the structure of farce; it is simply a self-delusion used to make oneself feel right while doing the wrong thing. To herd together, to scapegoat others, and to make it work on the basis of some set of "principles" is a typical human technique for self-justification of pride and selfishness. That the code is such a sham is one of the great ironies of Hemingway's treatment of these characters.

In the center of the "in-group" barricade is, of course, Lady Brett, who to a great extent is not only the center of the conflict but the central character in the novel. Hemingway treats her with a delicate balance of sympathy and antipathy. She displays a number of attractive qualities which are often attached to the traditional heroine, including beauty, wit, and pluck, and Hemingway reveals to us that her current unstable condition has been caused, at least in part, by two devastating experiences with romantic love. (His picture of Brett and her husband on the floor with a gun between them is a wonderful multiple irony, joining a number of other romantic images satirically employed in the book and reminding us also of the forest lovers in the story "The Three-Day Blow.") To the shockable reader, Brett is the center of the novel's "sordidness"; to the young at the time of the novel's publication, she was the literary prototype of the liberated woman (having actually been patterned after one); and to the stubbornly romantic, she remains, regardless of her faults, the heroine who is tragically victimized by the modern world. Indeed, one can classify readers into types rather easily by the way they react to Brett— matching quite well the power she seems to have for segregating the characters within the novel itself.

However, despite the extenuating background for her current irresponsibility and despite her undeniable attractiveness, Brett is clearly in Hemingway's mind "a case," a waste of a fine spirit and a fine body. Regardless of her admirers both in and out of the novel, she *is* a Circe, as that damned literary fellow, Cohn, observes, and is the closest thing to a villain that the novel contains. She embodies all the sins of character that Hemingway publicly abhors and sometimes unconsciously displays, which may account for a certain amount of ambiguity in the attitude he has toward her and even toward her sins. Nevertheless, she is one of the primary targets for the satiric attack of the novel's title, since having decided she is "lost," Brett feels that she cannot be held responsible for her desperate behavior and the grief that she causes. She is out of the same mold of self-pity that later produced a hundred B movie heroines who are "jinxed" and "no good for anybody, even myself."

In response to her negative challenge, Jake, Mike, and Cohn (as well as Romero) all come to measure their manhood against her as a kind of catalyst. And their manhood is not measured by *cojones* (another misleading cliché of Hemingway criticism)—at least not in the usual sense of this vague Spanish colloquialism— but on the basis of the strength to see themselves clearly and the strength to bind themselves to an ideal worth living by.

That Mike and Cohn fail in these terms has already been demonstrated. Jake, however, is a developing character whose awareness and commitment is shaky until the end of the novel, where there is some evidence that he becomes self-aware and really aware of Brett for the first time. I have already spoken of the self-pity he is drawn into in the first section of the novel where his intercourse with Brett is largely that of trading sighs for what cannot be. Book I ends with a fairly good summary of their previous meetings: " 'Oh, darling,' Brett said, 'I'm so miserable.' I had [Jake thinks] that feeling of going through something that has all happened before." (p. 64) When one reads at the end of the passage (p. 65), "The door opened and I went up-stairs and went to bed," there is a strong suggestion that there will be a repetition of the suffering that Jake underwent the night before, when he left Brett, only to have her come up to his apartment at four-thirty the next morning, briefly parting from the Count waiting in his limousine in the street below, to see Jake and to report on her evening with the Count and his impressive ten thousand–dollar proposition. After she has left a second time, even after he has come face to face with what she really is, Jake cannot lose hold of the sentiment that had gripped him before her appearance:

> This was Brett, that I had felt like crying about. Then I thought of her walking up the street and stepping into the car, as I had last seen her, and of course in a little while I felt like hell again. It is awfully easy to be hard-boiled about everything in the daytime, but at night it is another thing. (p. 34)

Jake's feeling of going through something that has happened before and his suffering because of the way Brett steps into the car are all elements of comedy—if we can keep our distance.

Day is the time for those who have at least some measure of awareness to measure their feelings and values against the reality of things, and it may be that those who build their daytime bridges to reality with the strongest awareness are those who are troubled least with "night thoughts." Thus it is that a character in Hemingway's fiction may secure his stability (as in "Big Two-Hearted River") or redeem his sense of proportion through contact with nature.

It is this function that the pastoral interlude in the first part of Book II performs for Jake. Akin to the contrast pointed out by Carlos Baker between the priest's mountains and the narcotic, self-indulgent cities of the plain in *A Farewell to Arms,*[9] a sharp contrast is drawn between the clarity of the day experience on the Spanish fishing trip, and the confused chaos of the nightmare of Pamplona (it is stylistically— and in terms of a weird, disconnected content—a true nightmare). In Pamplona there is a constant conflict of egos floundering about, creating friction, betrayal, and degradation. In the mountains the characters feel free. Perfect harmony exists as Bill and Jake share with each other. It is the only real demonstration of "love" in the novel, and the fact that it comes between man and man, rather than man and woman, does not necessarily imply that Hemingway prefers men or that he feels women can be dispensed with. Instead, it is a further element of criticism directed toward the confusion of roles and the corrosive power of romantic illusion which have destroyed the simplicity and directness of the relationship between man and woman.

When Harris the Englishman comes, there is simply an expansion of sharing. All three men are not only intensely aware of their own and one another's well-being, they are all committed to an internal ideal of behavior based on their awareness. This is almost directly opposed to the jealousy and strife in Pamplona, and significantly, at the center of all of the trouble is Brett, the woman who refuses to accept her role as a woman. The only valid internal ideal held by the group in Pamplona is that of the aficionado held only by Jake, which Jake betrays by being seduced through his false sentimentalization of Brett. He is overcome, despite the dirty role she wants him to play, by feelings of yearning generated in a situation that is a parody of courtly love. He cannot have her; therefore he wants her. However, the lover here is not frustrated by circumstances that have committed his loved one to someone else (she is extremely available), but rather by his own physical disability. A great love story is being enacted by a man who has lost his maleness and a woman who dresses and talks like a man and who is filled with lust. What is more romantic than being asked to pimp for the woman you have put on a pedestal? The power of self-delusion is powerfully reinforced by the number of times Brett hits Jake on the head with her velvet hammer only to have him come back for more. *Tristan and Isolde* has been transformed into a comic Punch and Judy show.[10]

It is only after returning to nature once more in San Sebastian to wash out his soul in the ocean and assess his gains and losses that Jake, to paraphrase his previous statement of philosophy, finds out truly what he has bought and what he has paid for (p.148). His illumination comes after he receives a telegram from Brett asking him to rescue her (she has cut off her affair with Romero) at a hotel in Madrid. It is a summons to a task that is a hideous parody of knight-errantry—the fair maiden is really a whore, and the castle in which she has been imprisoned is a second-rate hotel; the dragon who keeps the gate is an unpaid bill for two weeks of adultery with a squire almost half her age. Jake sends Brett a telegram in return announcing his arrival time, and with the bitterness of true self-perspective says to himself: "That seemed to handle it. That was it. Send a girl off with one man. Introduce her to another to go off with him. Now go and bring her back. And sign the wire with love. That was it all right. I went in to lunch." (p. 239.) "And sign the wire with love" is his realization of the folly of self-indulgence, lack of awareness, and commitment to an illusion. It is only by keeping this change in perspective in mind that the full irony of the final scene can be apprehended. Although remaining to a degree sympathetic and loyal, Jake allows his bitter detachment to become more and more obvious. The climax and point of the novel is that Jake finally becomes his own man. No one should believe that he joins together again with Brett, agrees with her that she has "acted well," and goes off on the merry-go-round once more. As far as Madrid is concerned, "all trains finish there" (pp. 239–40).[11]

The elements of Brett's repetitions in the last scene are interesting variations on the theme of egocentricity. Her only real acknowledgment of Jake as a human being with emotions comes toward the end of the scene, first with the question, "You like to eat, don't you?" and next the request, "Don't get drunk, Jake. You don't have to." In context, both appear to be feelers toward confirming whether the old sentimental magic is still working on Jake—"Am I really tearing you up inside?" Until this point, she displays a mixture of two emotions: self-pity for the loss of Romero and self-righteousness for her sending him off. Her most frequently repeated statement is that she is not going to talk about it. She continues to beat the drum of her great love and sacrifice on the brain of her companion, however, and at the thought of how good it feels not "to be one of these bitches that ruins children" (p. 243), she is overcome by a sense of her own nobility and bursts into a fit of crying. Now at this point the reader can join in her sense of martyrdom, her faltering attempts to repress emotion, her nearly unrecognized act of courage, and her sense of the loss of the one good thing that has entered her shattered life. If the reader does, then he must regard *The Sun Also Rises* as a sophisticated soap opera. The reader had better look at the details of Brett's character and behavior as Hemingway has drawn them. Then Brett's statement at the climax of her self-dramatization, "You know it makes one feel rather good deciding not to be a bitch," becomes almost comic except that the self-deception is so disastrous for others. When she says, further, that "It's sort of what we have instead of God," Jake sums up her choice to be lost and to glory in it when he replies, "Some people have God. Quite a lot." But of course, God has never "worked well" for her; how could He? So Jake suggests another martini as a more acceptable alternative.

The contrast between Jake's state of mind and awareness and Brett's is nicely set up in the last paragraph of the novel. She is resting *comfortably* against Jake in a taxi, while at the same time Jake perceives that *outside,* "It was very hot and bright, and the houses looked sharply white" (p. 247). Brett's attention is still inward, as reflected by her physical position, and her emotions still directed toward pity for herself and what she cannot have but wants: " 'Oh, Jake,' Brett said, 'we could have had such a damned good time together' (p. 247). And we know exactly what a damned good time he would have had too. The kind of good time he has already had, plus the happiness given to Mike, and Cohn, and Romero. For of course it is not just Jake's incapacity to have sex that encourages Brett to tromp all over him. To her, Jake is a valuable piece of property, a home base for self-pity that she can return to until the loss of Romero, or whoever it might be, has lost its poignancy.

However, Jake is no longer crouched into himself, as he was at the table in Pamplona, there wallowing.[12] He sees the sharp white of the houses (a clarity of vision reminiscent of the fishing trip and San Sebastian—but this time *in Brett's company*) and the raising of the traffic policeman's baton (a gesture of control and an indication that for Jake, at least, self-pity and illusion have been put in their place). " 'Yes,' I said. 'Isn't it pretty to think so?' " (p. 247) are Jake's last words, and implicit in his tone are the indications that the emotional price for such pretty pretenses is far too high in terms of value received for him to pay any longer.

NOTES

[1] The classic study of the courtly love tradition is C. S. Lewis's *Allegory of Love* (New York, 1958).
[2] Maria and Pilar, in *For Whom the Bell Tolls,* might be seen as exceptions to the above descriptions. Maria, however, although victimized in a sensational way before the novel's action begins, is not seen in the novel itself in the role of victim. On the contrary, her role is that of an emerging personality. Just as an unhealthy sex experience has "killed" her, so does a healthy sex experience give her back her life. A victim of mass rape, she loses her identity; a recipient of an individual's genuine love and concern, she regains it. She is a person of limited background, but still a recognizable identity with needs and an existence important to Jordan beyond his own life. Pilar, of course, is a wise mother figure, but almost a reversal of the expected "mother-knows-best" role in that she is crude and profane and is on occasion also wrong. Furthermore, throughout the entire novel she is guided by the wishes of the male protagonist. It is significant for the thesis I develop in this chapter regarding role-confusion to see that she becomes a man only by default when Pablo renounces his own manhood; when another man, Jordan, takes over, she becomes a woman again. Although she remains aggressive and opinionated, she never

becomes "mom"; Hemingway is at great pains to reinforce the idea that she is all the while a lusty, passionate girl inside.

[3] This tradition at the inception of the novel was carried on by the picaresque narratives, such as Nash's *The Unfortunate Traveller* and Fielding's *Tom Jones;* today, such picaresque novels as Heller's *Catch-22* and Bellow's *Henderson the Rain King* carry on the burden of the masculine tradition in the legitimate novel. It is interesting that Hemingway never wrote a novel in this vein.

[4] Mark Spilka, "The Death of Love in *The Sun Also Rises,*" in Carlos Baker, ed., *Ernest Hemingway: Critiques of Four Major Novels* (New York, 1962), p. 20. Spilka's article is probably the best ever written on this novel, but he takes Jake and Cohn much too seriously.

[5] Robert Penn Warren, "Ernest Hemingway," in John W. Aldridge, ed., *Critiques and Essays on Modern Fiction* (New York, 1962)—the basic essay on the Hemingway "code." Warren, very properly, gives a great deal of emphasis to discipline; I cannot agree, however, with the idea of Jake and Brett as "initiates." The idea of the "code" has been expanded and altered by many others; among the most interesting and complete re-examinations of the code is that presented by Earl Rovit in his fine book, *Ernest Hemingway* (New Haven, 1963) (see his chapter "The Code: A Revaluation").

[6] New York, 1958. I count some twenty-four direct and indirect references to Hemingway's uses of satire reported by Fenton. Hemingway's first published writing in the high school paper *Trapeze* was heavily influenced by Ring Lardner. Fenton notes that Hemingway's "careful adaptations of Lardner had been an invaluable opening exercise in some of the technicalities of idiomatic prose, as well as a profitable experiment in various levels of humor, burlesque, and satire" (p. 26). Later, even in the straight reporting of his job on the Kansas City *Star,* there was an opportunity for writing which allowed for the "now characteristic, undercut Hemingway climax, full of unstated, ironic implications" (p. 44). Still later, when working for the Toronto *Daily Star* and *Star Weekly,* where he had a great deal more freedom as a feature writer, Hemingway presented himself in his material primarily as a humorist: "Humor continues to be at least an important ingredient in all of his work for the magazine and, to a lesser degree, the *Daily Star,* during the next four years. His style and attitudes matured as he ranged experimentally through all the various levels of burlesque, mimicry, satire, and irony. All of these qualities have been important in his fiction" (p. 81). Fenton notes further in regard to this period that "the war, quite clearly, was a genuinely compulsive factor in all Hemingway attitudes in 1920. His instinct toward satire had been sharpened by his experiences in Italy and by the disillusioning contradictions he observed in Chicago and Toronto" (p. 84). A break in Hemingway's employment by the Toronto paper came when he went to Chicago to write for a promotional house organ, *Co-operative Commonwealth,* and while holding down a nine-to-five job wrote on his own in the evenings, firing out "satirical rewrites of world news to *Vanity Fair*" (which were not published). Two short sketches, one ironic and the other satiric, were published during this period in New Orleans by the *Double-Dealer* (p. 101). Quitting his job in Chicago and going back to work for the *Star Weekly,* Hemingway turned once again to satirical sketches and feature articles (p. 113). Finally, at the end of his book Fenton notes that "the interludes of buoyant humor and ironic wit" were basic to Hemingway's success as a correspondent and "he exercised them constantly." After his newspaper apprenticeship in the months that followed, "Hemingway was inclined to think of himself at least in part as a humorist. . . . and as late as July, 1925, when he was working on the first draft of *The Sun Also Rises,* he regarded that manuscript as in part a humorous one" (pp. 260–61).

[7] See *D.I.A.,* p. 7. Hemingway sees comedy as a parody of form, as something that pretends to be serious.

[8] See Arthur L. Scott, "In Defense of Robert Cohn," *College English,* XVIII (March, 1957), 309–14, for an excellent discussion of this point.

[9] *Hemingway: The Writer as Artist* (Princeton, 1963), Ch. V.

[10] Robert W. Lewis, Jr., has examined the courtly love pattern which recurs throughout much of the early and middle period of Hemingway's work.

[11] For the interpretation of this line and for the insight that this moment is the turning point for Jake, I am indebted to Rovit, pp. 155–58.

[12] Pp. 222–23. Bill identifies the period at Pamplona as a "wonderful nightmare"; Jake sits and gets drunk but does not "feel any better."

Bertram D. Sarason

LADY BRETT ASHLEY
AND LADY DUFF TWYSDEN

Unlike the historical drama or novel in which the living, or once living persons, are named by name, the *roman à clef* employs fictitious names for real persons; and part of the fun, of course, is to get the key to those who have been disguised.[1] More often than not, identities are fairly transparent, if not to the general reader, at least to some reviewers, and always to the author's intimate friends, some of whom might well turn up as among the fictive. And more often than not, their identities have been thinly concealed only to be heavily satirized or to have their intimate affairs intimately disclosed. Writers of such novels, one suspects, are hopeful of a *succès de scandale.* Ironically enough, those who have been the victim of the disclosed scandal frequently elicit our sympathy, or the scandal serves the purpose of raising from obscurity those whose reputations might never have spread beyond the circle of their acquaintants. In speaking of novels of this type, one must regard Hemingway's *The Sun Also Rises* as exceptional in at least one respect. The author has incorporated himself in the cast of characters, incorporated himself as the sexually incapacitated hero, Jake Barnes, and even consented to publicly identify the hero with himself. There are, indeed, people who exculpate Hemingway for his harsh treatment of Harold Loeb and Kathleen Cannell (the Robert Cohn and Frances Clyne of the novel, respectively) on the ground that he treated himself with far greater severity than these, his former friends.

The tendency of the foregoing remarks is not to encourage persons with a zeal for publication to defame themselves, or to encourage others to ask their literary friends to select them as fictional underdogs. In fact, if one were to respect current canons of criticism, particularly those of the New Critics, one should judge even a *roman à clef* with no heed to the key, with no concern for pairing up the living and the fictional, and with no obligation indeed for passing moral judgment on how justly the author has treated those identified. One should not go outside the text. One does.

From *Connecticut Review* 2, No. 2 (April 1969): 5–13.

For, perverse as it may seem to critical purists, the reader is not content solely to seek critical satisfactions; and even best-seller lists elicit widespread curiosity. We may concede at once that the private life of Ernest Hemingway has nothing to do with the value of this or that work he has written, but biographies of the writer continue to be written and read. It is asking too much of human nature to expect persons *not* to be interested in the author himself or the living characters who have been transmuted into a *roman à clef.* It is certainly to be expected that we will want to know how fair, or how malicious, the author has been to those persons. And if we pursue these interests in depth, we may find ourselves in areas remote from our original inquiry: the justice of the author's delineations. What we may discover is that characters fictionalized in a novel may become fictionalized still more in life. Hemingway, himself, it will be noted, underwent some such transmogrification. The myths created by an author about himself or other living persons are taken for reality and *that reality* is attested to by sober persons who not only confirm the author's fictive portrait, but improve upon it. In one way or another, the characters in *The Sun* acquired imaginative biographies—a myth here, a legend there.

Remember what consequences Hemingway brought on himself! Essays and critiques on the *real* Hemingway! Had he in fact like the hero of the novel, been incapacitated by a wound suffered in the war? Was he speaking of the shock to the entire man that he must have suffered at Fossalta when his body was host to some twenty dozen splinters of an exploded mortar shell? Or again, should we take the matter symbolically? Those who did, those especially with a Freudian orientation, concluded that Hemingway had problems, as the saying has it; and the analytic-minded sought to read Hemingway's assumed neurosis between the lines of his stark prose. Finally, when it became all too apparent—and very much more so since the appearance of Mr. A. E. Hotchner's book—that Hemingway the man, was, to put it mildly, on this side of exuberance, a new myth replaced the old ones. The biographers settled on the theory that, of course, Hemingway was both virile and intact, and that his fictional counterpart, the wounded, impotent Jake Barnes represented imaginatively the blockade to a love affair with Lady Duff Twysden (the Lady Brett Ashley of the novel) which had to be foregone because of Hemingway's loyalty to his wife, Hadley. More on this legend to come!

So, several myths have been generated from *The Sun Also Rises,* some, as we have seen, concerning the author himself. But the truth about the living characters is far more astonishing—if it be the truth. It is said that there was, in the Hemingway circle of the Paris of the 1920's, a friend of Hemingway's who had been wounded genitally in the then recent war. He was presumably the sitter for that aspect of the portrait of Jake Barnes, and Hemingway did blurt out before the novel was published that, along with Harold Loeb, that friend too was destined for the slash. To Hemingway's ultimate credit, it must be said that he kept the friend's identity a secret; for when Hemingway gave Herbert Gorman a key to the characters, he set himself up as the model for Jake Barnes. However, concealment stopped there; for Hemingway did identify, among others, the rapacious Frances Clyne of the novel with Kathleen Cannell. A goodly number of expatriates in the Paris of the 1920's actually believed that Kitty Cannell was a gold-digger. But assumedly Hemingway was writing about someone else, a young woman on the periphery of his and Harold Loeb's circle. That was a young woman associated with *Broom* magazine who had been spurred on by a lady novelist to trap Harold Loeb into marriage. The lady novelist does not herself appear in *The Sun Also Rises*. Those with a zest for scandal might regret the exclusion, for the lady novelist was to achieve some repute as a writer—one of her works commanded an introduction by T. S. Eliot. It is as an intrigant that she remains mute and inglorious.

Hemingway apart, Lady Brett Ashley is the character that became the most legendary in life. She was drawn by Hemingway from Duff Twysden, and many of Hemingway's contemporaries assumed a one-to-one correspondence between the fictive Brett and the living Duff. Inevitably, in the memoirs of those who have recorded their Paris days of the 1920's, Duff is encountered fulfilling precisely the role Hemingway imagined for her in *The Sun Also Rises* where her natural habitat is given as either the bedroom or the bar. Historians of the era make it their business to report every glimpse they have of her at the Dingo or the Dôme or the Select. And we are left to assume that if her drinking is a fact, her promiscuity follows; for the latter is not as easily eyewitnessed as the former. Someone presumably knowledgeable like Robert McAlmon made it a point to interlard the autobiography of his literary life with his having arranged to lease an apartment for the "Lady Brett of *The Sun Also Rises*" who "had acquired an American boy friend, much younger than she. . . ." Someone not knowledgeable at all like Jed Kiley told us that even before the novel was published, he had declared his night-club off-limits to her. "All that baby ever kept was the change when somebody gave her over two dollars." She was "hard-boiled," John Dos Passos wrote when he recalled meeting her in Pamplona (she was not even there at the time). And in 1927, a year after the novel was published, Matthew Josephson recounted "how accurately Hemingway had drawn his friends and acquaintances." Josephson had gone to the Dôme, when he met "a tall slender woman" and "a tired-looking Englishman whom she called 'Mike'." They all chatted together and then went to Jimmy's bar. But even before then, Josephson sensed they were Hemingway's characters; ". . . the bantering manner with its undertone of depression; it was all there."

The two characters that Josephson had met were, of course, Lady Duff and Pat Guthrie, the Mike Campbell of *The Sun*. At Jimmy's, Harold Loeb was to appear out of the blue. Mike showed "little signs of irritation" as if Robert Cohn of the novel had appeared, and Josephson felt later that he had been through "a spooky sort of cocktail hour. . . . The characters were real enough and definitely not ghosts." So Josephson, like other writers of memoirs, bore witness to the accuracy of Hemingway's portraits; and years later, when he met Lady Duff in Connecticut on an occasion when she was drinking gin and coffee, he remarked that, "Nothing could stop her drinking." His few glimpses—perhaps they were no more than the two recounted here—confirmed his earlier description of Lady Brett Ashley: "alcoholic." He made no comment on the other adjective he employed for the fictive Brett, namely, "libertine"; its accuracy for the living Lady Duff is left for us to assume. But it must be said that Josephson, unlike some others, was not being intentionally malicious. As Santayana has said of creators of myth, he made "epicycles, as it were, on the reflex arc of perception." He remembered the novel, he saw parallels in real life. Like the others, he established a correspondency.

Such correspondency, according to the writers quoted here, allegedly struck them in a few months, or the immediate year, or instantly following the publication of The Sun Also Rises. But these were not impressions that faded with or were modified by the passing of time. The foregoing quotations are all from books published in the 1960's. Nor were these writers the only corroborators of Hemingway's realism and the establishers of myths to come.

Historians of the '20's tell us that after the publication of The Sun Also Rises, Lady Brett herself became the ideal for Smith College girls whom she inspired to be depressed, and for whom she was the model for dissipation. Apparently, Lady Brett's influence was not limited to this side of the Atlantic. Robert McAlmon represented her to be the model of imitation for women of the Rive Gauche. One is tempted to imagine a bourgeois father and mother in the provinces wondering, "Where did we go wrong?," and one of them rejoining, "C'est la Brett," or a college president telling an irate Board of Trustees in Northampton, "Gentlemen, it's that Brett Ashley."

It was inevitable that the influential Lady Brett Ashley and the living Lady Duff Twysden came to be identified. The identification lingered and was reaffirmed through Hemingway's suggestive words to Hotchner, "Her pallbearers had all been her lovers. Brett died in Taxco, Mexico. She was forty-three ... On leaving the church, where she had a proper service, one of the grieving pallbearers slipped on the church steps and the casket dropped and split open." Many years before Hemingway related this anecdote, another one had already been circulating. The rumor was that all of Duff's pallbearers were so drunk that the coffin they bore fell and rolled down a Taxco mountainside. The facts are that Duff, who died at the age of forty-six, in St. Vincent's Hospital in Santa Fé, New Mexico in June, 1938 was cremated (probably in Albuquerque). There was no coffin, there was no service, there were no pallbearers. Professor Philip Young mentioned to me that the sort of stories circulating about Duff were reminiscent of those that were current after the death of Andrew Jackson; and one recalls funeral myths associated with the charismatic of an earlier day: Marlowe, Shelley, and Ben Jonson for example.

But even the seemingly realistic accounts of Duff Twysden—those that highlighted Hemingway's accuracy—are open to serious question. Most commentators who observed her failed to take into account the times in which she lived and the milieu in which she moved. "She was young then," Lady Duff's friend, the eminent photographer, Berenice Abbott said, "and in those days everyone was gay, everyone drank."

We must bear in mind that those who saw her in the Dingo or the Dôme or the Select were not there themselves as sightseers. They too drank, and some of them, like Robert McAlmon, could drink her under the table. But there is good reason to believe that her drinking was essentially of that time and that place—not necessarily a permanent trait of her character. As for her promiscuity, let it be said that many of those who commented on her were themselves "free," and certainly, if they themselves were not, they had friends who were, and after all, it takes promiscuous men to make for promiscuous women. Once again, we must remember that there was a revolution going on—the sexual revolution did not begin in the 1960's—and we have every right to think of Lady Duff as merely a participant in that revolution. However, the stories of her license might well justify the retort of Mark Twain when told of his death, "Highly exaggerated." That is to say, we only know of two incidents, a very brief affair with Harold Loeb, a more extensive one with Pat Guthrie. Jimmy Charters, the barman who liked Lady Duff, believed that she was madly in love with Guthrie, who, he said, deserted her for an American girl. Loeb thought she wanted something more than an affair; she wanted to marry him. No other lovers have ever been named, although her friends concede that she had many affairs. But such friends may have been carried away by the evocative power of the fictive Lady Brett. Their assumptions may be gratuitous. If the accounts about her were true, one must recall that almost everyone who knew her agreed that Lady Duff was charming and captivating. That type of attractive woman, of course, would have more possibility of erotic experiences than the run-of-the-mill woman—and more possibility for gossip. Furthermore, one who knew her in the Paris days, and who herself was of English descent, pointed out that Duff was déclassé; and because she was, she suffered for a while that special instability from which American women are exempt, and from which English women suffer markedly.

All this is by way of saying that the fictive Brett Ashley, having become the female symbol of the Lost Generation, the living Lady Duff became the viable symbol of that generation. Through the creative offices of Hemingway, she became in the public mind not a participant in an uprooted group, but its exemplar. Accordingly, many who knew Duff made their estimate of her so as to jibe with her symbolic status. In the minds of the writers of memoirs, she became an abstraction. Heaven knows, as Brett Ashley she talked little enough in *The Sun*. Her dialogue was often flip, always laconic. Her most extensive utterances—and her most memorable—were, "Oh darling, I've been so miserable." and "Oh Jake, we could have had such a damned good time together." No one ever heard her speak that way in real life; Josephson, of course, caught an "undertone of depression" when he heard her bantering. One can not find a single sentence quoted from the living Duff. Equally astonishing is the absence of a recorded incident, other than a quarrel with an Apache in some bistro—precisely what we would expect to be recorded—that would indicate that there were events in Duff's life other than those prescribed by the novel, drinking and promiscuity.

So, Hemingway's portrait was taken for granted, and it was made credible because Hemingway in the novel had used some incidents drawn from real life. Apparently what Jake Barnes told Robert Cohn about Brett Ashley in Chapter V had some basis in reality. Duff was about thirty-four years old when *The Sun* was published in 1926, she was about to be divorced from Sir Roger Thomas Twysden, she apparently had been divorced previously, and she hoped to marry Pat Guthrie. A similar background was given by Jake Barnes to Robert Cohn. Subsequent events of the novel, especially those involving a love affair with Robert Cohn, were likewise based on reality, although Harold Loeb has issued his version of the events to indicate that Hemingway's accounts were somewhat wide of the truth. Moreover, the one-to-one correspondence between the characters of the novel and their reality is currently being questioned. Recently, Kathleen Cannell has also disclaimed —and with justification—the accuracy of her portrait in *The Sun*. And even Mr. A. E. Hotchner has pointed out that the incident of the bullfighter, Pedro Romero, tossing Lady Brett a trophy did not happen in actuality to Duff, but to Hadley Hemingway, the author's first wife. (Harold Loeb asserted that the bullfighter, Cayetano, who was the model for Romero, figured in the lives of himself and Duff and Hemingway for only a fleeting moment.) But in the main, Hotchner's quotations from Hemingway tend to support the established image of Duff. To the myth of the pallbearing former lovers, Hemingway added the fiction that, "Those days with Lady Duff ruined poor Loeb for the rest of his life," implying that Duff was very much like Brett Ashley, who made castration her hobby. But in the novel, Brett Ashley is finally able to exercise discipline out of respect for the bullfighter Romero.

If that gesture was a saving grace for the lady of the novel, Hemingway allowed no such exculpation for Duff. Loeb, himself, in a recent article, has denied that he was ruined; and I myself have seen the letters written to Loeb—kind letters— written by Duff after their brief affair in the South of France. Perhaps this is the time to make one fact clear between the real and fictive Lady, and, indeed, between Hemingway the author and Hemingway the man. Some Hemingway biographers— and Harold Loeb himself—are to this day uncertain as to whether an affair between Hemingway and Duff had taken place. But it is quite certain that the Jake Barnes–Lady Brett Ashley affair occurred only in the pages of *The Sun Also Rises*. The living Hemingway, unlike the fictive Jake Barnes, was quite sexually competent. The living Duff Twysden, unlike the fictive Lady Brett Ashley, it remains to be added, was quite unwilling. Yes, she did tell Hemingway that she did not wish to break up a family—she told him this only to keep him at a distance, not out of regret. The excuse she gave was one of the oldest and the lamest, one of her friends told me. Hemingway was not her type, I was informed from still another source. That source was no other than the person to whom McAlmon referred as "An American boy friend, much younger than she...." That was her husband-to-be, not just a boy friend, with whom she planned to come to America, and with whom she lived happily for many years until her death in Santa Fe. He was a painter named Clinton King—by best accounts, her third husband.

In any event, the Kings came to America. Accounts of their life here are recounted from friends and acquaintances, some of whom had already thought of her in terms of the myth she had become through identification with Lady Brett Ashley. For example, Harold Loeb is quite certain that she met her husband-to-be by way of introduction from another painter, Sir Cedric Morris; but a close friend of Duff says that their meeting took place otherwise. King, that close friend said, was in a Paris bar, behind whose counter was a mirrored wall. In the mirrors he saw a beautiful face. It was Duff's and he fell in love with her. At once he introduced himself; they went off together; and eventually were married. So be it. Not really married, the friend added, "Duff would never do a thing like that." In the realm of fact was the King family's reaction. The Kings had a flourishing candy business in Texas, and the father was determined to stop the marriage. Lawyers were sent across the Atlantic to dissuade the young painter. Even five years later, to friends near Nyack, New York, he recalled with relish how he had defied the family. So, we can be quite certain they were married, and that they came to America with King losing his family's support. They were so poor thereafter, a friend of theirs said, that they had to live in a barn—the barn somewhat of an exaggeration, the dire poverty being just temporary.

Hereon, from all accounts, the Duff Twysden of legend—alcoholic and libertine, for whom false gaiety was a veneer for despair—is reported almost completely different. But even before her arrival here, Berenice Abbott repudiated Hemingway's fictive portrait. "He did not understand her at all. His portrait was superficial. Yes, he was fascinated by her old-world charm, her breeding and manners; but he saw her through the eyes of a boy from the midwest. He made her out to be a tramp—that was crazy. But he looked at women only sexually, not as people. I grant that she was on a binge once in a while, but she was not alcoholic. As I said before, everyone was drinking then. She was attractive and charming and so she had many admirers, but she had talents. I saw some of her paintings. They were good paintings." Harold Loeb, too, remembers her paintings, and he too did not think she was an alcoholic. And that was the testimony of her New York friend, Mrs. John Rogers, and the testimony also of Dr. and Mrs. Edward Harkavy, near whom she lived for several months in New City, New York and who were in a position to know.

Duff and Clinton King had come to New City, New York to head an art school shortly to be opened. They worked in the spring of 1934 with the owner, a Mrs. Romaine. Quite unforeseen, there was a squabble over who should pay the postage to mail out brochures, and all at once the project folded. In New City were Duff and her husband, stranded without a cent. The Harkavys did what they could. They gave them shelter in a shack (not a barn) they owned; they gave them the use of their vegetable garden; and they sent their Korean houseboy with a drink of gin per day. The Korean servant, who had a passion for the stuff, saw to it that the limit was strictly observed. Dr. Harkavy, a practising psychoanalyst, is certain that Duff was not an alcoholic, not merely because she survived on that ration, but because, he said, she had none of that apparent greed nor the strained look so characteristic

of alcoholics. Duff's friend, Mrs. John Rogers, also said that Duff was not an alcoholic; and when these friends were questioned about her fidelity to her husband,
they were all certain that she was faithful and that theirs was a very good marriage.
Apparently, during the many periods of occasional financial hardship, and an un-
detected tubercular illness, Duff was happy.

Mrs. Rogers vibrated smiles as she recalled Duff, "So captivating and witty. She
was always witty, always delightful." Dr. Harkavy recalled "darting eyes and a
mischievous look." His wife (known professionally as Millia Davenport) recalled one
of Duff's harmless, though complicated pranks. "One day, at a gathering on the
Carnochan Estate in New City, New York, a group had gathered to hear a lecture
and to see some slides on the flora and fauna of Africa. The novelist, Bessie Breuer,
was determined to impede the lecture and turn the gathering into a party. She
began to undress the speaker, and then broke out into the score of an Italian opera.
At this point, Duff unexpectedly dropped in; she sized up the situation immediately.
Assuming the role of a desperate impresario, she addressed herself to those
present and to an imaginary audience outside, imploring someone to volunteer to
fill a role left vacant by a suddenly stricken member of the cast. When by gestures,
she made it appear that no volunteer was available, she braced herself suddenly and
heroically joined Bessie Breuer in carrying on the opera. Duff was imaginative and
was also musical; and in a later year, on inheriting a small sum, she spent most of
it on the purchase of a piano." Dr. Harkavy recalled her always ready for sport. On
one occasion, there were at a party three newly arrived German psychoanalysts,
one of whom was Erich Fromm. Dr. Harkavy took an instant dislike to one of the
trio, a Dr. C.—who bore himself with a holier-than-thou attitude, and who seemed
to communicate the idea that he was the living Christ. Pointing him out to Duff, Dr.
Harkavy asked if she would be so kind as to bring this divinity down to earth. She
was to pretend to seduce him. But she did not have to. Dr. C. took one look at her
and became mere man. It was not, Dr. Harkavy emphasized, that she was another
Zelda Fitzgerald. "She liked fun," he said, "she wouldn't let a dare pass, but she
wasn't reckless, she wouldn't endanger her life."

This then is a different Duff than the incurable alcoholic, the libertine, morbid
character whom Hemingway depicted in The Sun Also Rises, and who was believed
to have been represented with complete accuracy by those who knew her in Paris
in the 1920's, and who recalled her in many parts of the world forty years later. The
real person was about 5', 7", slender, long-legged, with luminous eyes that were
always animated, a strong face—like that of a Norman soldier, Mrs. Rogers said.
She was not voluptuous as Hemingway described Brett Ashley to have been. She
did not have "curves like the hull of a racing yacht."

As we have seen, there were gross distortions made of the living Duff in the
creation of the fictive Brett Ashley. But even those who disbelieved Hemingway's
portrait—some of her friends and admirers in America—themselves created legends, or believed legends that they heard, or involved those who had once been
close to Duff in myth and legend. One apocryphal item has it that Harold Loeb

pursued Hemingway with a revolver, not as Hotchner passed on a similar item, just after the publication of *The Sun Also Rises,* but when Hemingway stole Duff away from Loeb. These fictions are part of a larger legend begun by Jimmy Charters in his *This Must Be the Place*—with a preface by Ernest Hemingway. Charters said that after the publication of *The Sun Also Rises* the real characters depicted in the book went after the author with a gun apiece. One addition to this legend has it that Kitty Cannell, having acquired a boyfriend over six feet tall, ordered him to clout Hemingway on sight (Mrs. Cannell has said there is not a word of truth in this story). Still another, and a more romantic version, has it that young Clinton King, then about twenty-two and some fifteen years the junior of Duff, beat Hemingway to a pulp in a Paris bar. Perhaps just as unfounded is the story that Duff was born a member of the minor Scottish nobility. With that story goes the expected sequel: the coming-out party, the superficial education, the marriage into which she was forced by her parents to a drunken nobleman. One variant has it that, in fact, she abandoned the groom at the wedding, and ran off with the best man—Duff herself told this to Harold Loeb. As one goes deeper into research for the facts of Duff's life, one finds dubious testimony on both the friendly and hostile sides. Even presumably objective records conflict. Her father's name on the records of St. Vincent's Hospital, Santa Fe, New Mexico is given as "Sterling." That does not correspond with the name of "Smurthwaite" given by *Burke's Peerage.* In fact, according to that source, her original name is given as "Mary Smurthwaite."

To be sure, one must distinguish between ordinary errors and unusual myths. But the myths are plentiful, and there is no question that they arose from the convincing magic of Hemingway's pen. We may, if we wish, regard that evocative power as a gift, or a by-product of genius. Or we may—the New Critics insist that we should—regard the whole matter as really a sociological phenomenon. But if great works of literature stimulate our imagination long after the book is closed, or the play over, the superior *roman à clef* too has this persisting power. It is, admittedly, another type of power. We are drawn, to be sure, not within ourselves, but out there—to the world of the living. And as we seek to establish if the fiction we have read corresponds to the way it was, or the way the characters were, we may find ourselves encountering newly generated fictions remarkable enough to shift us once again back to ourselves, so that the outcome may be a rekindling of our imagination. As for a particular living character, Duff Twysden, we find, as we shuttle between the realities and the myths about her—often uncertain as to what were the realities and what were the myths—we become aware that she had some special quality, that quality that absorbs us in spite of dry facts and statistics. Outside of the pages of *The Sun* she possessed what Henry James called, "The real thing." He meant it paradoxically, of course; it was that suggestive quality about a person that could transcend his existential certitudes so as to stir the artist's creative power. And it may be argued that the once-living Duff Twysden—or as she might be called, Mary Duff Sterling Smurthwaite Byrom Twysden King—possessed that compelling power even far more than her fictional counterpart, the famous Lady Brett Ashley.

NOTES

[1] I wish to acknowledge the kind help of several persons. Donald St. John of Franconia, New Hampshire, provided several bibliographical items for research. Professor Carlos Baker of Princeton University, and Professor Philip Young of Pennsylvania State University were available for consultation on one or two points concerning Lady Duff Twysden's biography. Several persons who knew Lady Duff or who knew about her were generous enough to discuss their information with me. They were Mrs. Marguerite Cohn of New York City, Mrs. William Rogers, Jr. of New York City, Mrs. Dana Burr of New York City, Miss Berenice Abbott, Abbot Village, Maine, Mrs. Kathleen Cannell of Boston, Massachusetts, Mr. Clinton King of Chicago, Illinois, Mr. Harold Loeb of Weston, Connecticut and Dr. and Mrs. Edward Harkavy of New City, New York. Assistance was also received from Sister Mary Joachim, Administrator of St. Vincent Hospital, Santa Fe, New Mexico, and from Dorothy Fribble of Nyack, New York. Mrs. Gail Bhonslay, of Armonk, New York helped edit the manuscript.

Carole Gottlieb Vopat

THE END OF
THE SUN ALSO RISES:
A NEW BEGINNING

While some critics, most notably Philip Young, feel that Jacob Barnes does not change at all in the course of *The Sun Also Rises,* and others, like Mark Spilka, John Rouch, and Richard Hovey,[1] conclude that Jake changes only to realize the full extent of his inability to change, a close critical reading of the end of the novel indicates that this position needs to be re-evaluated. Jake Barnes does indeed undergo profound change, and that change, which has taken place gradually and progressively throughout the novel, is summed up concisely and symbolically in the final pages of Book III.

Jake has undergone the shock of many recognitions before Book III opens. He has been changed by the events in Pamplona: the spectacle of Romero's utter masculinity; the revelation of his own shameful role as steer and pimp; the realization that he is in his romantic dreaming little different, although quieter, than Robert Cohn. More importantly, he has recognized that what he had been calling romantic love is instead compulsion and misery, a neurotic and scarcely controllable sickness which, rather than shore up his tentative masculinity, only serves to castrate him further. Jake has changed in his estimation of himself, his wound, his crowd, and his love for Brett Ashley, who he has been discovering is not so "absolutely fine and straight" (Ernest Hemingway, *The Sun Also Rises* [New York: Scribner's, 1926], p. 39).

In Paris Jake once accused Brett of liking "to add them up"; when she agreed ("Well, what if I do?"), he responded, "Nothing" (23). In Pamplona, however, when Brett reveals her feelings about Romero (Chapter XVI), Jake is not as warmly accepting of her behavior. He has learned too much about himself and her to accept the myth or excuse of their specialness. When Brett refers to their mutual illusion—that their affair, could it materialize, would be perfect—he contradicts her: "I'd be as big an ass as Cohn." He sees that to Brett he is no more than one of "them." Rather than her own true love he is her possession—"You're the only

From *Fitzgerald/Hemingway Annual 1972,* pp. 245–55.

person I've got"—and, as such, his status is no different than Cohn's or Mike's: "You've got Mike," he reminds her. Jake says he still loves her, but love is no longer blind. He interrupts her litany of self-pity in an attempt to make her pity others, as he does, and realize the effects of her actions upon them: "... It's been damned hard on Mike, having Cohn around and seeing him with you" (188).

Jake tries to teach Brett to control herself, to "go off like a cat," rather than act like a bitch. His many sleepless nights have convinced him that it is as impossible to select which feelings one will entertain as it is to stop feeling altogether. But he has also learned that while one cannot help feeling, he can help showing his feelings and, worse, acting upon them unwisely. Jake does not tell Brett not to feel; rather, he advises her not to act on her feelings: "Don't do it ... you ought to stop it ... you oughtn't to do it ... you don't have to do that..." (190). Jake has learned from Romero's example in the bullring that it is possible, although difficult, to control one's actions. This is, after all, what style is about. Rather than merely putting on a good show in public, as Brett and Mike define it, style is a way of life: disciplining and controlling one's self to exercise grace under emotional pressure.

But Brett is having none of it: "I can't help it. I'm a goner now, anyway. Don't you see the difference?" Jake refuses to allow her to abdicate responsibility for herself: "No." He forces her to admit that she is, indeed, making a conscious choice among a number of alternatives, that she is doing not what she must, but what she wants: "I've got to do something," she answers him, then admits, "I've got to do something I really want to do. I've lost my self-respect." Hers is less a problem of compulsion than of selfishness. Finally, she sees this too: "I've always done just what I wanted." "I know." Jake does, indeed, "know," for he has often suffered the consequences of her irresponsible self-indulgence. He does not try to convince her that she is anything but a bitch: "Oh, I do feel such a bitch." "Well" (191).

But while Jake may not support her, he continues to serve her. He gives up his role as conscience and becomes once again her steer: "What do you want me to do?" Unlike Brett, he often must do what he does not want to do. He cannot stand up to her, cannot interrupt her nor interrupt himself. Jake's own compulsiveness is part of the all-pervasive circularity, futility and repetitiveness that dominate the novel. Like the sun which rises and sets, like Brett, like Mike and Cohn, Jake seems condemned to go around in circles, unable to control himself or his violently self-destructive "steer" impulses. Forced to choose between his *afición*, or obsession, for Brett and his *afición* for the bullfights, he begins paying the bill for having Brett as a friend, attempting to give her "back her self-respect" at the price of his own. The bill comes immediately: Cohn calls him a pimp and knocks him out while Mike feigns unconsciousness to evade helping him, then later cashes in on the last remnants of Jake's friendship with Montoya to borrow a hundred pesetas. His old comrade, Bill, cannot comfort him, first advising him to search for the one drink "that gets it" then turning on him angrily when his suffering proves immune to drink: "Get tight ... get over your damned depression" (233). The bulls have no compassion for the steer they have wounded, for "old Jake, the human punching bag."

Jake's feelings of loss, despair, estrangement and futility descend upon him with the impact of a crushing blow, as though he has been wounded anew in another war. Or, rather, it is the same wound and the same war, fought this time on the battlefield of the fiesta, a continuation of the wound and war on the Italian front and the earlier injury and battle on the football field of which he is now reminded. As Mark Spilka points out in "The Death of Love in *The Sun Also Rises*"(89), "the war, the early football game, and the fight with Cohn have this in common: they all involve ugly, senseless, or impersonal forms of violence, in which a man has little chance to set the terms of his own integrity." The kick in the head in America, the blow to the genitals in Italy, and the visceral wounding in Spain are all evidences of the same wound: impotence, whether in sport, love, war or life, a wound simultaneously of the guts, the balls and the head. Jake has been wounded in the ability to take charge, to control and master, to live with that courage, dominance, independence and stamina which for Hemingway is the essence of masculinity, epitomized in the bullfighter's ability to "live his life all the way up" without fear or compromise. Jake's wound is such that he is unable to get it all the way up. He is unable to stand up to life, experience, women, his inner self. Instead, he is passive. He runs from confrontation, backs down from the bulls, trying to "play it along and just not make trouble." Where Robert is unable to get started and Brett unable to stop, Jake's own trouble is his inability to finish, to complete or follow through an action, as he is unable to refuse Brett's demands, although he knows they are degrading and destructive.

Now, in Pamplona, Jake feels the same sense of the world's irrevocable alteration, the same inner dislocation and estrangement he felt in the hospital in Milan or walking home from the football game, when "It was all different . . . and it was all new . . . it was all strange . . ." (199). He is suffering from emotional shell shock, from battle fatigue, and wants desperately to withdraw from the field, set down his suitcase and find a "deep hot bath to lie in." But as long as the crowd is around him to demand his service and his solace, he cannot set down his burden. Although injured himself, he continues to respond to their pain with compassion and responsibility. He climbs upstairs to visit the wounded Cohn, forgives him and shakes his hand. He gives Mike his own bottle of wine, opens and pours it for his shaky friend, then later tucks him into bed, comforting him as though he were a child: "You'll sleep, Mike. Don't worry, boy" (218).

But he himself cannot drink, sleep or wash away the consequences, the burden, of this fiesta. Although Brett seems able to bathe away, if only momentarily, her feelings of guilt and disgust, when Jake finds the "deep stone tub," "the water would not run." He is not too drunk to tot up and pay his bill. The celebration continues outside his window but "it did not mean anything." He sees that he has been blind ("Yes . . . I'm blind"), and knows that in some way his view of the world and of himself has changed, that both have come more sharply into focus: "The world . . . was just very clear and bright, and inclined to blur at the edges . . ." (234). The exact nature and effect of the change become clear to him in the peace and solitude of San Sebastian.

Away from Pamplona and the crowd, Jake is reintroduced to the pleasure of his own company. Apart from the brief, exhilarating thrill of the actual bull-fights, there was little pleasure for him in the fiesta. Even his joy in liquor had been lost, for he drank too quickly, solely to get drunk and without tasting the wine. Now, removed from the heat and noise, he realizes once again how good life can be when his emotions are under control. "Through with fiestas for a while," he appreciates the unadulterated pleasure of his quiet life: "It was pleasant to be drinking slowly and to be tasting the wine and to be drinking alone" (243).

Unlike Brett, who needs noise, crowds and company, if not an audience, Jake is not afraid of being alone nor does he, like Cohn, spend most of his time looking for ways to run away from himself. He enjoys being by himself, walking, reading, drinking, watching the crowds, listening to music. By himself he experiences regen-erative moments of utter quiet—of sleep, relaxation, solitude—which enable him to continue, rising fresh with the sun each morning, no matter what has happened the night before. Unlike Vicente Girones, he was not killed in the rush of bulls at Pamplona. Like Romero, who performs, although battered, or the bicycle racer, who, despite his painful boils, refuses to abandon a race he may win, Jake, although wounded, holds on. Unlike Brett, Mike or Cohn he is able to bear his own pain. He does not create scenes nor does he take out his frustration on others, use them, or attempt to make them pay for his hurt. He has a form of courage and self-control as valid, if not as spectacular, as Romero's: the courage to bear his feelings, the control to "not make trouble for people," a source of strength which is, like Romero's, inherent, not something he acquires, as Cohn learns to box. His inner life, of which he has been so afraid, provides him with strength as well as "trouble." It is turbulent but also abides, like the earth whose freshness he so enjoys; like the sea, whose haunting presence Jake is aware of throughout the novel, it is a source of life and pleasure as well as of "bad weather."

Jake rejects for the moment the simple, "safe, suburban" life of France as he rejects the simple-minded bicycle team manager who pompously announces that "following and organizing the road races had made him know France" (247). Jake wants to face the unknown, "in the destructive element immerse." He decides to confront the sea. Although he appreciates France as "the simplest country to live in" because "everything is on such a clear financial basis," he returns to Spain where "you could not tell about anything" (244). He is not as crippled as he thought and he can handle more than a life based solely on the simple exchange of values. He can get to know himself, can face his own sort of bulls within his own bullring. In San Sebastian he is not content merely to float on top of the calm water, but dives deep beneath the surface, "swimming down to the bottom ... with my eyes open ..." (245). He faces his wound and himself, and sees, finally, "how to live in it."

At San Sebastian he confronts his fears. He knows the destructive power of the ocean and his limits as a swimmer. He is a cautious man. Although "it felt as though you could never sink," the sea will kill him if he gets overtired or overcon-fident. He tries "to keep in the trough and not have a wave break over me" (248). Climbing up on the raft, away from land and people, he surveys the terrain: "On the other side of the narrow gap that led into the open sea was another high headland. I thought I would like to swim across the bay but I was afraid of cramp" (249). Jake would like to swim in the open sea, become as involved with life, with Brett, with emotions, as bullfighters can, but he is afraid of "cramp," of wounding. He is afraid of drowning in the open sea, of facing the bull head-on rather than vicariously, of a love affair, of women, of his unconscious, of a life without limits. Yet he also sees that there is no shame in facing his fears and limitations squarely, acknowledging them, and living with and within them as best he can. Indeed, there is a kind of courage in such a confrontation and realization. People who refuse to accept their limitations are, in the terms of the novel, either fools, drunks or dead men; they end up committing suicide with the bulls. Although he cannot swim in the open sea, there is still much that he can enjoy: "Then in the quiet water I turned and floated. Floating I saw only the sky, and felt the drop and lift of the swells. . . . the water was buoyant and cold" (248). Nor does his wound exempt him from the responsibility of living well. Unlike the others, he does not use his limitations as an excuse for self-indulgence and irresponsibility. He realizes that he must live in a limited world, but he also knows that within that world he can live with cleanliness, order, and style: "After a while I stood up, gripped with my toes on the edge of the raft as it tipped with my weight, and dove cleanly and deeply, to come up through the lightening water, blew the salt water out of my head, and swam slowly and steadily in to shore" (249).

Although not a bullfighter, a conqueror and destroyer of savage beasts, Jake is more than a taxidermist, a lover and collector of animals already slaughtered. While he does not have Romero's consummate ability to dare, disarm and destroy that which threatens him, he can have a richer life than the count, who in his avid pursuit of the safe and nonthreatening is "dead, that's all." The price of the count's carefully controlled life has been his reduction of other people to commodities, to stuffed dogs, with whom he never really engages, offering money but never himself. Jake, on the other hand, realizes the value of compassion, of giving and sympathizing as well as controlling. He does more than just "not make trouble for people"; he responds to them with a compassion, responsibility, understanding and forgiveness that set him apart from the rest of his careless crowd.

But San Sebastian is a place Jake visits; he does not live there. The seashore is a cool and peaceful interlude; in the interior, the war and hell of modern life burn undiminished. Jake's Rest and Recuperation leave is brief. A "military-looking" post-man summons him back into the battle, delivering his orders—two telegrams from Brett, with whom Jake has yet to make a separate peace. The old illusion of power and love momentarily reasserts itself, greeted this time with disgust at his role rather than romantic melancholy or self-pity: "Send a girl off with one man. Introduce her to another to go off with him. Now go and bring her back. And sign the wire with love. That was it all right." San Sebastian has been "all shot to hell" (250).

But when he awakens on the train the next morning to see "Madrid come up over the plain," the lessons of San Sebastian are still with him. Madrid is the city at "the end of the line," "the sun-hardened country" where "all trains finish" (251). It's the city where illusions end. In Madrid, Romero has paid the bill for his affair with Brett. Even Brett has faced an unpleasant truth about herself in Madrid: Romero, much younger than herself and ashamed of her, is not her "sort of thing." And in Madrid, this city of renunciation, Jake at last renounces his dreams about Brett. The old games, the old "lines," the old trains of thought, all "finish there. They don't go on anywhere."

On his way to Brett's hotel room, Jake passes "through the gardens, by the empty palace and the unfinished church on the edge of the cliff..." (251). He bypasses the relics of the past, the "antiquities" and "suitcases." He leaves behind his old longings for religion (the church) or romance (the gardens) or an external authority (the palace) to order his life, illusions which were in themselves incomplete and desperate ("empty . . . unfinished . . . on the edge of the cliff"). He leaves behind, as well, his dreams of the Garden: "Couldn't we just live together, Brett? Couldn't we just live together? . . . Couldn't we go off in the country for a while?" (57). Instead, Jake gets off in "the high, hot, modern town." He disembarks in hell, but it is a clean, well-lighted hell, one with room to breathe and light to see. The heat that bakes Madrid is the heat of the sun, not the dark, crowded, smoky denseness of the dream-ridden Parisian bals. Madrid is a hell of realization and self-knowledge, Jake's harsh moment of truth. No longer in France, the "easiest, simplest country to live in," Jake has said good-bye to all that, to the easy deceptions and cowardices of his life in Paris. He is in another country, and his illusions, those familiar stuffed animals, are dead.

Jake enters Brett's hotel room neither lover nor knight nor partner in the destructive dream business. He and Brett no longer form a working "we." Instead, he announces himself with "it's me." He sees Brett clearly and with detachment: "The room was in that disorder produced only by those who have always had servants" (252). Brett is, at last, a real and discrete person, not a symbol or token or projection of himself, as she has been. What Jake sees in the disordered bed brushing her short hair is not a "Circe" begrimed in her own wallow or a Siren who has been shorn. He sees no symbols but a suffering human being. He responds to Brett with pity: "She was trembling in my arms. She felt very small." He knows that while she is kissing him, she is "thinking of something else" (252). He knows he has no part in her sufferings. He is not the First Cause of them; she is not miserable for want of him. Her affair with Romero had nothing to do with him; he was only her "servant" to be "utilized" in getting her way. Brett, in her sick and selfish world, makes no distinction between servants and friends. But in her hotel room Jake knows he is no longer her servant, one who is compelled to obey; rather, he is her friend who chooses to comfort her: "Tell me about it." Jake consoles and defends her, agrees with her and supports her, lying for pity's sake: "You were probably damn good for him" (253). When her defensive self-deceptions break down, he holds her shaking and crying in his arms, wanting nothing from her for himself.

However, once Brett's vulnerability has been rearmored by Jake's compassion and a few drinks, she no longer needs his arm to uphold the supportive defense of her illusions, nor his hand to help her swallow them; "her hand was steady enough to lift [the Martini] after that first sip" (256). In the cool bar of the Palace Hotel Brett has found a safe and familiar harbor and no longer clings to Jake as though drowning in the open sea. Then Jake begins reestablishing his distance from her, disengaging himself from her company, refusing to slip back into his old role of steer-confidant-servant, that old "dead end." When Brett boasts that "deciding not to be a bitch" is "sort of what we have instead of God," Jake answers "Some people have God . . . quite a lot" (257), aligning himself not with Brett but with those many others whose lives have meaning, purpose and order ("God"). Jake has within himself what F. Scott Fitzgerald called the "fundamental decencies," honesty, carefulness, endurance, courage, which make him part of the "quite a lot" who "have God." Jake may be himself "the unfinished church on the edge of the cliff." Perhaps his wound is such that he will never finish, never complete nor be completed, like Romero, but he is still "a church."

Jake will be Brett's friend, but he will no longer be her barman, serving with "wonderful gentility" the "coldly beaded" illusions she requires in order to feel "set up" within a cool refuge from the heat and light outside. He will not be as he was in Pamplona, a polite servant who absorbs blame for the carelessness of others ("I should have asked, you know"), perpetuates their illusions ("As they were before?"), and knows when he isn't wanted, going "far enough up the bar so that he would not hear our conversation" (256). Living within her self-absorbed circle, for Brett all cities are the same, but Jake knows he is in Madrid: "You could feel the heat outside through the windows" (257). He knows that although Brett has no friends, there are many eager to be her servant. He knows that for her there is nothing special about him as there is nothing special about this particular barman nor about this particular bar: When Brett exclaims, "Isn't it a nice bar," he contradicts her: "They're all nice bars" (256).

Although Brett is comfortable drinking in the Palace Hotel bar, coming in from San Sebastian Jake has passed by "the empty palace." He gets hungry, too hungry to be satisfied with the "rotten" food the Palace offers: " 'Where will we have lunch?' I asked Brett. . . . 'Here? . . .' 'It's rotten here in the hotel' " (257). His appetites are too strong to be satisfied with the chilling, romantic concoctions served up by the empty palace; although lethe and nepenthe for Brett, they are hemlock for him. Demanding more substantial nourishment, he takes himself to "one of the best restaurants in the world." Jake does not need to settle for "rotten" food and deadly games. There is a world beyond Brett and the empty Palace bar, a world of appetites he can satisfy, in which there is more and better to sustain him than Brett or the empty palace can provide: "We had roast young suckling pig. . . . I ate a very big meal and drank three bottles of *rioja alta*" (257). Although Brett "never ate much," Jake's world is rich in sensations: "I like to do a lot of things." He refuses to enumerate or discuss those "things" for Brett; they are a world in which she does not belong, pleasures she does not enjoy.

Brett, feeding off martinis and men, is never satisfied and always ravenous; Jake, satisfying his hunger in more substantial ways, eats, and is fulfilled: "I feel fine." Brett continues to batten upon her illusions, preferring stuffed dog to roast young suckling pig. She is convinced that Jake is getting drunk because they love but cannot have each other, that his suffering is breaking down his self-control. Jake is drinking a great deal but for no reasons she would understand: "How do you know?" Giving up the illusion hurts; it is, indeed, painful to realize not only that he is not loved but that he probably never will be. Yet the pain of starvation and the steady diet of humiliation and shame were more painful still. He sees that he cannot subsist on a dream which has ceased to nourish him, can no longer phantasize that he is full. Malnutrition is another way of committing suicide with the bulls; Jake has realized that, as Brett says, he doesn't "have to."

In telling Brett that he is "not getting drunk," he is telling her that he can control his behavior, that he is no longer compelled by her. He can drink his wine without getting blind. He can enjoy and complete his meal. He can control his behavior and his emotions so that the pleasure of his sensations is undiluted: "I'm just drinking a little wine. I like to drink wine" (258). He cannot control the bulls but he can control himself. He can control the destructive compulsions which ruin his life.

Brett does not get the message for she still hasn't seen Madrid: "I haven't seen Madrid. I should see Madrid." Jake offers to show her the town, but does not run immediately to service her, refusing to interrupt his pleasures to take care of her needs. He finishes his wine first. He takes care of his own appetites; he takes care of himself. When he does enter the taxi, *he* "told the driver where to drive." In control of himself and this situation, he can end his destructive liaison with Brett: " 'I'll finish this,' I said" (258).

He and Brett are still close, still sharing the same war world, still forming their own community. Yet while in the cab in Paris, "our lips were tight together," in Madrid Jake observes that "*Brett* moved close *to* me" but "*we* sat close *against* each other." Jake can feel where he stops and she begins. The community he chooses to form with Brett in Madrid is not the same as they shared in Paris. They no longer feed off the same fantasies and illusions, the same phases and phrases; they are no longer joined at the mouth. Instead, they are two separate people with two separate selves within two separate bodies which touch but never merge.

Brett does not realize the dream is over. She rests "comfortably" within the circle of Jake's arm, within the circle of the hired cab, within the circle of her compulsions, within the circle of her illusions: "Oh, Jake . . . we could have had such a damned good time together." However, Jake is not comfortable. Brett is "pressing against" him, the weight not only of her solid physical presence but also of her metaphysical demands. The policeman, the projection of that part of Jake's self capable of arresting his destructive impulses, stops him once again from destroying himself, from "committing suicide with the bulls." Jake has erect and vigorous within him—if not without—a source of masculinity too potent to allow him to be taken for a ride: "He raised his baton. The car slowed suddenly. . . ." Responding to Brett with pity and irony, compassion and control, Jake breaks the circle: "Isn't it pretty to think so?"

NOTES

[1]See, for example, Philip Young, *Ernest Hemingway: A Reconsideration*, rev. ed. (New York: Harcourt, Brace and World, 1966), p. 86; Mark Spilka, "The Death of Love in *The Sun Also Rises*," in *Twelve Original Essays on Great American Novels*, ed. Charles Shapiro (Detroit: Wayne State University Press, 1958), rpt. in *Hemingway and His Critics*, ed. Carlos Baker (New York: Hill and Wang, 1961), p. 91; John Rouch, "Jake Barnes as Narrator," *Modern Fiction Studies*, 11 (1965), 370; and Richard B. Hovey, *Hemingway: The Inward Terrain* (Seattle: University of Washington Press, 1968), p. 67.

Sam S. Baskett

BRETT AND HER LOVERS

In an early recognition of Hemingway's "literary" and "historical" accomplishment, John Peale Bishop observed in an essay taking its title from Emily Dickinson's "The Missing All," "It is the mark of the true novelist that in searching the meaning of his unsought experience, he comes on the moral history of his time."[1] Hemingway studies over the years have further secured this recognition, particularly for *The Sun Also Rises*. Given what has become the critical consensus that this first novel somehow expresses the way it was in Hemingway's early time, there has been surprising disagreement about just what is revealed by the distinctly different experiences of Jake Barnes, Pedro Romero, Robert Cohn and Bill Gorton, each of whom has received consideration as the moral center of a work that has also often been read as having no moral center. These contradictory readings have not been easy to reconcile, supported as they largely are by seemingly convincing evidence. Yet the counterpointed experiences of the novel's principal characters do resolve into a clearly discernible moral pattern if they are brought into sharp "literary" and "historical" focus, a pattern that in part constructs the time's moral history as well as embodies it.

This is to say that the several lovers of Lady Brett Ashley fix upon her as an uncertain image of great value: to paraphrase the Lady herself, she is sort of what they have instead of God. To their image of her they make such overtures as the time and their individual capacities permit, overtures recalling the question Frost's oven bird "frames in all but words / . . . what to make of a diminished thing": for the value each affixes to Brett is a function of his value of himself and the life he is able to live. From these combined self-definitions emerges the "meaning" of the novel, the significance of which is most fully realized in the context of the patterns of a number of other authentic American "fictions" of the early twentieth century.

Most radically, the pattern of the twentieth century has been sought by Henry Adams. Adams had been delighted to discover that Lucretius "In perhaps the finest

From *Centennial Review* 22, No. 1 (Winter 1978): 45–69.

[lines] in all Latin literature ... [had] invoked Venus exactly as Dante invoked the Virgin"—as one who governed the nature of things.[2] Turning to the twentieth century, however, he found that Woman as Force had been replaced by the dynamo. In the consummate poem which now seems to epitomize the emerging "modern" era, T. S. Eliot's Prufrock describes a circumstance of chaos counterpointed by his desire for a center of meaning symbolized by the attracting power of woman. Thus, a central autobiography and a central poem of the time Hemingway inherited present a compelling version of the same image which dominates *The Sun Also Rises.* That image is also dominant in the novel which impressed Hemingway as an "absolutely first rate work"[3] in May, 1925, two months before he began his own novel. In *The Great Gatsby,* he found a situation similar to the one he would employ, that of a woman idealized far beyond her "perishable"[4] features controlling the world of her "high-bouncing lover" of the epigraph. In her depletion, Lady Brett Ashley, of course, is more akin to Daisy Fay, as she is finally realized, than either to Adams's or Eliot's "one." How well both seemed to illustrate the extremity of the new age is apparent in Joseph Wood Krutch's *The Modern Temper,* published in 1929. The chapter "Love—or the Life and Death of a Value" describes a generation attributing to love "some of the functions of the God they had lost," although inexorably rationalism and physiology were stripping it of its "mystical penumbra."[5] Krutch thus points to a major transformation in the treatment of Woman by Fitzgerald and Hemingway as opposed to that of Adams and Eliot. For both the historian and the poet, at least in *The Education* and "Prufrock," are primarily concerned with Woman as symbolic of highest value, even if that symbol now seemed superseded or inaccessible. The two novelists, however, in a "time of troubles," were not only concerned with what R. P. Blackmur termed "a kind of irregular and spasmodic, but vitalized metaphysics," but also with "a broad and irregular psychology."[6] Daisy is elevated to the role of goddess in Gatsby's romping mind, but she continues to exist, and ultimately *only* exists on a human psychological plane. In the presentation of several "visions" of Lady Brett Ashley, however, Hemingway was to hold in more ambiguous, if precarious, balance the perishable and transcendent, as a complex parade of lovers offer her their varied services in keeping with such value as love retains in their scheme of things.

I

Brett's complicated characterization is enigmatically voiced in both French and English by Jake's concierge: "that lady, that lady there is some one. An eccentric, perhaps, but quelqu'une, quelqu'une."[7] Assuredly, Brett is "some one," in more than one language. As a type of the new woman of the 1920's, she radiates independence, intelligence and beauty. She sees through "rot," sharing with Jake a more profound appreciation of the "modern temper" than that of the other characters. Her appearance reflects the new idea of beauty, her short hair "brushed back like a boy's"—indeed, Jake claims proudly, "She started all that." In a striking image that suggests both her femininity and her impersonality, she is described as being "built with curves like the hull of a racing yacht, and you missed none of it with that wool jersey" (22). Apparently her own woman, in only a few weeks she engages sexually with at least two men in addition to her fiancé. Under the gaiety of Mike's quip that their hotel is a brothel is the serious theme of Brett's debasement of sex. Half asleep, Jake can confuse her voice with that of Georgette, the *poule* he takes to dinner.

Yet in her feminine attractiveness, debased or otherwise, Brett remains essentially unfathomable, somehow apart, as Jake states expressly. She has a way of looking "that made you wonder whether she really saw out of her own eyes. They would look on and on after every one else's eyes in the world would have stopped looking." This is surely extraordinary seeing, both in relation to Brett and in relation to Jake as he sees Brett seeing. Jake immediately adds the ordinary, human dimension, however, appearing to recognize that the powers he attributes to her are illusory: "She looked as though there were nothing on earth she would not look at like that, and really she was afraid of so many things" (26). But Brett, even when she is most "afraid," at least until the final scenes, is principally a contained figure to whom her suitors react, rather than a human being whose motives are susceptible to psychological analysis.

Brett's "mystical penumbra" is greatly intensified by a number of suggestions that she is more than "just personal," even to Jake, "my own true love . . . [my only] friend in the world" (55, 58). In a passage of over one hundred words excised from the manuscript, Jake makes this dimension of their "own true love" even more explicit in an aside to his reader, disclaiming any psychological understanding of Brett or of his unbelievable passion for this person who determines his world. Perhaps Hemingway felt that enough evidence of Brett's strangeness remained in the novel, for there are many motifs suggesting her uniqueness, even apart from her magnification by her different lovers. For example, ironically enough, her promiscuity, which seems almost maternal, never casually salacious. She rejects the count's offer of high-priced prostitution, even though she finds him entertaining and she always needs money; she is "looking after" (203) Mike; she goes with Cohn because she thought it would "be good for him" (83); she sends Romero away not to be "one of these bitches that ruins children. . . . It's sort of what we have instead of God" (243–45); and, as Chaman Nahal has convincingly argued, on one occasion, in a passage exquisitely handled by Hemingway, she affords Jake some sort of sexual gratification so that he will "feel better" (55).[8] In some of these instances she acts for reasons not fully specifiable, at least as the data is given in the novel, but surely her motives go beyond simple self-gratification on any level, motives somehow related to the symbolic beauty of one who "started all that."

In another persistent motif, Brett seems to seek absolution for her actions through her compulsion to bathe, a persistence that expresses a desire for purification transcending cleanliness. But Brett's extraordinary qualities are most directly suggested in Pamplona, where on one occasion she walks through the crowd, "her head up, as though the fiesta were being staged in her honor" (206). Earlier, on the afternoon of "the big religious procession" when "San Fermin was *translated* from one church to another,"[9] Brett is stopped inside the church because she is hatless. Clearly she is the wrong image for the church, too much a disheveled Venus to be allowed in the presence of the Virgin. Even appropriately attired, "I'm damned bad for a religious atmosphere.... I've got the wrong type of face" (208). Outside, however, in the street that runs

> from the chapel into town.... lined on both sides with people keeping their place ... for the return of the procession.... dancers formed a circle around Brett and started to dance.... They took Bill and me by the arms and put us in the circle. Bill started to dance, too. They were all chanting. Brett wanted to dance but they did not want her to. *They wanted her as an image to dance around.* (155) [Italics added]

The interpretation is Jake's, of course, but Brett's actions here, as throughout much of the novel indicate that, try as she will to be merely a dancer, she possesses an aspect, however "wrong" that causes her to be an image "translated" from one sort of "church" to another—the otherwise empty space between the "chapel" and "town" around which a number of people dance in the absence of the return of "the big religious procession."

II

Six men in *The Sun Also Rises* offer Brett such love as they have: Bill Gorton, Count Mippipopolous, Mike Campbell, Pedro Romero, Robert Cohn and Jake Barnes. The first three listed are without illusions, governed as they are not by an ideal but by the nature of things in naturalistic versions of the formula Adams had learned from Lucretius and Dante. To them, there is no supreme value and Brett, far from incarnating such an ideal is a sexually tantalizing woman whom each in his own way wants to possess. It is easy to overlook the fact that at first Bill is much taken by her. Appreciative of the "Beautiful lady.... Going to kidnap us" before he has even met her, he responds to her spirited, openly flirtatious manner with a wittily veiled allusion to fornication[10] and a promise to join her later. In only a few minutes, he has decided she is "Quite a girl" (74–76), but on learning of her engagement to Mike he backs away, and there are no more charged exchanges, even rarely any conversation, between them. His immediate and total withdrawal expresses both his attitude toward Brett and his general approach to life. It is revealing that his friend Edna wishes that Bill had been present when Cohn fights Jake and Mike. "I'd like to have seen Bill knocked down, too. I've always wanted to see Bill knocked down. He's so big" (191). Through the ironic code he tries to teach Jake, Bill remains "big" by limiting his risks, with Brett or anyone else. Having casually noticed the "Beautiful lady," he as casually dismisses her from his concern, despite an encouragement that would have fulfilled Cohn's greatest dreams, when he realizes love for her would not be an uncomplicated "exchange of values" (72). And so he continues loveless, a quality apparent even in his relation with Jake, the person he is "fonder of . . . than anybody on earth." Ultimately, they don't really speak the same language. "You don't understand irony" (114, 116), he jeers at Jake jokingly, whereas Bill, entertaining, charming friend though he may be, lives through irony.

The count explains to Jake and Brett the "secret" of his enjoyment of life: "You must get to know the values." Having established his scheme in terms of what he can buy, he buys—champagne from his friend Baron Mumms, gourmet meals, a "houseful" of antiquities, eighteen eleven brandy, ladies with "class." Later, praying to "make a lot of money" (97), Jake is reminded of the count. When Brett amusedly queries whether love has any place in his values, a question in itself emphasizing her role in the novel—he responds that he is always in love. "That, too, has got a place in my values." Brett retorts, "You're dead," for she well understands that place: ten thousand dollars if she will go to Biarritz with him. To the count—who never "joke[s] people. Joke people and you make enemies" (58–62)—love is obviously a serious business; it is either purchasable or not. With his love, as with his wine, the count does not intend "to mix emotions up" lest he will "lose the taste." Despite his impressive wounds, the count is hardly the hero much critical commentary has made of him.

Like Bill and the count, Mike sets a high value on his fiancée's sexual attractiveness: she, to him, is "a lovely piece." His emotions, of course, are involved to an extent precluded by Bill's irony and the count's accountant practicality, but they arise from his need for a mutual dependence, rather than any commitment to ideal worth. As Mike writes to Jake, "I know her so well and try to look after her but it's not so easy" (126). Nor is it easy for Brett to look after Mike, in his view the original basis of their relation: "she loves looking after people. That's how we came to go off together. She was looking after me" (203). At the end, although she cannot bring herself to marry him, she plans to go back to Mike, and they doubtless will live in a brothel of sorts, alcohol and good-natured carelessness Mike's only defense against their mutual inadequacies in "looking after" each other.

Bill, the count and Mike remain unchanged by their "love" for Brett. Cohn, on the other hand, is vulnerable to passion and transformed by it. Boyishly cheerful, "he had been moulded by the two women who had trained him." His present "lady"—so designated four times in one page by Jake—had taken him in hand: "Cohn never had a chance of not being taken in hand. Also he was sure he loved her" (5). "[L]ed . . . quite a life" (7) by this demanding mistress, he is also the servant of a romantic imagination, stimulated by his reading of "splendid imaginary amorous adventures . . . in an intensely romantic land"—as a guidebook to what life holds in Jake's appraisal, "about as safe as it would be . . . to enter Wall Street direct from a French convent, equipped with a complete set of the more practical Alger books" (9). In this unique figure facetiously suggesting an "exchange" of financial and religious values, Jake dramatically presents Cohn's danger, and his own as I will consider presently. It is a danger arising from utter commitment to a supreme value, all the more dangerous because so immaturely conceived,[11] as opposed to the relative safety of the other "lovers" just discussed who contemplate a more or less "[s]imple exchange of values" (72) for the fulfillment of their different ideas of satisfaction.

Cohn is thus by temperament recklessly ready for "amorous adventures" of greater intensity than that afforded by his liaison with Frances, who, even though she is unaware of Brett, describes what Cohn is looking for.

> I know the real reason why Robert won't marry me ... It's just come to me. They've sent it to me in a vision in the Café Select. Isn't it mystic? Some day they'll put a tablet up. Like at Lourdes.... Why, you see, Robert's always wanted to have a mistress ... And if he marries me ... that would be the end of all the romance. (51)

The "mystic" vision, recalling Adams's allusion to the power of belief in a divine mistress revealed at Lourdes, is not Frances's, of course, but Cohn's; for from the first, he looks at Brett as Moses looked "at the promised land" (22), a vision superseding his desire for romantic life in South America. He is ready to fight the next day when Jake calls her less than perfect. Cohn finds in her a certain indescribable "quality": "I shouldn't wonder if I were in love with her" (38). Even in such a detail as his tennis game he is changed by his love. Formerly he had "loved to win"; now he doesn't care when "People beat him who had never had a chance with him" (45). Faced with her profanation of what he regards as a sacramental union, he calls her Circe, but never denies her power over him, following her around "like a poor bloody steer" (142), in Mike's drunken analogy. Cohn does not think of himself as a steer, however, and he ultimately does "battle for his lady love" (178) until he is routed from the ambiguous world represented by Brett.

Concerned as he is with being a writer, Jake confesses in Chapter VI to a difficulty in showing Cohn clearly, giving as the reason, "I never heard him make one remark that would, in any way, detach him from other people" until he fell in love with Brett. Again, "If he were in a crowd nothing he said stood out" (45). Yet manifestly Cohn does stand out for Jake—he begins his novel with him, is concerned to show him clearly and comes to be "blind, unforgivingly jealous of what had happened to him" (99). One explanation, beyond jealousy, for Jake's blindness toward Cohn is that in him he may well see himself, both in his hopeless love and in the attitudes that make him vulnerable to such a love. Cohn has often been compared to Gatsby in his "romantic readiness," but in this respect neither is Jake totally unlike Fitzgerald's hero. The yacht image by which Jake first describes Brett suggests not only her feminine attractiveness, but a realm of inaccessible beauty, much as Dan Cody's yacht seen "over the most insidious flat on Lake Superior" represents to Gatsby "all the beauty and glamour in the world" (98, 101), the vision he was later to translate into Daisy's "white face." Jake's romantic readiness is in evidence throughout much of the novel. For example, he shares Cohn's interest in the "innocent occupation" of reading "romantic" books. Even if he does not take *The Purple Land* as "literally" as Cohn does, its "splendid imaginary amorous adventures" are his assessment; moreover, any possible irony in this description is undercut by his enjoyment of a similarly "sinister" book at Burguete, "a wonderful story" about a woman and "her true love" who waited twenty-four years for her husband's body to be recovered from a glacier. This protracted postponement of consummation mirrors Jake's spellbound attendance on his "own true love," revealing as it does that whether he fully realizes it or not he is in effect taking such a work as "a guide-book to what life holds" for him.

Of course, he does realize, particularly at night, that such "waiting" is unsatisfactory. "What do you do nights, Jake?" asks his fellow correspondent. What he does is to take a *"poule"* to dinner, having "forgotten how dull it could be" (16). This is not the first time, the point is clear, that, waiting for Brett, he has made such a futile gesture to quicken his life. "You're getting damned romantic" (23), Brett quips insensitively. More characteristically, Jake cries about what he cannot have. "It is awfully easy to be hard-boiled about everything in the daytime, but at night it is another thing" (34). Decidedly, he is not "hard-boiled" with Brett. The two most obvious instances in which he seems to allow Brett to wrench the course of his life into her service are his taking her to Romero and his unquestioning obedience to her call at the end. But throughout the book, and over a considerably longer period than Cohn, he slavishly makes himself fully available to Brett, as she requires his services.[12] Although in his "hard-boiled" moments Jake recognizes Brett "only wanted what she could not have" (31), when they are first alone in the Paris taxi, he is unable to resist offering himself abjectly to her. He kisses her, professes not to understand when she draws back, begs her to love him and questions hopelessly, "Isn't there anything we can do about it?" then answering, "And there's not a damn thing we could do." He rouses himself, "We'd better stay away from each other," and almost immediately, "It's good to see each other" (26–27). After the episode in Jake's bedroom previously noted, he entreats Brett to live with him, saying he could bear her being unfaithful, unaware she has promised to go to San Sebastian with Cohn. Jake persists:

> "Can't we go together?"
> "No. That would be a hell of an idea after we'd just talked it out."
> "We never agreed."
> "Oh, you know as well as I do. Don't be obstinate, darling."
> "Oh, sure," I said. "I know you're right. I'm just low, and when I'm low I talk like a fool." (56)

In this infatuated state dancing to the tune of "You can't two time——," Jake summarizes his predicament: "I had the feeling of a nightmare of it all being something repeated, something I had been through and that now I must go through again"

(64). Although Brett is the most frustrating aspect of his life, he cannot do without her whenever she will suffer his attendance.

Irrevocably committed to his unavailing love, Jake is forced to see his attitude in perspectives provided by the calculating appraisal of the count, the lusty dependency of Mike, the romantic worship of Cohn, the passing interest of Bill. However, none of these "lovers" is able to function as his "tutor"—to employ Earl Rovit's general term[13]—with the possible exception of Bill Gorton. The count, Mike and Cohn provide in their various ways clearly negative examples: ultimately, Jake is unable to take any of the three seriously as living a satisfactory life. Bill's stance is more problematical, especially since he is so convinced of its efficacy and since he so insistently concerns himself with what might be called "The Education of Jacob Barnes." When he arrives in Paris at the beginning of Book II, he immediately senses his friend's depression, and, without knowing the cause, light-heartedly undertakes a cure, continuing intermittently until he learns the dimensions of Jake's malaise at Burguete. Claiming to be on an extended spree, actually Bill is in complete control, and his barbed alcoholic prolixity turns out to be brilliantly pointed in their first scene together. As a writer, he first tells Jake a "travel story," moralizing "Injustice everywhere," a clear antidote to the self pity he must have discerned in him. He then takes another tack, this time as a "nature writer." Walking down the Boulevard, they come first to a statue of two men whom Bill identifies as inventors of pharmacy, and then to a "taxidermist." Bibulously inspired, he is up to the connection, urging Jake to buy "Just one stuffed dog" as a cure of sorts. "Certainly brighten up your flat.... Mean everything in the world to you . . . Simple exchange of values. You give them money. They give you a stuffed dog." Jake pretends to believe that Bill is drunk, but when Brett joins them and flirtatiously remarks, "You've a nice friend," he responds wryly, "He's all right.... He's a taxidermist," signalling his awareness that Bill has been trying to stuff him, to fill up his hollowness and "brighten up ... [his] flat" (71–75).

In this and ensuing conversations, Bill lays down a barrage of imperatives, functioning, as Morton L. Ross has noted, "very much as does the preacher in Ecclesiastes," his "sermon" consisting principally of "commandments" which he announces as "universal guides to action";[14] but it should be kept in mind he is only addressing Jake. Many of his instructions have often been read as facetious chatter, but even what seems mere badinage is charged with thematic significance. Whatever the degree of flippancy, his advice may be collected under four major precepts which are the basis of his life, the life he is urging on his best friend: Utilize a little; Never be Daunted; Show Irony and Pity; Do not Question. The reason for his instruction is obvious. For clearly Jake is not fully utilizing; he is often daunted; instead of showing irony and pity when he's "feeling" he is only "hard-boiled" in the daytime and self-pitying at night; and he continues to be "pretty religious."

Explicitly, Jake neither accepts nor rejects Bill's "commandments." In the Paris street scene, as noted, he evasively accuses Bill of being a hundred and forty-four drinks ahead of him. He is more relaxed at the Burguete inn, away from Paris and

Brett, literally warming up to Bill's friendly advice, as echoes of Ecclesiastes, here-tofore unnoticed, make clear.[15] This feeling of warmth is quickly dispelled the next morning, however. Jake gets up early to dig fishing worms for both of them. Returning, he encounters a renewed ironic onslaught. "What were you doing? Burying your money? . . . You go out and dig some more worms and I'll be right down. . . . Work for the good of all! . . . Show irony and pity." Bill thus jibes that Jake is still not properly utilizing: the skilled fisherman uses flies; the knowledgeable buyer does not bury his money.[16] Jake, unable to claim Bill is intoxicated in this instance, is reduced to retorting, "Oh, go to hell!" and leaving the room thumbing his nose as Bill launches into his irony and pity song of "feeling" to the tune of "The Bells are Ringing for Me and My Gal." At breakfast, however, under Bill's urging, he attempts to "Say something pitiful"; "Robert Cohn." Bill approves and extends his instruction. "That's better. Now why is Cohn pitiful? Be ironic," but Jake has had enough. "Aw, hell! . . . It's too early in the morning" (113–114). At lunch Bill returns to his exhortation, giving his mock sermon,

> "Utilize a little, brother. . . . Let us not pry into the holy mysteries . . . with simian fingers. Let us accept on faith and simply say—I want you to join with me in saying—What shall we say, brother? . . . Let us kneel and say: 'Don't eat that, Lady—that's Mencken.' "

Jake attempts to "join" Bill repeating part of the lesson, "Utilize a little," in reference to a bottle of wine, although he ignores the other ironic reference to communion: "Don't eat that, Lady." and as Bill continues his anti-questioning preachment with the inspired conceit that Bryan, Mencken and he "all went to Holy Cross together"—sacrilegious hilarity coupling simple fundamentalism, strident skepticism, traditional Catholicism and mocking irony—Jake is reduced again to accusing Bill of being "cock-eyed." His tutor, however, pushes on with sober understanding to Jake's two overwhelming questions: Brett and "what it was all about" (148). For the first time Bill asks Jake directly, "Were you ever in love with [Brett]?" and then, immediately, in an apparent *non sequitur,* "[A]re you really a Catholic?" (122–24).

The two questions are closely related to Jake's condition, of course. The love he passionately desires to realize with Brett and the divine love of those who "have God . . . [Quite a lot]" (245) are both unavailable to Jake.[17] In this intimate scene he admits the dual source of his most fundamental "feeling," but despite this intimacy his answers are reserved. He admits to being in love with Brett, "Only I'd a hell of a lot rather not talk about it"; and he is "[t]echnically" a Catholic, although he disclaims any knowledge of what that equivocation signifies. Jake's brusqueness seals off Bill's probing, and he shifts from jabbing irony to sympathetic support, even to the extent of carrying the despised fishing worms.

How much of Bill's tutelage Jake finds acceptable is only gradually apparent. And two central episodes indicate that he must learn more profoundly from other sources: the fight with Cohn and the last day of bull fighting. In the Cohn encounter Jake pays the price of not following Bill's precepts, becoming in the latter's telling phrase, "Old Jake, the human punching-bag" (199). His love for Brett has now led him to act as a "pimp" and then to try to fight Cohn. Quickly knocked unconscious, he is revived with "a carafe of water on my head" to find "everything looked new and changed. I had never seen the trees before. . . . It was all different." In this awakening, he is a way he has not been before; he still cares, but he is now more irreversibly aware of the unreality of his dream of Brett and all she represents to him. The experience is intensified by his recollection of the effects of another head "wound," of having been "kicked in the head" in a youthful football game and returning to full cognizance carrying his suitcase through his home town, only "it was all new. They were raking the lawns and burning leaves. . . . It was all strange" (191–93).[18] Now in this similarly transformed world he has a feeling of carrying a "phantom suitcase," the baggage of his new awareness he must carry for the rest of his life, the burden of full consciousness that Bill is determined to avoid.

Stunned as he has been by Cohn, Jake must descend still further from his romantic expectations. After reluctantly shaking hands with his kindred adversary, he wants "a deep, hot bath to lie back in . . . a hot bath in deep water" but, significantly, "the water would not run" (193–95). More or less in a state of shock, still unable to cope with his feelings, he goes to bed. The next day, waking with "a headache" he must cope with even more: the articulation of his new awareness in the art form of the bull fight. Jake had loyally defended Bill's understanding of bull fighting to Montoya, who had merely repeated "But he's not aficionado like you are" (131). Montoya is astute in perceiving that Bill is an interested spectator rather than a passionate enthusiast. There are no knowledgeable exchanges between Bill and Jake at the fights as there had been in the "country" around Burguete; in fact, a number of comments reveal his limited appreciation. And during the afternoon of Romero's triumph, described in a passage of over nine pages, Bill's only recorded response is the scarcely insightful, "There he goes" (219), as Romero kills his first bull. Jake's appreciation of bull fighting as tragedy is on an entirely different plane, one prepared for by his observation on the second day of the fights. "Romero's bull-fighting gave real *emotion*," not "a fake *emotional feeling*, while the bull-fighter was really safe" (168). Through this vocabulary, bull fighting is linked to Bill's song of "Irony and Pity," "When you're *feeling*. . . . When they're *feeling*" (114) [All italics added]. The last day of the festival this motif is continued and charged with greater emphasis by the appearance of *sensation* three times on the same page, the only occurrences of the word as opposed to over forty instances of some form of *feeling*. With this underscoring, the concept of tragedy is specifically introduced.

> Belmonte, in his best days, worked always in the terrain of the bull. . . . This way he gave the *sensation* of coming *tragedy*. People went to the corrida to see Belmonte, to be given *tragic sensations,* and perhaps to see the death of Belmonte . . . the element that was necessary to give the *sensation* of tragedy. . . . (213–214) [Italics added].

Jake goes to the bull fights to see great matadors work "in the terrain of the bull" and thus to be given the traditional "tragic sensations" of pity and fear. What he must be struck by, however, is the pointed contrast with the way he had been living his life, in self pitying, futile aspiration, rather than "all the way up" (10) as he had once characterized the life of the bull fighter to Cohn. "Everybody behaves badly," he tells Brett. "Given the proper chance, I'd be as big an ass as Cohn" (181), and the "phantom suitcase" he now carries is part of his new recognition of himself in this light, in expecting from Brett, and from life, what he is not going to get. Romero, however, does not "behave badly" in or out of the ring, and as a bull fighter, through his "greatness" he enables his audience, including Jake, to experience the "sensations" of tragedy. Romero, in keeping with his name either as "pilgrim" or "pilot fish," provides Jake with a momentary vision of the stance he would like to be able to assume, not in the bull ring but in his entire life. In this sense Romero, in another dimension than Bill, serves as Jake's tutor.[19]

But what of Romero outside the ring? There remains to consider him as Brett's lover. After saying that Romero had the "greatness," Jake adds, "He loved bull-fighting, and I think he loved the bulls, and I think he loved Brett" (216). Certainly he responds to Brett's encouragement, even though he has earlier been informed that Mike is doing "[n]othing. . . . waiting to marry this lady" (176). In contrast to Bill, he is undeterred by this information. And he performs for her in the bull ring, maneuvering the action in front of her, presenting her with the ear he is awarded for his triumph. But he is distinctly not a knight like Cohn, "ready to do battle for his lady love." His performance as a matador, as well as his fight with Cohn, is first of all for himself and only incidentally for Brett. He even has a bit of condescending humor as he presents the ear to her. "'Don't get bloody,' Romero said, and grinned" (221). He defines himself not primarily as Brett's lover as do Cohn and Jake, but as a bull fighter, with no commitment of any sort between himself and his vocation. Jake makes the distinction: "He loved bull-fighting . . . and I think he loved Brett."

In what way does he love her? After "a final look to ask if it were understood" (187), he proceeds sexually in accordance with that understanding. His initial tentativeness arises both from his natural disbelief that this woman from what must seem another world is available, and also from his youth. He is repeatedly designated a "lad," "boy," "kid," or "child" by Montoya, Jake and Brett. Montoya is particularly concerned with his immaturity outside the ring. "'Any foreigner' can flatter [a boy like that]" (172). Learning that this nineteen-year-old primitive wanted to marry the thirty-four-year-old sophisticate, Jake summons enough humor to say, "Maybe he thought it would make him Lord Ashley." After Brett sends him away, she feels good at not ruining "children." And Romero, surely dimly understanding that he is out of his element, does go—back to *his* true love, bull fighting. He would have married her, Brett tells Jake, "to make it sure I could never go away from him," after she had grown her hair out and "gotten more womanly, of course." Romero, in his boyish self-confidence, wants Brett for his woman. He has only "been" with two before, Brett says, and until this experience "never cared about anything but bull-fighting" (242–45). But he only wants to marry Brett if she will fit *his* naïve image of a wife, the wife of a matador committed to his vocation. We do not fully know Romero's story, of course, but there is nothing in what we do know to suggest that Brett determines his world in the way she does that of Cohn and Jake: she is not his goddess. It is as impossible to consider his momentary expression of youthful male ardor for a sexually exciting woman as committed love as it is to understand how he has been read as fully heroic.

This is not to deny that he passes his first test of true "greatness" in the bull ring on the last day of the festival. But, as Cohn responded to Jake's rather rigid aphorism that only bull fighters live life all the way up, "That's an abnormal life" (10). What, to consider an example given dramatic focus in the novel, are we to make of Belmonte, a significant figure in Jake's education who has received little attention?[20] Not one of Brett's lovers, he *is* Jake's unwitting tutor—an example of heroism, loving nothing, "going through his pain." Once, one of the greatest matadors, he can no longer live in his vocation "all the way up," providing an answer to Romero's youthful confidence, "I'm never going to die" (p. 186). In his prime strong and fully accepting of danger, he is now old and sick, avoiding risks by picking bulls for their "safety." "[N]ot sure that there were any great moments," "He no longer had his greatest moments in the bull-ring." Where then, the phrasing seems to ask, does he have "his greatest moments"? Jake has just observed him in such a moment. Belmonte, having failed in the eyes of the crowd with his second bull, smiled contemptuously

> when he was called something particularly insulting, and always the pain that any movement produced grew stronger and stronger, until finally his yellow face was parchment color ... he passed through into the callejon and leaned on the barrera below us, his head on his arms, not seeing, not hearing anything, only going through his pain. When he looked up, finally, he asked for a drink of water. He swallowed a little ... took his cape, and went back into the ring. (214–15)

Observing such greatness as Belmonte can now achieve in the tragic human circumstance figured forth on the "parchment color" of death with which he, and Romero, as well as Belmonte are all ultimately faced, Jake is surely "given tragic sensations." Jake's identification with Belmonte is emphasized not only by the phrasing, "going through his pain," which recalls his earlier description of having been through a nightmare "that now I must go through again," but also by the fact that there is no indication that his perception of Belmonte's agony is shared or even perceived by anyone else—Bill, Brett or the crowd.

After the bull fights are over, it is not surprising that Jake, feeling "like hell," under Bill's ministrations gets "drunker than I ever remembered having been." Bill wants him thus to get over his "damn depression" (223), that is to follow the advice he has been giving—to go through less pain. Jake has cause for his deepest depression. Brett has gone off with Romero, reinforcing the finality of his earlier "nightmare" that his dream has become. Also, in the same afternoon he has been "given" two different sets of "tragic sensations." He has experienced the classic tragic emotions evoked by Romero's public artistry transmuting the dangers of life to a higher form. But he has also identified with the private agony of Belmonte "looking at nothing," his "great moments" in the past. Jake recognizes that there are unlikely to be any "great moments" for him, that his life is to be in considerable part his going through a pain that will never be completely alleviated by pleasure, God, love or by any other opiate, reality or value. This recognition of himself and his world has not exhilarated him, but it has transformed him, even more dramatically than Robert Cohn's blows. At such a "boundary situation"[21] he is no longer "blind." He now looks "strange" to himself in the mirror and his "world was not wheeling anymore. It was very clear and bright, and inclined to blur at the edges" (224). Strengthened by this tragic perception of his life as he must live it, not the "abnormal" life of Romero, but the "normal" life of Belmonte, he is now able to rejoin Bill soberly, eat some proffered soup and start living his life as best he can, at the end of his line.

Jake has not thus facilely achieved tragic dimensions, but the issue of tragedy as opposed to therapy has been raised in the novel. Hemingway, of course, explicitly raised it himself, in two different letters shortly after publication. "It's funny to write a book that seems as tragic as that and have them take it for a jazz superficial story," and three days later, the book was not "a hollow or bitter satire, but a damn tragedy with the earth abiding forever as the hero."[22] These remarks, together with the several references to tragedy in The Sun Also Rises—even without anticipating the discussion of bull fighting as tragedy in Death in the Afternoon—call attention to the movement of the novel, and the life of its narrator, in the direction of the tragic vision. At the beginning, Jake, in Rovit's terminology, is the tyro, but by the end he has learned much from three tutors, Bill, Romero, and Belmonte; from the negative examples of Cohn, Mike and the count; as well as from the head blows of Cohn, Brett's lover most like himself. The extent of his development and its limitation, is apparent in the final scenes.

In Book III, which opens just after Jake's "world was not wheeling any more," it is "all over." Specifically, it is the fiesta that is finished, but more widely, it is the entire sequence of events that has wrought a change in Jake and his world, most particularly, his love of Brett. He says goodby to Bill in France, and Jake goes back to Spain, "recover[ing]" an hour": they are different countries and times. Jake proceeds steadily and quietly through the routine of his days in San Sebastian, seeming to gather strength from swimming in the "green and dark" water, from vistas of a "green mountainside" and "a green hill with a castle." Very explicitly, after Jake has filled out his "police bulletin" and is swimming in the sea, there is imagery of depth, anticipating the elevation of the Madrid scenes.

> Then I tried several *dives. I dove deep* once, swimming *down* to the *bottom.* I swam with my eyes open and it was green and *dark.* The raft [with two lovers on it] made a *dark shadow.* I came out of water beside the raft, pulled up, *dove* once more, holding it for length, and then swam ashore. (234–35) [Italics added]

Both his state of mind and the natural scenery suggest something of the mood of the episode at Burguete, but there is a difference. In San Sebastian, he sustains himself, unsupported by Bill's noisy camaraderie, and he seems more in control of his universe.[23]

This serenity is put to test when Brett summons him to Madrid. At first, he seems in danger of reverting to the self-pitying attitude in Paris:

> That seemed to handle it. That was it. Send a girl off with one man. Introduce her to another to go off with him. Now go and bring her back. And sign the wire with love. That was it all right. (239)

Here again is the familiar tone of helpless, desperate commitment. Jake seems ready to resume his dance around Brett's image, transfixed in a desire that can neither be denied nor satisfied—in effect endowing Brett with a "mystical penumbra" and making his worship of her serve for his "big religious possession." Jake is different, however, as a careful reading makes clear. Brett is now reduced to "a girl" in difficulty, and "love" is a "sign." For better and worse, Jake is no longer dancing around Brett's image in quite the same measures. Immediately after sending the telegram "I went in to lunch," not only an indication of his new equanimity, but an illustration of his determination to "utilize" as best he can, to be further shown in the climactic scenes in Madrid. These passages are carefully prepared for by Jake's journey to the "end of the line" through symbolic scenery intensified by the concentration of a number of images of elevation as well as by reverberations in the words here italicized, of portions of Section V of *The Waste Land*. He sees Madrid "come up over the *plain,* a compact white sky-line on the top of a little *cliff* away across the sun-hardened country. . . . we climbed up through the *gardens,* by the *empty palace* and the unfinished *church* on the edge of the *cliff,* and on up until we were in the high, hot modern town." Unable to work the "elevator," he walks up to the second floor of the Hotel Montana—*"Mountain"*—to be admitted by a maid with a *"sullen face"* (239–40). The "arid plain" is now behind Jake, and he is ready to set his lands in order by shoring up his ruins with such fragments as he has. He proceeds to exemplify in his actions and attitudes several of the commandments of his "nice friend," the "taxidermist." He takes Brett to Botin's, "one of the best restaurants in the world," where, as the name translates, he collects his "bounty" or "spoils of war" in a sumptuous meal. "I like to drink wine," he tells Brett, "I like to do a lot of things" (245–46). Just how much he enjoys "utilizing a little" remains uncertain, but in sharp contrast to his behavior in Paris, he is "undaunted" in Brett's presence.

More significantly, as he "feels"—some form of the verb occurs seven times in two pages—he stabilizes his world with irony and pity. His tenderness toward Brett is continually apparent, as he supports her firmly while asking nothing. "Tell me about it. . . . You were probably damn good for him. . . . You ought to feel set up. . . . Dear Brett" (241–43). And, as noted, he can even be ironical about Romero's motives for wanting to marry Brett. All of his remarks to Brett, as well as all of his actions show attitudes designed to palliate the pain each is going through. In Paris, Jake had been the weaker of the two, but in Madrid, following some of Bill's instructions, he is much stronger. And so in the magnificently evocative last lines of the novel, he can sum up the growth he has achieved in his response to Brett's shallow *cri de coeur,* "we could have had such a damned good time together," with "Yes. . . . Isn't it pretty to think so?" (247). Yet there is more to his response than irony and pity, for as he had signed his wire "with love," so this response also bears the mark of love. Jake now sees his love more clearly for what it is—even his comforting response is punctuated as a question. But in seeing his love in its diminishment, he still holds on to it, not desperately but with perspicacity. "Feeling" however diminished is preferable to calculated "simple exchange." Jake is now able to act for the first time as a Hemingway hero, having made his play, to back it up.[24]

Bill had been concerned, of course, to get Jake not to make this play, the play for the love of Brett, the play for ultimate rather than simple "exchange." Aware that Jake could never have had a "damned good time" with Brett—with her his destiny would always be most likely that of the "human punching-bag"—Bill also believes that Jake's search for answers will be equally fruitless. In short, as a substitute for frustrated faith, human and divine, in whatever formula of precarious consubstantiation, he has recommended taxidermy and self-protection. Tutored as he has been by all of his experience of a world that is neither his own nor himself, and true to his own feelings, Jake, however, must make a more complicated play, a search for love as a value that transcends both utility and fantasy, even as Brett's mystery disperses under his more penetrating gaze.

By the final scenes in Madrid, Jake is able to hold himself steady in the paradox of wanting everything and having nothing except himself—Emily Dickinson's paradox of "The Missing All"—both states expressed in his absurd, magnificent passion for Brett, and captured in his final words. He is not yet a tragic hero pushing resolutely toward a victory of spirit against the inevitable defeat of circumstance, but he is at his own "boundary situation." If he is not, like Santiago, "beyond all the people in the world," he is farther out than he has been before. Much closer in time and situation to Nick Adams in "Big Two-Hearted River," who "wanted to be a great writer," he is not yet ready to fish "In the swamp [where] . . . the fishing would be tragic. In the swamp fishing was a tragic adventure. Nick did not want it." Neither does Jake seem to "want it" as he holds himself tautly against the pressures of his life in the final scenes of the novel.

III

But Jake obviously does "want it." His experiences do not end in Madrid, in the taxi with Brett. They end with his seeking out the meaning of his impossible/possible love for Brett through the writing of *The Sun Also Rises,* even as Nick Carraway's "lost words" are recaptured in the telling of Gatsby's story. Recognizing that he may indeed have to live without the love of God, or any sufficient image thereof, the predicament cited as characteristic of the "modern temper" by Krutch, he still refuses to deny the attracting power of both. "[T]o find, / Not to impose . . . / It is possible, possible, possible. It must be possible," Stevens was to write in *Notes toward a Supreme Fiction,* and Jake from this position sets out to order his "poem of the mind." The overtones of Stevens are far from gratuitous: Stevens himself recognized the affinity in a 1942 letter stating that although Hemingway was not usually regarded as a poet, he considered him "the most significant living poet as far as the subject of EXTRAORDINARY ACTUALITY is concerned."[25] In the process of writing the "poem" of his life, Jake composes, in effect, his "love song"—the uniqueness distinguishing his human syllable from that of Brett's other lovers whom he knows in secret kinship. Faced with playing things as they are, he finally neither asserts in foolish desperation as Cohn, nor abdicates his full human responsibility as do the other lovers in their separate ways. Rather as the artist he set out to "create in honesty"[26] a world in which he can live as a moral being. Bill had taunted him at Burguete with not knowing irony and pity. "And you claim you want to be a writer, too. You're only a newspaper man. An expatriated newspaper man." Bill is a writer, and a successful one; but he limits himself to "travel stories" and "nature-writ[ing]." Tragedy is beyond his reach. Jake, however, will not accept such limitations. Unlike Bill, and Cohn, another writer of limited vision, he really is ultimately concerned with "an abnormal life," one lived "all the way up." *The Sun Also Rises* is a record of how he attempts to learn to live that life. Seeing all around him, as well as inside himself, evidences of the death of value, Jake chooses, even in recognition of that extinction, to create his own "All"—*The Sun Also Rises*—and in the act of so doing comes on a "moral history" that at once follows the pattern of the age but also deepens and enriches its tragic colors.

NOTES

[1] "The Missing All," *Virginia Quarterly Review,* 13 (Winter 1937), 118. Cited in Carlos Baker, *Hemingway: The Writer as Artist* (Princeton, N.J.: Princeton University Press, 1972), p. 75.

[2] *The Education of Henry Adams* (New York: The Modern Library, 1931), p. 384.

[3] Carlos Baker, *Ernest Hemingway: A Life Story* (New York: Charles Scribner's Sons, 1969), p. 146.

[4] F. Scott Fitzgerald, *The Great Gatsby* (New York: Charles Scribner's Sons, Student's Edition, 1953), *passim,* but especially pp. 111–12.

[5] *The Modern Temper* (New York: Harcourt, Brace and World, Inc., 1929), pp. 73, 78

[6] R. P. Blackmur, *Anni Mirabiles: 1921–1925* (Washington, D.C.: The Library of Congress, 1956), p. 26.

[7] *The Sun Also Rises* (New York: Charles Scribner's Sons, The Scribner Library Edition, 1954), p. 53. Subsequent citations in text.

[8] *The Narrative Pattern in Ernest Hemingway's Fiction* (Rutherford, N.J.: Fairleigh Dickinson University Press, 1971), pp. 42–45.

[9] In the only other use of the word in the novel, four pages later, when Brett wants a bath, Bill Gorton offers, in diction so awkward as to demand attention, "Let's *translate* Brett to the Hotel" (159) [Italics added].

[10] The language refers to Eliot's epigraph to "Portrait of a Lady" taken from The Jew of Malta: "Thou has committed / Fornication: but that was in another country, / And besides, the wench is dead."

[11] William Bysshe Stein has discussed Hemingway's treatment in his short stories of the "illusion of redemptive passion [which] identifies the arrested adolescence of the American adult" in "Love and Lust in Hemingway's Short Stories," Texas Studies in Literature and Language, 3 (Summer 1961), 239.

[12] It is a possibility previously unremarked that the reasons he has withdrawn $600 from his account since the first of the month—twice Cohn's monthly allowance from his mother, a fact rather nastily set down by Jake—is that he is providing Brett with considerable sums. It is surely significant that as meticulously as he keeps his accounts, even noting a two-franc trip, he does not itemize this large expenditure. Interesting in this connection is the fact that about the time he had finished the first draft of The Sun Also Rises, Lady Duff Twysden asked to borrow 3,000 francs from Hemingway. Baker, Ernest Hemingway: A Life Story, pp. 155–57.

[13] Ernest Hemingway (New York: Twayne Publishers, Inc., 1963), pp. 53–77.

[14] "Bill Gorton, the Preacher of The Sun Also Rises," Modern Fiction Studies, 18 (Winter 1972–1973), 520.

[15] As they enter the town there are eight separate references to the cold. At the inn they drink hot rum punch against the cold; and the evening concludes, "After supper we went upstairs and smoked and read in bed to keep warm. Once in the night I woke and heard the wind blowing. It felt good to be warm and in bed" (108–111). In the relevant verses of Ecclesiastes, "Two are better than one; because they have a good reward for their labour. For if they fall, the one will lift up his fellow: but woe to him that is alone when he falleth; for he hath not another to help him up. Again if two lie together, then they have heat: but how can one be warm alone?" Ecclesiastes 4:9–11.

[16] In addition to the four commandments I have listed, Ross includes "Work for the good of all." Yet in the "fishing worm" context this is heavily ironic, and, furthermore, there is no evidence that either Bill or Jake is ever concerned with any common good.

[17] Stein has noted how Hemingway is concerned in his short stories with the "degradation of the Passion by sexual passion." Again, "in dramatizing the absurdities of modern love—the nostalgia for passion—[Hemingway] succeeds in defending the principles of his crypto-Catholicism" (236, 239).

[18] Both experiences of this new, strange world are described in terms evoking Gatsby's new world after he realizes no call is coming from Daisy. "He must have looked up at an unfamiliar sky through frightening leaves and shivered as he found what a grotesque thing a rose is and how raw the sunlight was upon the scarcely created grass. A new world, material without being real ... that ashen, fantastic figure ... the amorphous trees ..." (162). Mark Spilka, whose remarks are usually illuminating and always pro-vocative, does not see this passage as indicative of Jake's awakening. "Barnes seems to have regressed here to his youthful football days.... Cohn has also regressed to his abject college days: they are both emotional adolescents, about the same age as the nineteen-year-old Romero." "The Death of Love in The Sun Also Rises," Twelve Original Essays on Great American Novels, Charles Shapiro, ed. (Detroit: Wayne State University Press, 1959), p. 251. I am, of course, arguing that it is precisely at this point that Jake is advancing beyond Cohn and Romero.

[19] Noting the translation of Romero's name, Bruce L. Grenberg goes on to state that Romero provides Jake with an ideal. But, as he properly notes, "His heroism per se cannot be translated directly into the modern world Jake occupies." "The Design of Heroism in The Sun Also Rises," Fitzgerald/Hemingway Annual (1971), pp. 283–84.

[20] Most commentators have ignored Belmonte. Rovit, whose reading of Hemingway generally and The Sun Also Rises particularly, is most persuasive and stimulating in almost every instance, unaccountably dismisses Belmonte. Belmonte is a "tutor" and "code-hero" (55) and yet "One of the few extraneous scenes in The Sun Also Rises ... concerns itself with the appearance of Juan Belmonte in the Pamplona bull ring" (32). On the contrary, I read his introduction as absolutely crucial to Jake's tragic development.

[21] In noting the use of this term by Kierkegaard, Jaspers and Tillich among others, Richard B. Sewall writes, "The tragic vision impels the man of action to fight against his destiny ... the artist in his fictions toward ... 'boundary-situations,' man at the limits of his sovereignty.... [T]he hero faces as if no man had ever faced it before the existential question—Job's question 'What is man?'" The Vision of Tragedy (New Haven: Yale University Press, 1959), pp. 5, 151.

[23] The contrast between the two similar times is shown in at least two incidents. At Burguete, he had remained dry, fishing from the dam with worms—Bill had used flies and "was wet from the waist down." Now he swims feeling that he "could never sink." Earlier, he and Bill had stumbled into a bit of sexual double-entendre involving pedals, joysticks, and bicycles that both immediately back away from as too

painful for Jake. At San Sebastian he maintains an "ironical" equanimity when similar references come up in the conversation with the bicycle-riders and their girls.

[24] Again, I am indebted to Rovit's discussion, in this instance of Colonel Cantwell's definition of a "tough boy," pp. 59–60.

[25] *Letters of Wallace Stevens*, ed. Holly Stevens (New York: Knopf, 1966), pp. 411–12.

[26] Blackmur, p. 8.

Patrick D. Morrow

THE BOUGHT GENERATION

"Last week he tried to commit suicide," one waiter said.
"Why?"
"He was in despair."
"About what?"
"Nothing."
"How do you know it was nothing?"
"He has plenty of money."

—Ernest Hemingway, "A Clean, Well-Lighted Place"

For almost a generation now, critics have noted the importance of money in *The Sun Also Rises*,[1] In his 1963 Twayne United States Authors Series book on Hemingway, Earl Rovit proposed that the hierarchy of the characters' financial values correlated exactly with the hierarchy of their moral values.[2] This idea has been widely accepted. Claire Sprague in a 1969 article supports this argument, noting that in *The Sun Also Rises* "how one gets and spends money becomes a subject index to character...."[3] Sprague also asserts that Jake "chooses to believe in value, chooses to erect a rigorous personal code which his literal account-keeping parallels."[4] Richard Sugg's 1972 article, "Hemingway, Money, and *The Sun Also Rises*," agrees with and amplifies the above, then moves on to explain how Hemingway uses financial transactions to reveal Jake as the novel's uncontested moral hero.[5] Finally, in a 1979 article, Nancy Comley proffers a diagrammed schema "to show how this concern with money manifests itself in an economic structure of exchange values which the Hemingway hero learns to apply to his life, most especially to his emotional relationships."[6] This linear critical development has certainly provided worthwhile insights into the role of money in *The Sun Also Rises*, but the topic is hardly a closed account.

From *Genre* 13, No. 1 (Spring 1980): 51–69.

123

Money is not merely an issue or a revealing metaphorical and moral pattern in *The Sun Also Rises;* money is an obsession in this novel. By my count, *The Sun Also Rises* contains 142 direct references to money, including such varied forms of monetary transactions as paying bills, tipping, betting, bribery, and borrowing and lending, in addition to several metaphorical uses and philosophical discussions of money (see Appendix). That is a rate of almost one direct monetary reference for every other page in the Scribner paperback edition of the novel.[7] By my count there are an additional 71 indirect references, such as characters ordering drinks without direct mention of paying for them. In *The Sun Also Rises,* then, there is some kind of monetary reference for every 1.2 pages.[8] Two questions arise at once from this data: what would account for Hemingway's intense concern with money in *The Sun Also Rises,* and what is the meaning of money in this novel?

As Carlos Baker's biography, *Ernest Hemingway: A Life Story,* clearly reveals, Hemingway's mind was much on money during the composition period of *The Sun Also Rises* (1925–26).[9] For years he had been under parental scrutiny and fire for not settling down to a reliable job that would provide a good, decent living.[10] Ernest, however, was much more his parents' child than they realized. Young Hemingway was very concerned with receiving monetary validation for his short fiction as well as gaining favorable contractual arrangements for future novel-length works. On the two trips to Pamplona that Hemingway made during these years, he became very intrigued with the "fiesta" mentality of deferred financial and moral maintenance. His new friends, Harold Loeb, Lady Duff Twysden, Don Stewart, Pat Guthrie, and Kitty Cannell, indulged in a constant round of party now, pay later. This all must have been both very attractive and very shocking to Ernest Hemingway, middle class midwestern young man. The dissipates he had seen earlier in Paris and Germany were faceless fools; these people were his friends and confidantes. The esoteric Duff Twysden not only shadowed Hemingway during this period, but twice in secret messages requested large sums of money from him. Whether or not he gave her any francs is unknown, but she was paid off by being the unmistakable main model for Lady Brett.[11] Hemingway's attitude toward these people was, as Malcolm Cowley said of the expatriates' attitude toward their war experiences, "spectatorial."[12]

Hemingway's other financial dealings through these years indicate his resistance to *carpe diem,* to speculative or spendthrift behavior. He damn well intended to work hard making a good living writing—not what people wanted to read, but what he knew to be truth. During this period Hemingway also first developed his natural talent for driving a hard bargain coupled with an unerring eye for the good deal. Without an agent, and with only *In Our Time* for collateral, he shrewdly played Knopf, Harcourt, and Boni and Liveright against each other to secure a fine financial arrangement for *The Sun Also Rises* from yet another publisher, Charles Scribner.[13]

Hemingway's guilty break-up with wife Hadley began during the writing of *The Sun Also Rises,* and there may have been a financial dimension to their split. The direct cause of the Ernest-Hadley break-up was Hemingway's second wife, Pauline Pfeiffer, whom Baker describes as a *Vogue* fashion editor searching Paris for a husband, the eldest daughter of "a landowning squire in Piggott, Arkansas."[14] In addition, Pauline's multi-millionaire and childless Uncle Gus took a strong liking to Ernest even before meeting him.[15] Was it from sympathy, guilt, or both that Hemingway assigned all immediate and future royalties from *The Sun Also Rises* to Hadley and their son? As we read through Baker's biography, Hemingway's attraction to what Auden called "the parish of rich women"[16] becomes all too evident. Nasty, satirical, and complex, *The Sun Also Rises* has a definite autobiographical dimension, and money loomed as a large and disturbing issue for Hemingway in 1925–26. Thus the beginning of Hemingway's life-long monetary conflict, pointedly summarized by Scott Donaldson: "On the one hand, [Hemingway] learned from his environment that it was right and manly to make money.... On the other hand, Hemingway had also been indoctrinated to think that easy money could ruin a man."[17]

Perceived as recurring metaphorical pattern, the monetary references in *The Sun Also Rises* reveal not only a vertical, hierarchical objective correlative to character morality, but also a constant circular, senseless, and frustrating motion by the characters. As such, money is a major component of the novel's circular formal and thematic essence. Its story is about a circle of people who journey in a circle within a circle (Paris, San Sebastian, Bayonne, Pamplona, Burguete, Pamplona, Burguete, Pamplona, San Sebastian, Madrid, Paris). Circular objects, from lights and tables to coins to the bull ring, form much of the setting. Hemingway even puns on this metaphor with his constant references to rounds of drinks. Money establishes the moral dimension of *The Sun Also Rises* as circular.

A whirl of speculation is the order of the day in *The Sun Also Rises*. Despite all the buying and selling of goods, the money spent buys few articles of substance. Expensive and frequent purchases of alcohol lubricate this *La Dolce Vita* world where everybody parties, but no one has any fun. Like alcohol, transportation is purchased for diversion, and throughout the novel there are several aimless taxi cab and automobile rides. At least transportation does provide movement to a new hotel room or café for the old diversions. There are no investments in the novel, and the monetary waste is continual, increasingly appalling as the novel progresses. While the concept of making money is mentioned several times in *The Sun Also Rises*, there is *no* mention of money in terms of future security. Rather, more money ensures that the "entertaining" circular movement of life without purpose can continue.

Several ideas about money recur during the course of *The Sun Also Rises*. One is the idea that money is the way to buy and control friendship. For example, Robert Cohn offers to pay Jake's way to South America (p. 10). The rich Cohn defines himself largely by using money as magnanimous gesture, a way to obligate, to control. Similarly, Count (another Hemingway pun?) Mippipopolous offers Brett ten thousand dollars if she will accompany him to Biarritz (p. 33). "The high priest of materialism," as Delbert E. Wylder calls the Count,[18] wishes to join and encumber the younger generation by financial obligation. With more success, Brett buys the friendship of Jake's concierge for two hundred francs (p. 55). A desperate Pedro Romero presses money on Brett in the hope of establishing physical control and obligation over her (p. 242). In addition to subsidizing Brett, Jake overtips at a hotel in order to buy the help's friendship in case he should happen to stay there again (p. 233). Money is the key link among the novel's characters, their primary foundation for establishing relationships.

Even art and religion are measured in terms of money in *The Sun Also Rises*. Robert Cohn writes, according to Jake, a very bad novel, but ironically Jake is impressed that the book made so much money (p. 8). Jack also admires Bill Gorton because of all the money he has made on his books (p. 70). No mention is made about the quality of Gorton's writing. Journalist Jake writes for money to buy time for indulging in seemingly masochistic diversions. Jake, who professes to be Catholic, goes to a church where he quite sincerely prays to make a lot of money (p. 97). When he mentions money in the prayer, though, he loses track of his prayer (as he has lost track of his faith), and becomes ashamed of himself. The bullfighters Belmonte and Mercial have corrupted their art for money (pp. 214–15); Romero is the true artist, not connected at all with money—until his encounter with Brett. Most of the characters at one time or another believe in and act on the notion that money purchases exemption from personal and moral responsibilities.

The only chapter in which money is not a factor is Chapter Twelve, where Jake and Bill go on a fishing trip to Burguete. Money does get mentioned early in the chapter when Bill inquires after he has seen Jake digging for worms, " 'What were you doing? Burying your money?' " (p. 113). This is exactly what Jake has done; he buries all mention of money during their trip to the Irati River. Hemingway chooses to show nature as incorrupted in this section, a healing wilderness for troubled men. The stream, as a non-circular encounter between man and nature, is one place where money has no use or value.

This pastoral interlude or counter-action in *The Sun Also Rises* supposedly features the novel's one truly admirable character, Wilson-Harris.[19] He actually functions, however, not as a minor code hero, but as an echo of Jake's worst characteristics. Duplicitous as his name reveals, Wilson-Harris insists on buying friendship with alcohol (p. 128) and gifts (p. 130). He makes what should be at least for Jake a brutally ironic statement: " 'I say. You don't know what it's meant to me to have you chaps up here. . . . I've not had much fun since the war' " (p. 129). Ever the affected Englishman, fawning continual compliments, Wilson-Harris is defined by his sentimental loneliness. His congeniality masks the magnanimous gestures of a man who pays to keep Jake and Bill for himself. Not surprisingly, Wilson-Harris declines an invitation to return to "civilization" and join the circle for the festival.

Money serves as a continual means for Hemingway to define and develop his characters within their circles of frustration. Narrator Jake Barnes, mutilated by a grotesque war accident, feels sexual desire, but is physically incapable of having sex.[20] Money appears to be Jake's only means for overcoming his impotence and achieving some measure of power. He pays the majority of the expenses in the book and is also the prime lender; rarely is he repaid in cash. To Lady Brett Ashley, his primary client, he gives all that he possibly can, and is compensated by her off-hand requests for more and more financial support. As the various café scenes indicate, money is typically the medium for their emotional exchanges. Jake even grants money sacred sanction and authority by substituting money for grace in the first church scene (p. 97). Jake may be so obsessed with money partially because he sees its function in an honest perspective. Without money, he and the other "cult" members would have absolute *nada;* with it, there are at least amusing diversions and some measure of feeling.

Jake's sidekick, Bill Gorton, is more bemused visitor than loyal group member. Only loosely an expatriate, he is also the only member of the party not emotionally involved with Brett. Bill does express some interest in Edna, the tourist and "groupie" picked up in a Pamplona bar. She has known Bill before, and acts most impressed with his apparently independent ways and means. But Bill's real interests and values lie elsewhere. Gorton is a financially successful nature writer, and his behavior at the fiesta demonstrates his eager willingness to enjoy the corruption of civilization and success. Bill's monetary philosophy can best be established by his own words: " 'Simple exchange of values. You give them money. They give you a stuffed dog' " (p. 72). Money equals value; money *is* value.

In Pamplona, Jake continues to buy and Lady Brett enjoys being purchased. Not valuing loyalty very highly, throughout the novel Brett entertains herself by the way a variety of men speculate over her. She uses Robert Cohn and Pedro Romero, and then sells them out by repossessing herself. She uses Mike Campbell as something of a sympatico sponge and reliable sexual toy while maintaining Jake as a crying towel and source of instant income. She could be considered parasitic, living off three men's money in the same careless manner in which she employs their bodies and attentions. Brett is the group's prostitute in that most all her relationships sooner or later become based on money. Her "intended," Mike Campbell, is both a financial and moral bankrupt. He too lives on credit, continually depending on his friends to bail him out of embarrassing situations. A practiced free-loader, Campbell even manages to have Brett pay most of his Pamplona hotel bill (p. 230). Mike hints that he was cheated monetarily by his former partner, just as in Pamplona he is cheated emotionally by Brett (p. 79). Mike whines and whines, the complete, even willing professional victim. As deadbeat, Brett takes the opposite tack, protesting loudly against her most insistent emotional and financial creditor, Robert Cohn.

The other two men in Brett's life besides Jake and Mike, Robert Cohn and Pedro Romero, fancy themselves idealists, but actually find their fulfillment as well in being victims. Cohn is a corrupted idealist, smugly believing that no one appreciates his true worth. He plays a system of romantic chivalry with the group, expecting and receiving ridicule and rejection. At the same time, Cohn attempts to proffer money as a way to obligate other characters, and as a way to rid himself of problems, such as how to placate his enraged fiancée in order to have a seacoast fling with Brett. Once again, money resolves a difficult personal and moral situation in *The Sun Also Rises* (p. 49). The immature Cohn is concerned with appearances and "getting away with it," shunning substantial values at all cost. Of course Cohn, the sad, ineffectual woman-haunted Princetonian, is most debilitated by being a Scott Fitzgerald hero in an Ernest Hemingway novel. As the logical polar opposite to Cohn, Pedro Romero appears at first to be incorrupt and incorruptible. However, he picks up enough of Lost Generation life to realize the potential in Brett's passion for him. When Romero finds that he cannot possess Brett, he finds a mutually agreeable indirect means of payment for services rendered. He, too, comes to know how these expatriates value money.

The circular movement of money and characters in *The Sun Also Rises* positions Jake and Brett as antagonists at the center in the novel's ring of action. An initiation novel *The Sun Also Rises* is not. Both these antagonists have been wounded, and out of their experiences have developed clearly defined moral codes. Brett believes in and acts on extrinsic values, a code of survival through sensation and appetite. As Brett puts it, "I've always done just what I wanted" (p. 184). Brett values not abstract concepts but what she wants to have. She accepts the depravity of man, exists only in the present tense, lives for disorder and uproar, and, as a creature of process, values most what she cannot have. But Brett also possesses a compelling contrary dimension, a great capacity for nurturing and love, and she is never more human and appealing than when she exhibits this vulnerability.

In terms of character development and values, the issue of money reveals much about Brett Ashley, Jake's formidable love and opponent. Robert Cohn first sees her as a lovely creature resembling Snow White (p. 39), then views her, with Mike's drunken approval, as Circe (p. 144). Jake typically sees her as the irresistible tormentor, fate, the bitch goddess. Critics frequently lose objectivity with Brett and empathize with these male characters' feelings about her. For example, Sheridan Baker states that "Brett must have an ever new man [sic] to replace the one she drains,"[21] and Robert W. Lewis portrays Brett as the woman in Ecclesiastes whose "heart is snares and nets."[22] Brett, however, has her own values, and it is the males' continual egocentric mistake of substituting their own projections of Brett's identity for her actual identity that causes so much masculine misery in the novel. Highlighted by contrast to Edna and Frances, Lady Brett is defined not by men, but by her own self-validated morality of appetite and survival. Brett is the best and most powerful practitioner of traditional male values, and this strength is nowhere more in evidence than when the males insist on celebrating her as their female goddess (p. 155). The *riau-riau* establishes Brett's complete control of the situation. Hardly a passive female, alternating between feeling states of male adoration and self-martyrdom, Brett surrounds herself with male strays who define themselves by being dominated victims.

Hemingway is aware of the humor this role-reversal situation can provide. We note the following exchange between Brett and Jake in the Café Select.

> I [Jake] said good night to Brett at the bar. The count [Mippipopolous] was buying champagne. "Will you take a glass with us, sir?" he asked.
> "No. Thanks awfully. I have to go."
> "Really going?" Brett asked.
> "Yes," I said. "I've got a rotten headache." (p. 29)

Jake will come to imitate more than Brett's British speech mannerisms. Established early in *The Sun Also Rises*, Brett's ability to generate, sustain, and be the center of situation after situation borders on the charismatic. Brett's outrageous behavior, her wardrobe and hair style, her calling herself a "chap," her skill and pride in being a "good drunk," her cavalier assumption that she can always get money—all demonstrate the validity of her strategy that to be a successful female, one must compete to be the most successful male.

Brett seeks not happiness but freedom. To this end she willingly rents herself out to attractive and useful landlords, but she is dominated and bought by no man. True to her values, she never once accepts money as payment for sex. Brett views the prostitute Georgette with scorn, nastily calling Jake's evening with her "restraint of trade" (p. 22). The novel's absorbing and futile quest by the leading male characters to become sole owner of Lady Ashley climaxes with her rejection of Pedro Romero. Like the other males, Romero is capable of seeing only his personal projection of Brett, but not Brett. He wishes to make an honest woman of her, reforming her by means of marriage, motherhood, and long hair. As Brett tells Jake near the end of *The Sun Also Rises:*

> "I didn't know whether I could make him go, and I didn't have a sou to go away and leave him. He tried to give me a lot of money, you know. I told him I had scads of it. He knew that was a lie. I couldn't take his money, you know. . . . He really wanted to marry me. So I couldn't go away from him, he said. He wanted to make it sure I could never go away from him. After I'd gotten more womanly, of course." (p. 242)

Brett typically acts in the plural; she sends for Jake, but plans a return to Mike Campbell. Brett tells Jake she is not a bitch and " 'It's sort of what we have instead of God' " (p. 245) partially because she would like to believe these words, but especially because she likes Jake, is sensitive to his problems, and knows he needs to hear this. More than any character in the novel, Brett has the capability to balance a show of pity and irony. Jake celebrates his quasi-repossession by indulging his appetite and by buying Brett all the booze she can drink and food she can eat. Brett intimidates and disorients the male characters in *The Sun Also Rises* to such an extent that none of them thinks to analyze her motives and behavior with the intention of developing effective strategies for either friendship or revenge.

As Brett's antagonist, Jake, with his capacity for being nurtured, believes in the intrinsic values of the *afición:* purity and skill are inherently beautiful and good. With a shaky faith, he wants and needs to believe in loyalty, justice, love, and the fundamental good will of mankind. We note the careful accounting of his bank balance (p. 30), his notion of fair payment (p. 148), and realize that he is the party of order. But Jake's vulnerability is his contradictory attraction to and need for the dominating Brett Ashley and her values. This vulnerability exists because Jake has been so terribly wounded. A Catholic, however fallen-away, he knows that he must have done something terribly wrong to have received such a punishment. Having no idea what he did to deserve this *corida,* Jake sometimes manufactures evil— betraying Montoya, pimping, getting drunk, acceding to Brett—in an attempt to believe that behind his being wounded, cause and effect firmly stand. Thus, Jake can perceive himself as an evil hero. However sympathetic or admirable, Jake is badly debilitated. This is a Fisher King, not an heroic young knight, that Hemingway sends into the arena to do battle against Duessa.

It *is* rather pleasant to think that after the fiesta, Jake recovers his lost values while vacationing in San Sebastian, so that when he encounters Brett in Madrid, he has come to his senses with a self-awareness born out of tragic recognition, and can rise above further involvement in her romantic conspiracies. As we have seen, such forms the prevailing critical view. Hemingway himself insisted that *The Sun Also Rises* was not a satire but a tragedy.[23] If Hemingway's book follows the tragic novel convention of a fallen, wounded hero rising to self-knowledge, a morally admirable perspective, and a consequent series of actions, then Jake must be congratulated for achieving an heroic stature in the *dénouement.* However, partially through the money metaphor, Hemingway undercuts this uplifting pattern to reveal not an emerging hero, but a continuation of frustration in this world where extrinsic values dominate. Drunk in Pamplona, Jake muses about money and life, ending his reverie by stating: "Maybe if you found out how to live in it you learned from that what it was all about" (p. 148). Jake comes to realize that "how to live in it" (extrinsic values, i.e., money) and "what it was all about" (intrinsic values, i.e., honor) are at irreconcilable odds. Like Krebs of "Soldier's Home," Jake resigns himself to being overwhelmed by a stronger force (Brett). Hemingway's pronouncement on *The Sun Also Rises* as a tragedy rings true when we realize the tragedy of the novel is that Jake cannot act on his beliefs. Typical of the twentieth-century American novelist, Hemingway saves most of the blow from this realization not for his protagonist, but for his audience.

In the opening of Part III, the scene immediately following the Pamplona festival's ending, Jake makes a number of decisions that indicate not resolve or enlightenment, but a serious depression. First of all, he determinedly insists on staying alone in San Sebastian, the scene of the earlier Cohn-Ashley "crime." Interestingly, although Jake notes that he has been to this hotel before (p. 234), he never names the hotel, possibly because while there, Jake acts like a sanitarium patient rather than a spa vacationer. Jake is comforted by watching the visiting nurses, immediately imposes a daily routine of therapeutic swimming and sitting, and refuses to join the community of bicycle racers. Jake's self-absorption is overwhelming. Typical of institutional life, meals constitute the high points of his days. He acts drugged and tense, at the edge of breakdown, not unlike Nick in "Big Two-Hearted River." Jake's languid days of isolated insulation do afford protection against the outside world of Spain, where "you could not tell about anything" (pp. 233–34). His regrets about returning to Spain concern consequences, phrased in a nostalgic financial metaphor about France.

> Everything is on such a clear financial basis in France. It is the simplest country to live in. No one makes things complicated by becoming your friend for any obscure reason. If you want people to like you you have only to spend a little money. (p. 233)

When Brett's telegrams arrive, Jake laments "that meant San Sebastian all shot to hell" (p. 239). This expression of surprise is an act. Having learned from Mike Campbell that Brett is broke (p. 230), Jake knows that she will be in touch with him shortly. Certainly Jake could wire Brett to go to hell and continue his quasi-hospitalization, but like an heroic rescue agent, he rushes to her aid at once. Again, action is "'put on the bill'" (p. 239). What Brett does need is a paying audience. Page after page she has demonstrated her ability to rescue herself.

Far from establishing a clean, well-lighted place of heroic action for Jake, the final scene ironically demonstrates the novel's enduring French values: *plus ça change, plus c'est la même chose*. What does the last scene change except location? In Madrid, Jake still pays and Brett still buys. When Jake first meets Brett in the sleazy Hotel Montana, he notes that her "room was in that disorder produced only by those who have always had servants" (p. 241). Jake continues his role of servant par excellence by patiently listening to Brett's sad tale of her latest affair; by paying for drinks and meals; and by booking them on the Sud Express for a night trip back to Paris. Jake would have paid for Brett's room, but Romero has already made this contribution as Brett's severance payment.[24] At Botin's, "one of the best restaurants in the world" (p. 245), Brett becomes concerned with Jake's sudden conspicuous consumption (including five bottles of *rioja alta*), fearing another unpleasant scene of drunken, weepy pouting (cf. pp. 54–56). Brett soothes by words but abuses by actions, a much more effective strategy for achieving her goals than the explosion of verbal indictment that Frances practices. In the end, both Jake and Robert Cohn "take it." The final tipping, the furtive taxi ride, and that hideously ironic upraised baton of the mounted policeman establish at the novel's finalé not a sense of recognition or resolution, but a continuing wandering. Like Francesca and Paolo, swept on hot winds without touching through their circle of Dante's Hell, Jake and Brett are driven through summertime Madrid on the winds of money. Instead of establishing a security in space, money in The Sun Also Rises is most useful for killing time. Rather than establishing superiority or even disengagement, Jake capitulates by joining Brett and her extrinsic values of meaningless motion and immediate gratification.

The use of money, then, is a major means for Hemingway to show the corruption of this modern world where values are relative, transitory, and for sale. Far from praising this lost generation, Hemingway damns their meaningless exchanges and lack of purpose, the absence of a moral center in their world. He attacks their irresponsibility by dramatizing their fruitless, circular quests for happy diversions. Jake requires diversion to forget his faded Catholicism and his painfully impotent love for Brett. Brett requires diversion to cover up her exploitations and encroaching middle age. Mike needs diversion because he is both a moral and financial bankrupt; diversions occupy his time and give some vague sense of direction to his life, namely a moving on to wherever he can still obtain credit. While a means, money is not—as Bill Gorton claims—an end in *The Sun Also Rises*. Despite the many equations of money to value in the book, money is not in itself valuable to the characters, but only the means for continuing their dissipation. If money is not a value in itself, if it is not a center for *this* group, then Hemingway's characters literally have lost all values. Far from being hostages to fortune, these characters, however wounded, create their own tragedy and hell.

The Sun Also Rises is a cyclical, cynical young man's book. Jake, Brett, and, by insinuation, Mike are the only characters left at the end of the novel because, in spite of their singular and collective guilt, they all accept and function well in the never-ending cycle of borrowing on time. Neither of the romantics, Robert Cohn and Pedro Romero, ever comprehends this cycle: they are both idealists, albeit corrupt ones. Bill Gorton is eliminated from the cycle because he is only a visiting expatriate, soon off to America. The concept of "paying the bill" works in tandem with the novel's cyclical process. Jake pays for his impotence and loss of religion; Brett pays for her manipulative behavior; Mike, Cohn and Romero pay for thinking they can possess Brett; Mike pays for his insolvent status; Cohn pays for behaving badly; Bill Gorton pays for his stagnancy. All the characters pay for their lack of purpose, their lack of definite goals, and their values which center around vanities.

Payment in *The Sun Also Rises* is not rendered in such concrete terms as cold cash; rather, the characters are mortgaged to frustration. As this cyclical pattern indicates, appropriately consummated by Jake's tipping a waiter and ordering a taxi as the novel closes, these characters can never gain on their moral deficit, but shall continue, gradually and voluntarily, to slide into the self-destruction of a material and moral receivership.

NOTES

[1] In addition to the critics noted, Scott Donaldson has an extensive analysis of Hemingway and money in *By Force of Will: The Life and Art of Ernest Hemingway* (New York: Viking, 1977), pp. 10–59.
[2] Earl Rovit, *Ernest Hemingway* (New York: Twayne, 1963), pp. 151–52.

[3] Claire Sprague, "*The Sun Also Rises*: Hemingway's 'Clear Financial Basis,'" *American Quarterly*, 21 (Summer 1969), 259.

[4] Sprague, 265.

[5] Richard P. Sugg, "Hemingway, Money, and *The Sun Also Rises*," *Fitzgerald/Hemingway Annual*, (1972) (Washington, D.C.: NCR/Microcard Editions), pp. 257–67.

[6] Nancy Comley, "Hemingway: The Economics of Survival," *Novel*, 12 (Spring 1979), 244.

[7] Ernest Hemingway, *The Sun Also Rises* (New York: Charles Scribner's Sons, 1954). All further references to *The Sun Also Rises* are from this edition; pages cited are included in the text. I am indebted to my English 352 class (Fall, 1977) for first showing me the extent to which monetary references appear in *The Sun Also Rises*.

[8] *The Sun Also Rises*, of course, was written under the shadow of *The Great Gatsby*, the most famous modern novel about the American obsession with money. Hemingway's next novel, *A Farewell to Arms*, rarely has any mention of money.

[9] Carlos Baker, *Hemingway: A Life Story* (New York: Bantam, 1970), pp. 197–229.

[10] Donaldson, p. 15.

[11] Baker, p. 202.

[12] Malcolm Cowley, *Exiles' Return* (New York: Viking, 1951), p. 38.

[13] Baker, pp. 210–11.

[14] Baker, p. 184.

[15] Baker, pp. 246, 260.

[16] W. H. Auden, "In Memory of W. B. Yeats," *The Collected Poems of W. H. Auden* (New York: Random House, 1945), p. 50.

[17] Donaldson, pp. 58–59.

[18] Delbert E. Wylder, *Hemingway's Heroes* (Albuquerque: The University of New Mexico Press, 1969), p. 61.

[19] Gerald T. Gordon, "Hemingway's Wilson-Harris: The Search for Value in *The Sun Also Rises*," *Fitzgerald/Hemingway Annual* (1972) (Washington D.C.: NCR/Microcard Editions), pp. 237–44.

[20] See George Plimpton, "An Interview with Ernest Hemingway," *The Paris Review*, 18 (Spring 1958), 76–77.

[21] Sheridan Baker, *Ernest Hemingway: An Introduction and Interpretation* (New York: Barnes and Noble, 1967), p. 50.

[22] Robert W. Lewis, Jr., *Hemingway: The Art of Love* (Austin: University of Texas Press, 1965), p. 34.

[23] In a letter to Maxwell Perkins, dated November 19, 1926, Hemingway stated that *The Sun Also Rises* was not "a hollow or bitter satire, but a damn tragedy...." Quoted in Carlos Baker, *Hemingway: The Writer as Artist* (Princeton, N.J.: Princeton University Press, 1956), p. 81.

[24] Hemingway may have used the name "Pedro Romero" not only in honor of the first great Spanish bullfighter, but because Romero is a common Sephardic name. The subtle irony of casting *both* Cohn and Romero as Jews would likely have appealed to young Hemingway's sense of humor.

APPENDIX

Direct References to Money in *The Sun Also Rises*

Ref. No.	Page No.	Book I
1	4	Jake tells of Cohn losing most of his first fortune.
2	5	Cohn establishes small "review of the Arts" with remnants of his fortune; the magazine becomes too expensive.
3	5	Cohn's mother has given him a $300 per month allowance.
4	6	Cohn buys a newspaper.
5	9	Cohn gambles and wins big at bridge.

6	9	Cohn reads *The Purple Land* "as though it had been an R. G. Dun report."
7	9	Jake turns down Cohn's proposed trip to South America: "Too expensive."
8	10	Cohn offers to pay Jake's way to South America.
9	10	Jake notes that Cohn has "plenty of money."
10	15	With Georgette, Jake pays for several "saucers."
11	17	Georgette notes about artists: "Still, some of them make money."
12	22	Brett arrives: "I say, give a chap a brandy and soda."
13	22	Jake refers to his evening as "priceless."
14	22	Referring to Jake spending the evening with Georgette, Brett says: "It's in restraint of trade."
15	23	Jake leaves a 55 franc note in an envelope for Georgette.
16	24	Jake tips a waiter.
17	26	Brett: "Don't we pay for all the things we do, though? . . . I'm paying for it all now."
18	28	Jake pays for a taxi ride with Brett.
19	29	Count Mippipopolous buys champagne.
20	30	Jake works on his bank statement.
21	32	Brett discusses where the Count got his money.
22	32	Brett states that the Count is "putting up" (i.e., supporting) the artist, Zizi.
23	33	Brett reports that the Count offered her $10,000 to go with him to Biarritz or another spa.
24	35	A street vendor urges tourists to buy his wares.
25	37	Jake offers Krum two francs for a taxi ride.
26	38	Jake notes that Mike Campbell will "be rich as hell some day."
27	42	Jake notes that Harvey Stone won 200 francs from him when they gambled.
28	42	Harvey laments that his money hasn't come.
29	42	Jake gives Harvey 100 francs.
30	46	Frances notes that she does not "have enough money to lunch at the Ritz."
31	46	Jake buys the latest *Paris Times*.
32	47	Frances notes that, in giving up alimony to obtain a speedy divorce, she has no money. Cohn, she notes, does have money.
33	48	Cohn will give Frances 200 pounds.
34	49	Frances reacts to this severance payment.
35	49	Frances states that her mother put all her money into French war bonds.
36	53	Mme. Duzinell had once "owned a drink-selling concession."
37	54	Brett reports giving Jake's concierge 200 francs.

Book II

67	90	Bill does need a fishing rod, so one is purchased, plus two landing-nets.
68	91	Car is hired.
69	91	Gambling for beers (probably paid for by Cohn).
70	91	Hotel payment is rendered.
71	94	Driver is paid.
72	95	Bill bets Cohn on Brett's arrival; discussion of the bet.
73	96	Jake checks on his bull-fight subscription and finds it paid up.
74	96	Jake tips a porter.
75	97	Jake prays for money in a church.
76	98	Cohn says the bet on Brett's arrival is off. Cohn would like to bet on the outcome of a bull-fight.
77	99	Of bull-fights, Jake notes: "You don't need any economic interest."
78	99	Jake buys three bus tickets to Burguete.
79	100	Cohn reimburses Jake for bus ticket.
80	106	Drinks, and a misunderstanding with the tip (Bill and Jake).
81	106	Drinks (with the Basques).
82	107	In America, Jake says, good wine is available if you pay for it.
83	109	Jake and the inn manager discuss Burguete hotel rates; they agree on a price.
84	113	Bill inquires if Jake is burying his money.
85	115	Bill says: "One group claims women support you."
86	123	"You're in the pay of the Anti-Saloon League."
87	124	Bill: "All our biggest business men have been dreamers."
88	127	Jake tips young lady who delivers a telegram.
89	128	Cohn's cheapness with the telegram is noted.
90	128	Jake and Bill pay for a telegram to Cohn.
91	129	Wilson-Harris, Jake, and Bill purchase wine in a pub.
92	136	Mike discusses payment of his tailor.
93	136	Mike discusses his bankruptcy.
94	137	Drinks.
95	138	Price of wine advertised in a shop is discussed.
96	142	Mike says Cohn will buy a drink.
97	144	Brett wonders if drinks have been paid for.
98	148–49	Jake's "getting your money's worth" speech.
99	151	Café prices, before and during the festival.
100	156	Jake offers to pay for some wine, but is refused.
101	156–57	Jake buys two wine skins (botas).
102	157	Jake pays to fill the wine skins with wine.
103	157	A man buys Jake a drink.
104	159	Dinner (with prices doubled for the festival).
105	161	Jake gives "an extra ticket to a waiter to sell."

Book III

Linda Wagner-Martin

WOMEN IN HEMINGWAY'S EARLY FICTION

When F. Scott Fitzgerald commented to Hemingway that Catherine Barkley in *A Farewell to Arms* is less successful than some of the women from his early short stories, he showed again his acute literary judgment. As Fitzgerald phrases it, "in the stories you were really listening to women—here you're only listening to yourself."[1] Whatever the reason for the distancing that was to mar Hemingway's portrayal of women characters from 1929 on (except for Pilar, Maria, and Marie Morgan), there is little question that Hemingway was at his most sympathetic and skillful in drawing the female leads of the short stories of *In Our Time* and *Men without Women* and of *The Sun Also Rises*. His manuscripts show that Hemingway was also comfortable with those portrayals, seldom making changes—except very minor ones—between what appears to be first draft and final versions.

One of the most striking characteristics of Hemingway's women in his early fiction is their resemblance to the later, mature Hemingway hero. It is primarily Brett Ashley's similarity to Jake Barnes that marks her as an aficionado of life (her phrase describing Count Mippipopolous as "one of us"[2] indicates that she knows the parallels, and bases her judgments of people on criteria similar to those Jake uses). But in fact, in Hemingway's earlier stories—"Up in Michigan," "Indian Camp," "The End of Something," "The Three-Day Blow," and "Cross-Country Snow"—the women have already reached that plateau of semi-stoic self awareness which Hemingway's men have, usually, yet to attain.

When Marjorie understands her rejection in "The End of Something," she behaves so admirably that Nick feels the impact of his loss doubly, and continues to mourn it throughout "The Three-Day Blow." " 'I'm taking the boat,' " she called to him as she moved away, out of reach of both touch and sound. What the expected female behavior was is indicated a few lines later as Bill appears on the scene:

From *College Literature* 7, No. 3 (Fall 1980): 239–47.

> "Did she go all right?" Bill said.
> "Yes," Nick said, lying, his face on the blanket.
> "Have a scene?"
> "No, there wasn't any scene."
> "How do you feel?"
> "Oh, go away, Bill! Go away for a while."[3]

If Hemingway/Nick were to choose at that moment, he would surely prefer Marjorie's pride and grace to Bill's insensitive smirking.

"The End of Something" is one of the earliest of Hemingway's well-made, well-imaged stories, In these, much characterization is accomplished through the attribution of the insightful perception. Marjorie, here, sees the old mill as both an emblem of their relationship ("There's our old ruin, Nick") and something magical ("It seems more like a castle"). In response to each suggestion, "Nick said nothing." An early version of the dialogue gives us Nick as a sharp-tongued anti-romantic:

> "What's that ruin, Nick?"
> "It's Stroud's old mill."
> "It looks like a castle."
> "Not much."[4]

An inability to see clearly, perceptively, is Robert Cohn's flaw by the time of *The Sun Also Rises;* finding these early male protagonists—Nick, Bill, Harold Krebs—marked by the same insensitivity provides interesting parallels. Truly stories of male initiation, the short stories of *In Our Time* and *Men without Women* tend to give us male characters who *need* that initiation. They learn from Hemingway's women. Or, tragically, they fail to learn.

In "Hills Like White Elephants" Hemingway employs exactly the same technique. Although the characters are introduced with apparent objectivity as "the American and the girl with him," Hemingway's sympathy is clearly with the girl—*Jig,* in the published story; *Hadley,* in the manuscript. The girl is perceptive, tranquil, troubled but not vindictive; despite all her conflicts and sorrows over the impending abortion, she behaves with "grace under pressure." Again, Hemingway conveys her superior vision through the title image:

> The girl was looking off at the line of hills.
> They were white in the sun and the country was brown and dry.
>> "They look like white elephants," she said.
>> "I've never seen one," the man drank his beer.
>> "No, you wouldn't have."

His literalness, his inability to respond to play are negative qualities in themselves, but the dialogue continues to give him even more abrasive responses:

> "I might have," the man said. "Just because you say I wouldn't have doesn't
> prove anything."
>
> The girl looked at the bead curtain. "They've painted something on
> it...."[5]

She deflects the argument, although the rest of the story is a marvel of dialogue
between the rational male ("It's perfectly simple.... It's really not anything. It's just
to let the air in.... It's really an awfully simple operation ... it's perfectly simple ...
it's the best thing to do ... It's really not an operation at all.... it's all perfectly
natural") and the distraught woman, who finally—three pages of his quarrelsome
reassurance later—manages to ask, with only a little loss of control,

> "Would you do something for me now?"
> "I'd do anything for you."
> "Would you please please please please please please please stop talk-
> ing?"

"I'll scream" the girl continues as he begins the repetitive reassurances, and one can
imagine the months of days and nights already given to this one-sided, clichéd
discussion. In lines deleted from the final version, Hemingway had the American go
to the bar and think, with dismay.

> There must be some place you could touch where people were calm and
> reasonable.[6]

In the revision of the early manuscript, Hemingway has carefully given the
perception of the title image to the woman. In the earlier and finally incomplete
version, the man and the woman shared the perception, but the image served no
purpose.[7] The story originally became trapped in the tavern and on the train, with
no mention of anything significant between the characters. We never know it is an
abortion story, and Hemingway abandons it, unfinished. The early version, as the
character's name indicates, was Hadley's story; the finished version carries an
epigraph line, "For Pauline—well, well, well."[8] Whatever else had happened to him
in the 1920's, Hemingway had found a structure that would make "Hills Like White
Elephants" work as a story of a strong, and sympathetic, female character.

One might surmise that "Cat in the Rain" is a continuation of the same story,
and that the young wife's frustration with her lonely and ultimately unsettled,
infertile existence stems from another impending abortion. The changes that Hemingway makes in the manuscript are all directed toward making George unsympa-
thetic, setting him in contrast to the gracious hotel keeper who understands the
woman's need to care for and to be cared for. In her climactic closing speech, when
she longs for stability and a home, Hemingway gives us the clue to her unhappiness:

> "I'd like to pull my hair back tight and smooth and make a big knot and
> wear a Spanish comb and have on a Yteb gown and a cat to sit in my lap and
> purr in front of the fire while I waited for someone to come home."

"You're a swell mixture," George said.

"I want a table set with my own silver and candles lit—and I don't want to know what's going to happen."[9]

The final version has, of course, deleted that last sentence (as well as rearranged the lines for rhythmic impact and thematic emphasis) but the poignance remains. George, hiding in his book, listening only in order to rest his eyes, parallels the reasonable American of "Hills Like White Elephants" and the adolescently selfish Nick and Bill of "The Three-Day Blow" and "The End of Something."

It can certainly be said that fascination with women characters, if not the characters themselves, dominate *In Our Time*. The original epigraph points to this fascination:

A GIRL IN CHICAGO: Tell us about the French women, Hank. What are they like?
BILL SMITH: How old are the French women, Hank?[10]

Although the interspersed vignettes might suggest more externally oriented themes of war and bullfighting, of the stories included in the collection, only five or six have a focus other than a woman character or a relationship. And even within the vignettes, a character's humanity is gauged by his or her sympathy toward the life processes—birth as well as death.

It seems very clear that, at this point in his career, Hemingway was as interested in women characters as he was in men—perhaps more interested. As he had written in 1956,

I have always considered that it was easy to be a man compared to being a woman who lives by as rigid standards as men live by. No one of us lives by as rigid standards nor has as good ethics as we planned but an attempt is made.[11]

And he continued in his 1959 "The Art of the Short Story," "It is hardest to do about women and you must not worry when they say there are no such women as those you wrote about. That only means your women aren't like their women."[12] The defensive tone in Hemingway's comments is probably explained by the negative criticism many of his woman characters—if noticed at all—had received. Not until Alan Holder's brief 1963 essay, "The Other Hemingway," had much attention been paid to his mastery of characterization of women.[13]

The fictionalization of Brett Ashley in *The Sun Also Rises* had in fact created many problems for Hemingway. Rather than being acclaimed as a warm, believable, brave woman, Brett was frequently maligned as unnatural, bold, nymphomaniacal.[14] Hemingway had never intended Brett to be an affront; she was to have gained readers' sympathy and admiration, and thereby buttressed the positive elements of Jake Barnes' persona. After such misreading, Hemingway may have been hesitant to trust his readers with what he thought were interesting women. Part of the submissiveness and languor of Catherine Barkley may have stemmed from what he thought was lack of appreciation of Brett's "nobility."

Also, had The Sun Also Rises been published as Hemingway had written it, much of the misreading of Brett would probably not have occurred. His deletion of the first chapter and part of the second—much material which explained and explored Brett as bereaved and betrayed war victim—left readers too little direction. Even though Fitzgerald's suggestion to cut this opening was made as a friendly gesture (to scuttle the random writing that plagued Hemingway at his most self-conscious), it has caused readers problems.[15]

The first chapter of the book—cut only after it was in galley proofs—was a positive presentation of Brett—broke, afraid of being alone. "This is a novel about a lady. Her name is Lady Ashley and when the story begins she is living in Paris and it is Spring. That should be a good setting for a romantic but highly moral story."[16] Hemingway then recounts Brett's grace, her style, her ability to weather all kinds of bad experiences: "Brett was a very happy person." We are treated to a description of her first husband's tying her up in her kitchen, to the financial uncertainty of her life. The first chapter closes with the foreshadowing for what was to be an atypical situation for Brett: "Brett was left alone in Paris. She had never been very good at being alone."

The irony of the novel (set in the spring, among people heading for a "fiesta" as the British title for the book emphasizes) echoes the strange experience of everyone's going on vacation, and Brett alone. What Hemingway was portraying was hardly a normal life for expatriates.

Chapter II, much of which was also omitted, focuses on Jake Barnes, but on Jake in relation to Brett. The chapter begins with Jake's statement that he cannot remain outside the novel because he is too much involved in the people he will tell about. . . . "I made the unfortunate mistake, for a writer, of having first been Mr. Jake Barnes." He continues,

> The thing I would like to make whoever reads this believe, however incredible, is that such a passion and longing could exist in me for Brett Ashley that I would sometimes feel that it would tear me to pieces. . . . whenever I had just left Brett . . . I felt all of my world taken away, that it was all gone, even the shapes of things were changed, the trees and the houses and the fountains. . . . Brett Ashley could do that to me.

And the reason for Brett's power over Jake is also described: "She never lost her form. She was always clean bred, generous and her lines were always as sharp."

Brett as Hemingway hero is not implausible, particularly given the frustration of Jake Barnes' wound and the impossibility of what they both come to see as a lasting relationship. If their love resembles that between Nick and his sister Littless in "The Last Good Country," that too may be intentional. For Hemingway, the prototype of marriage was that tragic relationship between his parents. Their marriage appeared early in his fiction with "The Doctor and the Doctor's Wife" (a story virtually untouched from manuscript to publication), "Indian Camp," and in the magnificent house-cleaning scene of "Fathers and Sons." As he wrote in the manuscript version of that story,

> ... father was very nervous. He was married to a woman with whom he had no more in common than a coyote has with a white French poodle....[17]

And in an even earlier version, "a man suffers in his own home. There is only one thing to do if a man is married to a woman with whom he has nothing in common ... and that is to get rid of her ... Whoever, in a marriage of that sort, wins the first encounter is in command."

Marriage for Hemingway—at least fictionally—was never an ideal state. Rather, his ideal seemed to be caught most effectively in the companionship of man/woman, boy/girl, brother/sister—a relationship bound by caring and sacrifice but not by obligation and power. Brett and Jake are, finally, only companions— exiled as effectively from the people who accompany them to Spain as if they were geographically alone. The geographical isolation Hemingway leaves for Littless and her brother, as he hides from the game wardens for fishing out of season. A story of peril and macho bravado, "The Last Good Country" conveys the tender rapport between brother and hero-worshipping little sister. It is also a story of Nick as initiator rather than initiated. "We're partners," Littless says, as she accepts her brother as guide and protector. Yet when Nick longs to kill the boy who turned him in, he realizes that Littless's greater moral consciousness will protect him, will keep him from harming anyone:

> she can feel it because she is your sister and you love each other....[18]

"The Last Good Country," though unfinished and hence never published until the Nick Adams stories were collected, also moves through images, and one passage in particular gives the sense of Nick's love for Littless, his affinity with nature, and his admiration for personal qualities like pride and grace:

> They went along down the creek. Nick was studying the banks. He had seen a mink's track and shown it to his sister and they had seen tiny ruby-crowned kinglets that were hunting insects and let the boy and girl come close as they moved sharply and delicately in the cedars. They had seen cedar waxwings so calm and gentle and distinguished moving in their lovely elegance with the magic wax touches on their wing coverts and their tails, and Littless had said, "They're the most beautiful, Nickie. There couldn't be more simply beautiful birds."
>
> "They're built like your face," he said.
>
> "No, Nickie, Don't make fun. Cedar waxwings make me so proud and happy that I cry."
>
> "When they wheel and light and then move so proud and friendly and gently..."[19]

It also works to create that image of Utopia that Hemingway will repeat throughout his work—the undiscovered, untouched country (or sea); the place free from corruption, malaise, personal dishonesty; the place clean and well lighted; the place—whether geographical or anatomical—found through initiative (travel, exploration, sexual discovery); the country that gives answers instead of only dilemmas.

The pervasive imagery begins here, in one of the few pieces of Hemingway's fiction which include a gentle and loving male and female relationship. But that there are few Hemingway stories in which male-female love is idyllic, that his second story collection was titled *Men without Women,* lies less in his attitudes toward his women characters (at least in his early fiction) than in his characterization of male characters as adolescent, selfish, misdirected. There is evidence of much sympathy on Hemingway's part of the women he portrays in this early fiction, and his focus is not to narrow—to concentrate almost obsessively on the reflexive self—until after *A Farewell to Arms.* It is as if the young Hemingway believed in the romantic, mystic ideal of a genuine love, of a man's finding ultimate completion with a woman, until the catastrophe of his father's death. He saw that at least in part as a result of his mother's rigid incompatibility, her continuing lack of love. As he wrote in an unpublished essay.

> We are the generation whose fathers shot themselves. It is a very American thing to do and it is done, usually, when they lost their money although their wives are almost invariably a contributing cause.[20]

Hemingway's manuscripts show how constant was his concern for his father's suicide, as well as for his evident unhappiness before it. The draft of "Cross-Country Snow," for example, continues past the ending scene in the published story, with Mike asking, "What's the matter George?"

> "Oh the family," George said. "You know . . . Oh, I wish my father wasn't such a damn fool."[21]

Another unfinished story had as protagonist a boy named Edward Thompson who hates his mother and fights with kids who say that his father killed himself ("Suicide is a lonely way to die but it is least annoying to the family if there is some semblance of accident").[22] "There are too many people alive for me to write about my father yet," he notes in the manuscript of "Fathers and Sons," and then continues:

> I loved him very much and I was fourteen before I knew that however he had made his life, I must make mine differently if I was to come through since his own life by then was ruined. . . . You could believe nothing your parents told you after a certain age because you had the example of their lives before you and you knew that whatever happened to your own life it should not be like that.

Marred, saddened, mistrustful of marriage because of his childhood experiences, Hemingway gave up most attempts to draw sympathetic women characters after he wrote the vehicle for expressing his own deep bereavement. *A Farewell to Arms* is not a romantic novel; it is instead a novel about loss. And the loss is that of his father, not of Catherine or a child. His notes on the manuscript of the novel express this transfer of emotion:

> I loved my father. Very much ... The novel was begun the winter of 1928 in Paris ... that fall went to Chicago—saw my father—Drove to Key West with Sunny—she told me about my father—went to N.Y. to get Bumby—wrote father on train—informed of death in station—went to Chicago then to Kansas City to rewrite.[23]

Unable to trust that better experiences would be his, Hemingway transferred that emotion into some of the most powerful of his fiction—the loss of Santiago, of Robert Jordan, and particularly of Thomas Hudson in *Islands in the Stream*. It is Hudson who relinquishes all relationship with women, reaching humanity through his love for his sons—the male tie again reinforced. As Hudson thinks of his boys,

> He had replaced everything except them with work and the steady hard-working life he had built on the island. That is, he thought he had. I would rather love a good house and the sea and my work than a woman, he thought. He knew it could never be true. But he could almost make it. ...[24]

Truer than he may have known, Fitzgerald's words of analysis, that Hemingway had stopped listening to his women characters. In his early fiction, Hemingway's attention was on women as themselves. In the later novels and stories, because his attention had been usurped by the deaths of his father and other men, women characters exist primarily to give the Hemingway character another dimension. The angle of vision is skewed, oblique; it still reflects, but less accurately. And Robert Lowell's theory—that any good poet creates for us *his* world—is once again borne out: the last Hemingway world was utopian, full of seas and energy and words, but strangely devoid of women.

NOTES

[1] F. Scott Fitzgerald, letter to Hemingway, Hemingway Collection, John F. Kennedy Library; used by permission of Collection.

[2] Ernest Hemingway, *The Sun Also Rises* (New York: Charles Scribner's Sons, 1926), 60. Hereafter cited in text.

[3] Ernest Hemingway, *In Our Time* (New York: Charles Scribner's Sons, 1925), 34, 35.

[4] Manuscript version of "The End of Something," Hemingway Collection, Kennedy Library.

[5] Ernest Hemingway, *Men without Women* (New York: Charles Scribner's Sons, 1927), 39.

[6] Manuscript version of "Hills Like White Elephants," Hemingway Collection, John F. Kennedy Library.

[7] Early version begins: "The train moved through the hot valley. Fields of ripe grain started at the rails to stretch across the valley. Far off beyond the brown fields a line of trees grew along the course of the Ebro and beyond the river rose abruptly the mysterious white mountains.

"We had called them that as soon as we saw them. To be disgustingly accurate I had said, '*Look* at those god damn white mountains.'

"Hadley said, 'They are the most mysterious things I have ever seen.'

"They were white mountains, not white with snow or any artificial aid but white themselves furrowed and wrinkled by the rains like all good mountains and they were very wonderful strange shapes and there were two ranges of them, one on each side of the broad brown and green valley of the Ebro. On a cloudy dark day they might have been gray as a white elephant is gray in a circus tent, but in the July heat they shown white as white elephants in the sun. . . ."

[8] On finished manuscript as if epigraph, Hemingway Collection, Kennedy Library.

[9] Manuscript version of "Cat in the Rain," Hemingway Collection, Kennedy Library, pp. 8–9.

[10] Epigraph to original *in our time* (Paris: Three Mountains Press, 1924), printed under title on title page.

[11] Ernest Hemingway, *By-Line: Ernest Hemingway*, ed. William White (New York: Scribner's, 1967), 461.

[12] Ernest Hemingway, "The Art of the Short Story," unpublished essay, Hemingway Collection, J. F. Kennedy Library, p. 4

[13] Alan Holder, "The Other Hemingway," *Twentieth Century Literature* (1963), 153–57.

[14] For example, see *Chicago Daily Tribune* (Nov. 27, 1926), p. 13; Herbert J. Muller, *Modern Fiction: A Study of Values* (New York: Funk & Wagnalls, 1937, pp. 383–403); Henry Seidel Canby, *American Memoir* (Boston: Houghton Mifflin, 1947, pp. 339–44); R. W. Stallman, *The Houses That James Built and Other Literary Studies* (East Lansing, Mich.: Michigan State University Press, 1961), 173–193; Sidney P. Moss, "Character, Vision, and Theme in *The Sun Also Rises*," *Iowa English Yearbook*, No. 9 (Fall, 1964), 64–67; and others.

[15] Letter from F. Scott Fitzgerald, reprinted in "Fitzgerald's *Sun Also Rises*: Notes and Comments," *Fitzgerald/Hemingway Annual*, 1971, pp. 1–9.

[16] *The Sun Also Rises* manuscript, Hemingway Collection, J. F. Kennedy Library.

[17] Manuscript version, "Fathers and Sons," Hemingway Collection, Kennedy Library.

[18] Ernest Hemingway, "The Last Good Country" in *The Nick Adams Stories*, ed. Philip Young (New York: Charles Scribner's Sons, 1972), 113.

[19] Ibid., 107–8.

[20] From Hemingway's anti-Humanist essay, Item 811, Hemingway Collection, Kennedy Library.

[21] Manuscript version of "Cross-Country Snow," Hemingway Collection, Kennedy Library.

[22] Manuscript version of unpublished story about Edward Thomas, Hemingway Collection, Kennedy Library.

[23] Manuscript of *A Farewell to Arms*, Hemingway's notes; Hemingway Collection, Kennedy Library.

[24] Ernest Hemingway, *Islands in the Stream*, discarded manuscript, p. 16; Hemingway Collection, Kennedy Library.

Roger Whitlow
BITCHES AND OTHER
SIMPLISTIC ASSUMPTIONS

Just as Catherine Barkley, Marie Morgan, Maria, and Renata are generally considered mindless and subservient sex creatures (Marie somewhat less than the others), so conventional critical wisdom tells us that Brett Ashley, Margot Macomber,
Helen ("The Snows of Kilimanjaro"), and Dorothy Bridges are Hemingway's bitch-
women. Because critical wisdom is often largely the perpetuation of "party lines"
of interpretation, however, I would point out that the "bitch" designation has been
far too glibly attached to the four women in question here, that all of these so-called
bitches are considerably more complicated than the label implies, and, most important, that some of the women—including the infamous Margot Macomber—are
actually morally superior to the male characters with whom they are associated and
by whom, in large part, they are judged.

Brett Ashley

Like other Hemingway heroines, Brett Ashley has been denounced as a weak
character. Allen Tate has called her "false," and has claimed that she is more
caricature than character.[1] Edwin Muir has claimed that Brett "is the sentimentally
regarded dare-devil, and she never becomes real."[2] The more serious and frequent
critical charges against Brett Ashley, however, are that she lacks the characteristics
of a woman and, worse, that she is a "bitch." On the first charge, Theodore
Bardacke claims that says that Brett is a "woman devoid of womanhood."[3] Jackson
Benson says that Brett is "a female who never becomes a woman."[4] Mimi Gladstein
says that Brett has a "bisexual image."[5] And, the most pointed, Pamella Farley calls
Brett "a perversion of femininity."[6] (Much has been made lately, incidentally, based
on "quick studies" of Hemingway's unpublished manuscripts, of Hemingway's own
alleged bisexuality and general confusion of sex roles, and, given the contemporary

From *Cassandra's Daughters: The Women in Hemingway* (Westport, CT: Greenwood Press, 1984), pp.
49–58.

preoccupation with such matters, much more is surely going to be said about it.)[7]

A careful reading of *The Sun Also Rises,* however—the only one of his books that Hemingway was almost completely satisfied with[8]—reveals that Brett was an individual whose female sexual appeal and general attractiveness were exceptional, despite her bobbed hair and her occasional association with homosexuals. From the beginning of the book, men find her irresistible. When Jake, as narrator, first introduces Brett, he says, "Brett was damned good-looking. She wore a slipover jersey sweater and a tweed skirt, and her hair was brushed back like a boy's. She started all that [that is, the new female hairstyle]. She was built with curves like the hull of a racing yacht, and you missed none of it with that wool jersey" (p. 22).[9] Robert Cohn, too, is immediately captivated by Brett, and a short time later, he says, "She's a remarkably attractive woman" (p. 38).

Every significant male character in the novel at one time or another comments on Brett's female attractiveness. When he is introduced to Brett, Bill Gorton says, "Beautiful lady" (p. 74), and later he says, "She's damned nice" (p. 76). Mike Campbell says, "Brett, you *are* a lovely piece. Don't you think she's beautiful?" (p. 79)—a refrain that he reiterates through the rest of the novel. There are Jake's repeated narrative descriptions: "Brett wore a black, sleeveless evening dress. She looked quite beautiful" (p. 146) and "Brett was radiant" (p. 207) and, finally, the near-uncontrollable infatuation of the nineteen-year-old bullfighter, Pedro Romero, for Brett. Hemingway makes amply clear, in short, that this is an exceptionally appealing woman—bright, beautiful, and sexual—and to call Brett "non-feminine," or "bisexual," or a "perversion of femininity," is to measure her by a standard of "womanhood" which is confining indeed.

A more unfortunate and inaccurate form of party-line criticism on Brett Ashley, however, is that which glibly labels her a "bitch." This assessment apparently began with Edmund Wilson and his interpretation of Brett Ashley as "an exclusively destructive force,"[10] and has been perpetuated almost uniformly by critics of the last four decades, including such notables as Philip Young,[11] Joseph Warren Beach,[12] Leslie Fiedler,[13] and John Aldridge, who describes her as a "compulsive bitch."[14] Almost to a person, the critics of the Brett-the-bitch school rely on Brett's own pronouncements for their interpretation, particularly the assertion that Brett makes to Jake after she leaves Romero: "You know it makes one feel rather good deciding not to be a bitch" (p. 245). This is, in fact, the single most quoted passage in criticism of the novel.

Superficially, Brett's behavior might be construed as "bitch-like." She does pursue courses of action which run counter to the wishes of the men with whom she is associated. In the early scene in the cafe, when Cohn, just introduced to Brett, fawningly asks her to dance, she lies, "I've promised to dance this with Jacob" (p. 22). Later, Jake and Brett discuss Brett's fiancé, Mike Campbell, and Brett says, "Funny. I haven't thought about him for a week"; when Jake asks if she has written to Mike, Brett replies, "Not I. Never write letters" (p. 63). When Brett insists that Mike tell the story of the questionable way he received his war medals, Mike says to Cohn, "Brett will tell you. She tells all the stories that reflect discredit on me" (p. 135). Recall, in addition, Cohn's label of Circe for Brett ("she turns men into swine" p. 144) and, most important, the way Brett torments Jake by repeatedly not appearing for dates and by repeatedly describing her affairs with other men, and one can see how she, and the critics following her lead, might think of herself as a bitch.

I would strongly assert that such a charge, however, is not valid, and for three major reasons: 1. Brett and the other characters in the novel live in a milieu in which relationships and responsibilities are intentionally loose and disordered, and her behavior merely reflects this milieu; 2. While Brett's behavior toward men is sometimes thoughtless, it is never cruel; and—central to an understanding of Brett's character—3. she is a woman, who, like Catherine Barkley, has a mind disordered by the impact of the war. Unlike Catherine, she cannot find the route to psychological health with the result that she consistently pursues a course of self-abuse, indeed of self-destruction.

To interpolate an historical note about the milieu: Many have recently pointed out that the twenties were not nearly so grim as Hemingway and the other expatriates portrayed them—nor, for that matter, nearly so glamorous as Scott Fitzgerald portrayed them either. For all the talk of a "lost generation," James T. Farrell claims that the years of the twenties, during which *The Sun Also Rises* is set, actually "fall within the most hopeful period of the post-Versailles world."[15] Contrary to the notion that all was either despair or glamour in the twenties, and contrary to Robert Spiller's assertion that in Hemingway "an era had found a literary voice for its skepticism and its faith,"[16] historian Roderick Nash summarizes his excellent argument that the Hemingways and the Fitzgeralds were writing decidedly "minority reports" on the decade that made them both famous:

> At the fringe of the American intellectual community stood a few really shaken minds for whom either the old absolutism nor the new relativism and scientism sufficed as a basis for belief. Yet even these disillusioned few refused to exist with no values at all. Instead they began the American exploration of a point of view later labeled *existentialism*. Axiomatic to this position was confrontation with human futility and the absurdity of life. For this reason these intellectuals' conception of themselves as a lost generation was essential. Such a pose was part of a deliberate artistic experiment, an attempt not to deny value but rather to create from their own frustrated lives existential situations in which radically new values could be formulated. Despair and disillusion were dramatized in order to accentuate the achievement of confronting reality. Ernest Hemingway, F. Scott Fitzgerald, Joseph Wood Krutch, and the malcontented minority they represented were lost only by traditional standards. In their own terms they were finding new ways of defining and keeping a new faith.

As for popular thought in the 1920s, there has likewise been overemphasis on the revolutionary and bizarre. We have read (and with the aid of records, television, and motion pictures, heard and seen) so much about the flapper, the bootlegger, and the jazz band that our conception of the era is greatly distorted. The 1920s were more than these things, just as the 1960s have been more than the jet set, hippies, and *Playboy*. We have forgotten F. Scott Fitzgerald's 1931 admonition that the jazz age concept he coined applied only to the "upper tenth of [the] nation." Perhaps even this was generous. The point is that evidence for generalizing about the mood of the decade is frequently incomplete, often by design. The twenties have been given little chance except to roar.

In fact, popular thought in these years was remarkably conservative. Beneath the eye-catching outward iconoclasm, the symbolic revolt, was a thick layer of respect for time-honored American ways, means, and rationales. The same nervousness that induced intellectuals to search for certainty prompted the general public to cling to familiar ideas with nearly hysterical intensity. It is difficult to square the popular taste of the 1920s in heroes, literature, religion, and politics, for instance, with the stereotype of the jazz age.[17]

Perhaps because of this conservatism of the twenties, many critics have been unable to empathize with the characters found in Hemingway's "minority report," and some have been quick to denounce the Hemingway milieu itself. The denunciations range from Henry S. Canby's claim that the characters of *Sun* are "lovable but futile revellers who ran from cocktail to cocktail up and down France, self-tortured, but flippant, as unmoral as monkeys,"[18] to Ernest Boyd's claim that the characters are "tragic comedians" and Hemingway himself is "a student of expatriate alcoholism,"[19] to Philip Young's charge that *Sun* is action "which goes no place,"[20] to Cleveland Chase's assertion that "it would have been difficult for Mr. Hemingway to have chosen a more dreary or aimless setting for a novel,"[21] to T. S. Matthews' comment that the action of *Sun* is "concerned with flotsam in the eddy of a backwater."[22] Even Hemingway's mother was not to be denied a critical shot at the fictional world her son created: "Why does he want to write about such vulgar people and such messy subjects?"[23]

The subjects are, to be sure, "messy." And the characters are vulgar, though, to be fair, they are vulgar in the same ways that children and adolescents are often vulgar. They bicker about trivia as children might. In the cafe at the opening of the novel Georgette says, in response to a question from Frances Clyne, "No, I don't like Paris. It's expensive and dirty," to which Frances replies, "Really? I find it so extraordinarily clean. One of the cleanest cities in all Europe" (p. 19). Quite childish, much like the later dialogue between Cohn and Jake about Brett, beginning with Cohn:

> "I don't believe she would marry anybody she didn't love."
> "Well," I said. "She's done it twice."
> "I don't believe it."

"Well," I said, "don't ask me a lot of fool questions if you don't like the answers."

"I didn't ask you that."

"You asked me what I knew about Brett Ashley."

"I didn't ask you to insult her."

"Oh, go to hell."

He stood up from the table his face white, and stood there white and angry behind the little plates of hors d'oeuvres.

"Sit down," I said. "Don't be a fool."

"You've got to take that back."

"Oh, cut out the prep-school stuff."

"Take it back."

"Sure. Anything. I never heard of Brett Ashley. How's that?"

"No. Not that. About me going to hell."

"Oh, don't go to hell," I said. "Stick around. We're just starting lunch."

Cohn smiled again and sat down. He seemed glad to sit down. What the hell would he have done if he hadn't sat down? "You say such damned insulting things, Jake."

"I'm sorry. I've got a nasty tongue. I never mean it when I say nasty things."

"I know it," Cohn said. "You're really about the best friend I have, Jake."
[P. 39]

The most adolescent scenes of all, however, concern drinking and the high-school-like glee with which the characters describe their drunkenness. Brett urges Mike Campbell to tell the others about his experience in court, and he responds, "I don't remember.... I was just a little tight," to which she responds excitedly, "Tight! ... You were blind!" (p. 136). Later, when Jake finds some of the others near the Bar Milano:

Outside the Bar Milano I found Bill and Mike and Edna. Edna was the girl's name.

"We've been thrown out," Edna said.

"By the police," said Mike. "There's some people in there that don't like me."

"I've kept them out of four fights," Edna said. "You've got to help me." Bill's face was red.

"Come back in, Edna," he said. "Go on in there and dance with Mike."

"It's silly," Edna said. "There'll just be another row."

"Damned Biarritz swine," Bill said.

"Come on," Mike said. "After all, it's a pub. They can't occupy a whole pub."

"Good old Mike," Bill said. "Damned English swine come here and insult Mike and try and spoil the fiesta."

"They're so bloody," Mike said. "I hate the English."

"They can't insult Mike," Bill said. "Mike is a swell fellow. They can't insult Mike. I won't stand it. Who cares if he is a damn bankrupt?" His voice broke.

"Who cares?" Mike said. "I don't care. Jake doesn't care. Do *you* care?"

"No," Edna said. "Are you a bankrupt?"

"Of course I am. You don't care, do you, Bill?"

Bill put his arm around Mike's shoulder. [Pp. 188–89]

As the fiesta is closing, Mike and Bill find Jake in his hotel room pretending to be asleep, and Mike says approvingly, "He's blind as a tick" (p. 224).

Before judging Brett a bitch, then, one must measure both the milieu she is part of and—some of the time it means the same thing—the individuals whose interests she frustrates.

We turn now to the men with whom Brett is associated and the ways in which she denies their wishes. There is Robert Cohn, with whom she eventually agrees to have a brief affair. Cohn is, as Hemingway obviously intends him to be, the complete ass. He fawns over Brett; he follows her almost everywhere; he says all the wrong things; and he is a bully. Though Brett, in order to talk to Jake alone, says to Cohn, "For God's sake, go off somewhere. Can't you see Jake and I want to talk?" (p. 181), her outburst is probably considerably less than Cohn deserves. Far from being cruel to Cohn, on several occasions she intervenes to prevent Mike from being cruel—saying to Mike's malicious goading of Cohn, "Shut up, Michael. Try and show a little breeding" (p. 141). Because of his cruel, drunken tongue, Mike Campbell, like Cohn, deserves whatever thoughtlessness Brett directs his way.

The matter of Brett's relationship with Jake and whether she is cruel to him must be taken up in the larger context of Brett's attitude toward herself and the self-destructive behavior which grows out of that attitude. Critics have almost uniformly taken Brett's "deciding-not-to-be-a-bitch" statement at face value and accepted her assumption that she has, therefore, been a bitch all along. When critics like Edmund Wilson claim that Brett is "an exclusively destructive force," they are reinforcing Brett's interpretation of herself—and it is a wrong interpretation. Brett hurts no one in the novel nearly as severely as she hurts herself. Her nymphomania, her alcoholism, her constant fits of depression, and her obsession with bathing are all symptoms of an individual engaged in a consistent pattern of self-abuse. Even in causing discomfort to Jake—much of which he sets himself up for—Brett causes even greater discomfort to herself. Before one too easily accepts Robert Cohn's view of Brett as the emasculating Circe, as critic Sheridan Baker and others do,[24] one must realize that Jake was not technically emasculated (as Hemingway made clear),[25] and that the injury the war (a male-mission enterprise) caused Jake is far more permanent and devastating than anything that Brett does to him.

The most significant symptom of Brett's pursuit of self-destruction is her nymphomania. Two of the basic interpretations of nymphomania are 1. that it is merely the open expression of the "natural" female sexual appetite of insatiation which, because of centuries of social restrictions (produced by male sexual limitations), is suppressed in most women;[26] and 2.—the more commonly held of the two—that it represents a woman's attempt to overcome social or sexual self-doubt, by demonstrating, through one sexual experience after another, that she is, in fact, attractive, desirable, wanted.[27] By the first interpretation, Brett's milieu could be said to allow freedom from most conventions, including those of female sexual suppression, but I am convinced it is the second of the interpretations of nympho-mania which more aptly applies in Brett's case. Her unsuccessful marriages, her engagement to a man she has no serious regard for, her inability to commit herself to anything meaningful—indeed her inability even to define what is meaningful—denote a mental confusion in Brett, on the matter of her own worth, which is compounded by her chronic cycle of drinking-drunkenness-recovery. Another, overlapping, cycle taints Brett's mind as well: alcohol-sex-guilt. Despite the osten-sible isolation of Brett and her group from the mores of the world at large, not even Brett can completely dismiss the attitudes (in this case, regarding female drinking and sexuality) of the prevailing culture which surrounds a subculture group.

Brett's mind is, then, seriously disordered and filled with guilt. But how does this condition reflect on Brett's relationship with Jake? Quite directly actually. As psychiatrist Eric Berne points out, guilty people feel a compulsion to provide themselves with punishment; they almost always "set the stage" of their lives so as to insure themselves of painful events, thus constantly providing themselves with the punishment that their mental states require.[28] Jake's physical condition provides precisely the kind of constant pain which Brett needs. When critics like Sheldon Grebstein claim that Brett is the "most dramatic example ... of how pure sex can waste lives,"[29] they overlook the rather obvious fact that Brett's sexual activity reflects not her threshold of lust but rather her threshold of self-abasement. Jake is the perfect vehicle. She can (with his encouragement) sexually tease him and herself. Midway through the arousal stage, she can step back melodramatically, acknowledge the impossibility of it all, and torment herself for initiating the action in the first place.

Such scenes of torment between Jake and Brett are common in the novel and much of the time they have the mock-seriousness of the soap opera. Near the opening, in the taxi, they kiss; then "she turned away and pressed against the corner of the seat, as far away as she could get." She says, "Don't touch me. . . . Please don't touch me" (p. 25). Later in the hotel, Jake asks, "Couldn't we just live together?" and Brett replies, "I'd just *tromper* you with everybody. You couldn't stand it" (p. 55). Still later in the cafe Brett tells Jake: "I'm so miserable," and then goes on to insure herself of a continued feeling of misery by telling Jake, "Good night, darling. I won't see you again" (pp. 64–65). Even the book's conclusion reflects the tease-withdraw-suffer syndrome that has become a routine part of Brett's relationship with Jake. In a tone of agony befitting television "daytime drama," Brett says, "Oh, Jake . . . we could have had such a damned good time together" (p. 247).

In Brett's relationship with Romero, we see two aspects of Brett's character that demonstrate that she is a self-induced "sufferer" but that she is *not* a bitch.

Early on she reminds herself, "That Romero lad is just a child" (p. 167), but adds, "And God, what looks" (p. 168). She ups the ante on her guilt not long afterward when she tells Jake (guilt coming from both directions this way), "I'm a goner. I'm mad about the Romero boy. I'm in love with him, I think," and follows immediately with the guilt pay-off when she says, "I've never felt such a bitch" (p. 184). Brett is better than she wants to think herself, however, for this time she would not be causing discomfort to someone who deserves it (like Cohn and Mike Campbell) or to someone who consistently asks for it (like Jake). To hurt Romero would be a bitch-like act and she cannot do it. Despite what she thinks, it is simply not her style. Brett is confused; she feels guilty (hence the obsession with bathing);[30] she is tragically self-destructive; but in no legitimate way can she be interpreted as a bitch.

NOTES

[1] Allen Tate, "Hard-Boiled," *The Merrill Studies in* The Sun Also Rises, ed. William White (Columbus, Ohio: Charles E. Merrill, 1969), p. 18.

[2] Edwin Muir, "Fiction [*Fiesta*, by Ernest Hemingway]," *The Merrill Studies in* The Sun Also Rises, p. 15.

[3] Theodore Bardacke, "Hemingway's Women," *Ernest Hemingway: The Man and His Work*, ed. John K. M. McCaffery (New York: Avon, 1950), p. 309.

[4] Jackson J. Benson, *Hemingway: The Writer's Art of Self-Defense* (Minneapolis: University of Minnesota Press, 1969), p. 30.

[5] Mimi Reisel Gladstein, "The Indestructible Woman in the Works of Faulkner, Hemingway, and Steinbeck" (Ph.D. diss., University of New Mexico, 1973), p. 115.

[6] Pamella Farley, "Form and Function: The Image of Woman in Selected Works of Hemingway and Fitzgerald" (Ph.D. diss., Pennsylvania State University, 1973), p. 32.

[7] See, for example, Aaron Latham, "Unfinished Manuscripts Reveal a Hemingway No One Knew," Chicago *Tribune*, October 17, 1977, Section 3, p. 20.

[8] Carlos Baker, *Ernest Hemingway: A Life Story* (New York: Scribner's, 1969), p. 312.

[9] *The Sun Also Rises* was originally published in New York by Scribner's in 1926. All page references apply to the 1926 edition.

[10] Edmund Wilson, *The Wound and the Bow* (Cambridge: Houghton Mifflin, 1941), p. 238.

[11] Philip Young, *Ernest Hemingway* (New York: Rinehart, 1952), p. 56.

[12] Joseph Warren Beach, *American Fiction: 1920–1940* (New York: Russell and Russell, 1960), p. 81.

[13] Leslie A. Fiedler, *Love and Death in the American Novel* (New York: Criterion, 1960), p. 307.

[14] John W. Aldridge, *After the Lost Generation* (New York: McGraw-Hill, 1951), p. 24.

[15] James T. Farrell, *"The Sun Also Rises," Ernest Hemingway: Critiques of Four Major Novels*, ed. Carlos Baker (New York: Scribner's, 1962), p. 4.

[16] Robert E. Spiller, *The Cycle of American Literature* (New York: New American Library, 1967), p. 207.

[17] Roderick Nash, *The Nervous Generation: American Thought, 1917–1930* (Chicago: Rand McNally, 1970), pp. 3–4.

[18] Henry Seidel Canby, "A Review of *A Farewell to Arms*," *The Merrill Studies in* A Farewell to Arms, ed. John Graham (Columbus, Ohio: Charles E. Merrill, 1971), p. 14.

[19] Ernest Boyd, "Readers and Writers," *The Merrill Studies in* The Sun Also Rises, p. 7.

[20] Philip Young, *Ernest Hemingway* (New York: Rinehart, 1952), p. 58.

[21] Cleveland B. Chase, "Out of Little, Much," *The Merrill Studies in* The Sun Also Rises, p. 10.

[22] T. S. Matthews, "Nothing Ever Happens to the Brave," *The Merrill Studies in* A Farewell to Arms, p. 10.

[23] Jackson J. Benson, *Hemingway: The Writer's Art*, p. 20.

[24] Sheridan Baker, "Jake Barnes and Spring Torrents," *The Merrill Studies in* The Sun Also Rises, p. 47.

[25] A. E. Hotchner, *Papa Hemingway* (New York: Random House, 1966), p. 49.

[26] Edward M. Brecher, *The Sex Researchers* (Boston: Little, Brown, 1969), pp. 191–94.

[27] H. L. P. Resnik and Marvin E. Wolfgang, eds., *Sexual Behaviors: Social, Clinical, and Legal Aspects* (Boston: Little, Brown, 1972), pp. 225–26.

[28] Eric Berne, *What Do You Say After You Say Hello? The Psychology of Human Destiny* (New York: Grove, 1972), pp. 31–32.

[29] Sheldon Grebstein, "Sex, Hemingway, and the Critics," *The Humanist*, 21 (July–August, 1961), p. 216.

[30] See *The Sun Also Rises*, pp. 53, 74, 83, 144, 159.

Milton A. Cohen
CIRCE AND HER SWINE

Midway through *The Sun Also Rises* appears a most revealing depiction of Brett Ashley: " 'He calls her Circe,' Mike said. 'He claims she turns men into swine.' "[1] Because the "he" is Robert Cohn, critics have not pursued this epithet as fully as they might. Cohn, after all, is the goat of the novel; his naïve romanticism verifies the weathered and weary cynicism of Jake, Brett, and Mike. Brett, conversely, is usually viewed the way she views herself: as one of the "us" who understand how the world works and form their values accordingly.[2] Yet Cohn's allusion is apt, even if it comes from an unappealing mouth. For the Circe myth not only informs Brett's beguiling characterization, it redefines her status, detaching her from the "us" group and relegating her to a Manichaean pole of evil, whose only counterweight of Hemingwayesque good is Pedro Romero.[3] Moreover, the myth clarifies the volatile sexuality of the story as a no-holds-barred struggle for domination, with debasement and emasculation falling to the losers.

The outlines of the Odyssean Circe myth are well known, as indeed they were to Hemingway, writing three years after Joyce's *Ulysses* was published.[4] Less well known, however, is how the theme of sexual domination and debasement suffuses every detail of the story, both literally and symbolically. The charms by which Circe lures Odysseus' men into her house are sensuous and hypnotic: her "lovely voice" echoing in her beautiful house, "her tranquil movement to and fro at her great and everlasting loom" (even then, a cliché for entrapment).[5] Her own identity is deliciously ambiguous. "It's either a goddess or a woman," Polites concludes—and falls into the trap. Circe opens her "polished doors," invites the men "to enter," and "ushers" them (all but the wary Eurylochus) into her "hall." Not only are the images unmistakably sexual, they show the nymph-goddess in complete control of this enticement and symbolic intercourse.

The drugged mixture Circe gives the men includes honey and wine—both ancient aphrodisiacs. Her coup de grace however, is a blow from her "long wand"

From *Arizona Quarterly* 41, No. 4 (Winter 1985): 293–305.

that turns them into swine. The pervasive phallic imagery in this story (Hermes, too, is a "god of the golden wand," and Odysseus opposes his sword to Circe's wand) symbolizes control. In enticing, then enslaving men with her sexual charms, Circe usurps the traditional masculine-aggressor's role; appropriately, then, her magical accoutrement, the wand, is phallic, her gesture aggressive. Conversely, her victims are not only debased, but emasculated. The mountain wolves and lions that prowl her palace grounds—animals of supreme virility—"rose on their hind legs to caress them [Odysseus' men] with much wagging from their long tails, like dogs fawning on their master. . . ." Similarly reduced, Odysseus' men comprehend their debasement with minds "as human as they had been before the change," but are utterly powerless to resist. Anguished by their impotence, "they shed tears in their sties."

Only the divine intervention of Hermes keeps Odysseus from the same fate. The god provides a magic herb to neutralize Circe's poisoned pottage; equally important, he teaches Odysseus how to tame this witch:

> When Circe strikes you with her long wand, you must draw your sword from your side and rush at her as though you meant to take her life. She will shrink from you in terror and invite you to her bed. Nor must you hesitate to accept the goddess' favours, if you want her to free your men and treat you kindly. But make her swear a solemn oath by the blessed gods not to try on you any more of her tricks, or when she has you stripped she may rob you of your courage and your manhood.

Sword against wand, strength against wiliness are the weapons in this struggle for sexual domination. As Odysseus executes Hermes' instructions, Circe immediately assumes a submissive posture: "with a shriek she slipped below my blade, fell at my knees and burst into tears." Just as Hermes foretells, she offers herself to Odysseus, but swears, at his insistence, to play fair. Now Odysseus can enjoy the spoils of his sexual victory: the tamed witch in "her beautiful bed," his men restored to their manhood "younger and much handsomer than before," and Circe's tireless hospitality in ministering to their every need. With a little help from the gods, a sexual tigress is turned into a purring pussycat.

Certainly, the Circe myth does not account for all aspects of Brett's complex characterization; nor does it ravel all of the story's thematic strands. But the two patterns correspond in several ways. Just as we first encounter Circe's house surrounded by the "fawning" wolves and lions, so we first see Brett surrounded by creatures that Jake (and Hemingway too) consider emasculate—homosexuals:

> As they went in, under the light I saw white hands, wavy hair, white faces, grimacing, gesturing, talking. With them was Brett. She looked very lovely, and she was very much with them. . . . Somehow they always made me angry. I know they are supposed to be amusing, and you should be tolerant, but I wanted to swing on one, any one, anything to shatter that superior, simpering composure. (p. 20)

Brett's physical charms are described in loving detail, but equally appealing is her vivacity. When she meets Bill Gorton, for example, she "smiled at him, wrinkling the corners of her eyes"—twice! (Indeed, this charming tic seems almost a Homeric epithet in its many recurrences.) Of course, what spices Brett's charm—and makes it so dangerous—is her sexual bravado: In both her dress and habits, she rejects the gestures of feminine subservience for those of masculine power. She wears her hair "brushed back like a boy's" under a man's hat, associates *only* with men, calls herself a "chap," and outdrinks any man in the story—no mean feat when drinking occupies so much of the action. Her sexual aggressiveness is equally unconventional: *she* chooses her lovers and has them on *her* terms. Like the sorceress whose ambiguous identity beguiles the sailors, Brett intentionally cultivates conflicting sexual images (well-displayed curves beneath a boy's haircut); like Circe, she is sexually aggressive; and like Circe (before Odysseus), she dominates her lovers.

Brett even shares some of Circe's occult powers. She weaves her web for Romero by reading his palm; and as she does so, "she was not at all nervous now. She looked lovely." Earlier, she has her fortune told by gypsies. Comfortable in a gypsy's tent, she is repelled by the Church—as witches are supposed to be. During the religious procession, she is barred from entering the San Fermin chapel for being improperly attired. In her other attempts to participate, she feels out of place, edgy. The confession she wants to observe is "in a language she did not know," Jake notes wryly. And when she tries to pray for her lover's success in the bullring, she cannot: " 'Come on,' she whispered throatily. 'Let's get out of here. Makes me damned nervous' " (p. 216). In fact, though Brett does exude a religious aura, only it is pagan and totemic: the religion of Dionysus. She is the pagan queen of the fiesta, as Jake observes her: "I looked and saw her coming through the crowd in the square, walking, her head up, as though the fiesta were being staged in her honor, and she found it pleasant and amusing" (p. 213). Just after she is barred from the Church,

> Some dancers formed a circle around Brett and started to dance. They wore big wreaths of white garlics around their necks. . . . They were all chanting. Brett wanted to dance but they did not want her to. They wanted her as an image to dance around. When the song ended with the sharp *riau-riau!* they rushed us into a wine-shop. (p. 160)

By juxtaposing this pagan ritual to the failed Church visit (just as he earlier contrasts her thwarted desire to witness Jake's confession to her successful visit to the gypsy camp), Hemingway leaves no doubt about Brett's magical, totemic powers.

Where Brett most differs from her mythic model concerns control and intent. Circe's enticements—the singing and weaving (knowing the men are outside), the invitation to enter, the deceptive hospitality—imply cool, calculated self-control. Brett is passion's slave. Just as her drinking is uncontrollable, so is her sexual desire. Thus her request to Jake for the Romero rendezvous is desperate and full of self-loathing: "I can't help it. I'm a goner. It's tearing me all up inside. . . . I've lost my self-respect.... God knows, I've never felt such a bitch!" (p. 190). Even while scarcely able to control her own appetites, however, Brett effortlessly—even thoughtlessly—entices and controls the men around her. Her motives are not malevolent, even have a curious altruism about them: she has nursed both Jake and Mike and goes off with Cohn because "it would be good for him."[6] But intentions are one thing, results another. Even without her wishing to exert it, Brett's charm draws in the unwary. Cohn, of course, is the story's object lesson, since Jake and Mike are already in her thrall:

> Dancing, I looked over Brett's shoulder and saw Cohn, standing at the bar, still watching her.
> "*You've made a new one there,*" I said to her.
> "Don't talk about it. Poor chap. I never knew it till just now."
> "Oh, well," I said. "I suppose you like to add them up." (p. 23, emphasis supplied)

Even Bill (who, somewhat like Eurylochus, manages to resist Brett's charm) feels her power to captivate in his very first glimpse of her: "Beautiful lady.... Going to *kidnap* us" (p. 76, emphasis supplied).

Debasement follows allure. Under Brett's spell, Mike, Jake, and Cohn are like snarling dogs around a bitch in heat, each wanting her for himself, each jealous of the others' claims on her, each (Jake and Mike at least) despairing that no one man can ever possess her. Indeed, animal metaphors abound in the fiesta section to suggest how debased, physically and spiritually, Brett's victims become. Following the unloading of the bulls, Mike calls Cohn a steer for following after Brett and "always hanging about so." Cohn, himself, seems to identify with this role, as he sadly remarks, "It's no life being a steer." He should know, for in several ways he emulates one.[7] The steer acts as buffer to the bulls to quiet them and keep them from fighting each other; for its efforts, it draws the bulls' wrath and is gored repeatedly. "Can't the steers do anything?" Bill asks; and Jake replies, "No. They're trying to make friends." Cohn's presence is scarcely calming—that pleasant task falls to Jake—but his steerish juvenility in mooning over Brett, in following her everywhere, and in foolishly assuming that their brief affair *means* something, goads both Mike *and* Jake to gore him with insult and Jew-baiting. Like the steer, Cohn accepts this abuse as his due, the price of his devotion to Brett: "His face had the sallow, yellow look it got when he was insulted, but somehow he seemed to be enjoying it. The childish, drunken heroics of it. It was his affair with a lady of title" (p. 184). Cohn, moreover, offers no insult in return, and, like the steer, wants only to be friends with his tormentors: "You're really about the best friend I have," he tells Jake, who pities him. Even his belated aggression is scarcely "manly." Before going off with Brett, he is ready to fight for his self-respect (however absurdly) against an imagined insult from Jake. Now her servile and self-appointed knight, he will fight only to protect his lady's honor.

Mike's debasement is simpler both in cause and effect. Engaged to a sexual dynamo, he must observe helplessly the proof of their hopeless betrothal in the person of Brett's former lover, Cohn, and her newest one, Romero. Besides drinking, Mike's only recourse is to attack the symptom, Cohn, since he himself is in love with the problem. Ironically, it is Brett who observes—appropriately, in bestial metaphor—how low Mike sinks in these attacks. She responds to his steer insult of Cohn by telling him to "try and show a little breeding." Mike's retort is richly ironic: "Breeding be damned. Who has any breeding, anyway, except the bulls?" (p. 146). As his behavior continues to deteriorate, Brett unwittingly confirms Cohn's depiction of her as Circe when she refers to Michael as a "swine" (p. 188).

Jake is clearly the character intended to gain our empathy; yet he too is not above tormenting Cohn and debasing himself. Unlike Mike, however, he feels guilty about it:

I was enjoying Cohn's nervousness. . . . It was lousy to enjoy it, but I felt lousy. Cohn had a wonderful quality of bringing out the worst in anybody. (p. 100)

Mike was unpleasant after he passed a certain point [in his drinking]. I liked to see him hurt Cohn. I wished he would not do it, though, because afterward it made me disgusted at myself. (p. 153)

As Jake well knows, though, the real source of his irritation is not Cohn himself, it is Cohn's affair with Brett and his pompousness about it:

Why I felt that impulse to devil him I do not know. Of course I do know. I was blind, unforgivingly jealous of what had happened to him. The fact that I took it as a matter of course did not alter that any. I certainly did hate him. (pp. 101–02)

Jealousy, vicarious cruelty, and self-disgust are one form of Jake's debasement. "Pimping" is another. Cohn's term for it may be extreme, but when Jake takes Brett to Romero, he violates both his self-respect and the qualities he most values in the bullfight. Earlier, he had shared Montoya's concern that Romero, the "fine boy," not be corrupted by foreigners. Indeed, Montoya trusted Jake's discretion and turned to him for advice in this very matter. Now, Jake knowingly betrays this trust: "He [Romero] sat down and looked at her across the table. I went out. The hard-eyed people at the bullfighter table watched me go. It was not pleasant" (p. 194).

The betrayal is only one of many, for Jake is always "on call" to Brett, to do her dirty work and bail her out of her perpetual messes. So he muses, as he wires her of his return: "That seemed to handle it. That was it. Send a girl off with one man. Introduce her to another to go off with him. Now go and bring her back. And sign the wire with love. That was it all right" (p. 250). What keeps bringing Jake back is the same thing that makes him hate and devil Cohn, and makes him betray his values and his self-respect: a tortured, hopeless love for Brett Ashley. His devotion to her is admirably selfless—true chivalry as opposed to Cohn's false chivalry—but it is also masochistic and debasing.[8]

In sum, Jake, Mike, and Cohn parallel the fate of Odysseus' crew in several ways. All are debased by their sexual attraction to an enchantress, metamorphosed into steers and swine. All comprehend their debasement and "shed tears in their sties." Jake cries alone in his room; Cohn cries both there and in public; even Michael approaches tears: " 'Jake,' Mike said. He was almost crying. 'You know I'm right. Listen, you!' He turned to Cohn: 'Go away! Go away now!' " (p. 184). Finally, it is no accident that Mike drunkenly shouts that "bulls have no balls"—to one who *does* have them, Romero.[9] For in their servility to Brett, all three lovers portray different kinds of the emasculation Hermes described to Odysseus: "when she has you stripped she may rob you of your courage and your manhood." For Jake, of course, emasculation is physical, not metaphorical: he cannot act on the sexual desire he feels for Brett. True, she did not cause his condition, and his learning to cope with it without complaint is, by Hemingway's standards, a manly virtue. Still, its presence emphasizes, by ironic contrast, Brett's sexual voracity, the hopelessness of their relationship, and thus his weakness in clinging to this futile, masochistic dream. Mike simply drinks himself into a sodden and, one surmises, impotent stupor to cope with the pain of Brett's promiscuity. Cohn's unmanliness appears not merely in his steerish passivity, but also in his adolescent romanticism that, in refusing to accept the world as it is, reduces him to tears when events do not fulfill his expectations. Thus, when his lady tells him off, and when Romero refuses to fight like a Princeton undergraduate, he can only blubber and leave in disgrace, "ruined." Above all, the emasculation of all three lovers appears exactly as it does in the swinish fate of Odysseus' crew: in their failure to resist the witch's spell; to change their debased state; to become controllers rather than the controlled.

Only Romero's machismo is proof against Brett's magic. His godlike perfection likens him to Hermes—a fair match against Brett's supernatural powers and one that reduces Jake's Odysseus to porcine POW. Hermes appears to Odysseus as "a young man at that most charming age when the beard first starts to grow." Romero is nineteen, and to Jake he is "the best-looking *boy* I have ever seen" (p. 169, emphasis supplied). The color imagery attending these two gods also matches. The herb Hermes gives Odysseus "had a black root with a milk-white flower." These are the only colors cited when Jake first sees Romero, despite the brilliant colors of the bullfighter's apparel: "His black hair shone under the electric light. He wore a white linen shirt . . ." (p. 169).

In the bullring, Romero displays Hermes' grace and swift dexterity: "I had her watch how Romero took the bull away from a fallen horse with his cape, and how he held him with the cape and turned him, smoothly and suavely, never wasting the bull. She saw how Romero avoided every brusque movement . . ." (pp. 173–74). Coupled with grace, of course, is his immense courage—the same courage that earned Hermes the epithet of "giant-killer." Indeed, Romero's icy bravery renders him "unattainable" to the bull—godlike—and permits him to prepare the kill with Olympian dispassion, as if he were conducting a ritual sacrifice (p. 174).

One other quality of Romero is worth noting. It appears in a small detail about his room: "There were two beds separated by a monastic partition" (p. 168). "Monastic" suggests that Romero's devotion to bullfighting is not only religious, but also ascetic and pure. His *afición*, therefore, is not for the flesh, as Brett herself confirms: "He'd only been with two women before. He never cared about anything but bullfighting" (p. 256). This uncorrupted innocence, coupled with his simple, traditional values (part of "the old thing" that Jake recognizes in him), makes sexual roles and behaviors for Romero as clear-cut as the black hair against his white shirt. Not for him the sexually ambiguous and inverted Parisian milieu where an impotent man introduces a prostitute as his fiancé, while his true love—a nymphomaniac— arrives in the company of homosexuals. Not for him men who lack cojones and women who dress like men. "He wanted me to grow my hair out," Brett confides to Jake afterwards. "He said it would make me more womanly" (p. 253). These qualities—beauty, grace, courage, and an untroubled, simple (some would say simple-minded) sense of sexual roles—compose the formula of Romero's "magic herb," the antidote that prevents him from falling under Brett's spell, becoming another of her swine. As Mark Spilka observes, "where Cohn expends and de- grades himself for his beloved, Romero pays tribute without self-loss. His manhood is a thing independent of women...."[10]

But it is not enough to conquer and dominate *this* Circe. For here, Hemingway radically departs from the Circe myth to remain true to his characters and to his times. Brett does not grow out her hair to fit Romero's image of femininity. Nor does she accept his money—another form of control. Nor will she allow him, any more than she did Cohn, to make an honest woman of her and tame her into monogamy. This Circe is not about to become Penelope: "He really wanted to marry me. So I couldn't go away from him, he said. He wanted to make sure I could never go away from him. After I'd gotten more womanly, of course" (p. 254). In fact, Brett sends Romero away, not vice versa. It is her first brave act in the story, the first in which she renounces her sexual magic and debasing power: "I'd have lived with him if I hadn't seen it was bad for him. . . . I'm not going to be one of these bitches that ruins children" (p. 254).

At best, then, their romance ends a standoff: Romero goes back to his bulls, uncorrupted by Brett's charms and certainly as manly as before. Literally and symbolically, he has "paid the bill" for his experience. Brett returns to her swine, to her hell of other people. Yet one senses that the standoff effects something of the liberating power that Odysseus achieves by dominating Circe. In deciding not to be a bitch, Brett has for once denied her appetite for a higher purpose. And Jake understands at last that, as all the symbols of this chapter suggest, he has indeed come to the "end of the line" with Brett. Only realizing this can he free himself of the illusion of the "damned good time" they could have had together, with the dripping irony of his final response: "Isn't it pretty to think so."

Perhaps the most intriguing aspect of the Circe-Brett parallel is that both witches base their fearsome powers on a dominating and voracious sexuality. As *they* wield the long wand, they debase and emasculate their lover-victims. Certainly, this view of woman as sexual menace, the vampire who drains the sexual life of her victims, was nothing new in Hemingway's time: Salome was to the arts of the preceding decades what the Gibson Girl was to American popular culture. Yet, it seems significant that Brett is the first and last major Hemingway heroine to possess this threatening power. The Catherines, Marias, and Renatas to come fade ever further from her high plateau of assertive individuality, fade ever further into the identity of their men.[11] So Catherine tells Frederic Henry: "There isn't any me. I'm you." And Maria echoes: "If I am to be thy woman, I should please thee in all ways."[12] In short, they are not women at all, only macho wet-dreams, empty vessels to be filled by the identities, values, and penises of their manly men. A bitch-goddess like Margot Macomber delineates the pattern perfectly: Her husband's cowardice is her mandate to rule and to assert her dominance by sleeping with a comparable power, Wilson. The cowardice gone, the mandate vanishes. An alternative solution to this bothersome problem of female identity was, of course, to avoid it altogether and write about "Men without Women": Nick Adams on the Big-Two Hearted or in the Alps, Santiago on the ocean, and many more. It is not by chance that at the calm center of The Sun Also Rises, the trout fishing at Burguete, male camaraderie flourishes with no women present. In any case, Brett's threatening and untamable energy enjoyed an exceedingly short, happy life. For Hemingway simply exorcised her sexual witchery from his prose.

NOTES

[1] Ernest Hemingway, The Sun Also Rises (New York: Charles Scribner's Sons, 1926), p. 149. Hereafter cited in text.

[2] The initiate-outsider division, so closely tied to the notion of the Hemingway "code," was probably popularized by Philip Young: "Lady Brett Ashley also knows the code and distinguishes people according to it; a person is 'one of us,' as she puts it, or is not.... the whole trouble with Robert Cohn ... is that he is not." Ernest Hemingway: A Reconsideration (University Park: The Pennsylvania State University Press, 1966), p. 83. Numerous other critics have accepted it, including Robert Penn Warren, Leo Gurko, and, more recently, Linda W. Wagner (" 'Proud and Friendly and Gently': Women in Hemingway's Early Fiction," College Literature, 7 [1980], 239–47). More recent studies of Brett, however, attest to the complexity and ambiguity of her character. Of these, the most balanced is Sam S. Baskett, " 'An Image to Dance Around': Brett and Her Lovers in The Sun Also Rises," The Centennial Review, 22 (1978), 45–69. Interestingly, Baskett asserts that "Brett ... is principally a contained figure to whom her suitors react, rather than a human being whose motives are susceptible to psychological analysis" (p. 48).

[3] Of the few critics who consider the "Circe" parallel at all, the most noteworthy are Carlos Baker, Hemingway: The Writer as Artist, 4th ed. (Princeton: Princeton University Press, 1972), pp. 87–88, and Leslie Fiedler, Love and Death in the American Novel, rev. ed. (New York: Stein and Day, 1966), pp. 318–20. Baker toys with Odyssean parallels, but declines to develop them, arguing that Hemingway's "esthetic opinions carried him away from the literary kind of myth-adaptation and over into that deeper area of psychological symbol-building which does not require special literary equipment to be interpreted" (p. 88). This seems a curious demurrer, considering the immense importance of the novel's prominent epigraph from Ecclesiastes and the later allusion to The Jew of Malta. In any case, "psychological symbol-building" and "myth-adaptation" need not be mutually exclusive ways of developing a theme. Fiedler certainly recognizes Brett's menace: "No man embraces her without being in some sense castrated, except for Jake Barnes who is unmanned to begin with; no man approaches her without wanting to be castrated, except for Romero, who thinks naïvely that she is—or can easily become—a

woman" (p. 319). But besides swinging a bit wildly (Romero, after all, is not castrated in *any* sense from his affair with Brett), Fiedler does not explore the Circean parallel, though he obviously shares its premises.

[4] Virtually as soon as Sylvia Beach published *Ulysses* in 1922, Hemingway read it and deemed it a "most god-damn wonderful book" in a letter to Sherwood Anderson, March 9, 1922 (*Ernest Hemingway: Selected Letters 1917–1961*, ed. Carlos Baker [New York: Charles Scribner's Sons, 1981], p. 62). It seems odd that Baker assumes that a young writer then developing his own style and freely adapting the innovations of others would not borrow techniques from Joyce as he had indeed appropriated them from Stein, Anderson, and Pound (see n. 3 above).

[5] Quotations from the *Odyssey* are from the translation by E. V. Rieu, published in 1946 by Penguin Books.

[6] Baskett, pp. 48–49. That Brett's escapades can be traced in part to a neurotic marriage to the ninth baronet Ashley also distinguishes her from Circe: a goddess requires no past to account for her caprices. Indeed, Hemingway may have sensed how much more vivid and memorable his character would be *without* a convenient case history. For, as Linda Wagner points out, the opening chapters he deleted "explained and explored Brett as bereaved and betrayed war victim" (pp. 242–43).

[7] Dewey Ganzel's brilliant study of Cohn as bull and Jake as steer (*"Cabestro* and *Vaquilla:* The Symbolic Structure of *The Sun Also Rises,"* Sewanee Review, 76 [1968], 26–48) is certainly valid. I would only argue that the characters are complex enough to play more than one role of the bullfight: the gored victim as well as the goring attacker.

[8] As with the initiate-outsider reading, the critical tendency to contrast Jake's "realism" to Cohn's self-deluded romanticism fails to distinguish between what Jake says and what he does regarding Brett. Martin Light, for example, writes that while Cohn wants to make an honest woman of Brett, "Jake, with common sense and a concession to fatality, accepts the nature of his condition and of Brett's character" ("Sweeping Out Chivalric Silliness: The Example of Huck Finn and *The Sun Also Rises,"* Mark Twain Journal, 17, No. 3 [1974], 21). More perceptive critics observe that Jake's desire to live with Brett in Book One is no less romantic and self-deluding than Cohn's chivalric notions. Indeed, Jake's subservience to her and his subsequent self-betrayals feed on his reluctance to abandon this dream (see Baskett, pp. 53–54, and Mark Spilka, "The Death of Love in *The Sun Also Rises,"* Twelve Original Essays on Great American Novels, ed. Charles Shapiro [Detroit: Wayne State University Press, 1958], pp. 241–42, rpt. in *Ernest Hemingway: Critiques of Four Major Novels*, ed. Carlos Baker [New York: Charles Scribner's Sons, 1962], pp. 19–20).

[9] In the first edition of *The Sun Also Rises,* the phrase appears as "Tell him that bulls have no horns" (pp. 181–82). By the time of the issuance of the Scribner Library edition in 1954, the phrase had been changed to Hemingway's original wording. An explanation is found in Hemingway's letter of July 24, 1926, to Maxwell Perkins of Scribner's:

> I imagine we are in accord about the use of certain *words* and I never use a word without first considering if it is replaceable. But in the proof I will go over it all very carefully. I have thought of one place where Mike when drunk and wanting to insult the bull fighter keeps saying—tell him bulls have no balls. That can be changed—and I believe with no appreciable loss to—bulls have no horns. (*Selected Letters,* page 211.)

[10] Spilka, p. 250 (Baker, *Critiques,* p. 23). Brett's decision to end the affair because "it was bad for him" does not necessarily contradict this view of Romero's invulnerability. Though she phrases her reason in the past tense, as a condition that has already occurred, she seems to refer to the future, i.e., that it *would* be bad for him. For she also reflects that "I don't think I hurt him any" (pp. 254, 253). We have no factual evidence that their brief affair corrupts Romero and a symbolic suggestion, in his paying the hotel bill, that it does not. Whether he could have withstood her corrosive powers in the future is a moot point.

[11] To be sure, some supporting female characters—Pilar is the best example—have distinct, powerful personalities. But one suspects that to the degree they assert themselves, they are (in Hemingway's view) surrogate men. Indeed, Pilar's nominal man, Pablo, abdicates his authority in weakness and drink, and Pilar acknowledges that she "would have made a good man" (*For Whom the Bell Tolls* [New York: Charles Scribner's Sons, 1940], p. 97).

[12] *A Farewell to Arms* (New York: Charles Scribner's Sons, 1929), p. 113; *For Whom the Bell Tolls*, p. 160. In the first printing of *A Farewell to Arms,* the phrase appears as "There isn't any me anymore. Just what you want." It was soon changed.

Wolfgang E. H. Rudat
BRETT'S PROBLEM

The question of why the main female character in *The Sun Also Rises* has the unusual first name Brett has always been somewhat of a crux in Hemingway scholarship. The following study is an attempt to answer that question and offer interpretations of seemingly unrelated passages from different parts of the novel, especially the conclusion—interpretations which will in part be based on the meaning of the name Brett and the allusive associations it evokes. In the process, my inquiry will discuss certain aspects of the genesis of the novel, and that discussion in turn will provide additional information which may be helpful interpreting the novel in its entirety.

I submit that Hemingway is punning on the German *Brett*—that is, *board*, *plank*—thus introducing the following sexual innuendo into the novel: Lady Brett is a plank nailed down by many men, but not nailed down for good by any of them. In fact, the pun on *Brett* lends special meaning to her family name "*Ash*-ley": that is, it compares Brett Ashley to a plank made of a wood that is known for its tough elasticity. Apparently unbroken herself, Brett has one lover after another bounce off her.

In the first longhand draft, which Hemingway finished in September of 1925, the woman's name was Duff. He replaced Duff, the name of a real person, (Lady) Duff (Twysden), with Brett when he was revising the draft in Schruns, Austria, during the following winter. Significantly, Schruns is a ski resort, and the colloquial German word for skis that is most commonly used in Austria is *Bretter/boards* (with *Ski* being the High German and "official" term). The pun thus adds a twist to the sexual innuendo pointed out in the preceding paragraph: Lady Brett is a ski which is set foot on by many men—but not by Jake Barnes, whom she truly loves but who is impotent as the result of a war injury.

Ironically, in his first draft Hemingway had presented Jake as an accomplished Alpine skier. As Frederic Joseph Svoboda notes in *Hemingway &* The Sun Also

From *Style* 19, No. 3 (Fall 1985): 317–25.

Rises: *The Crafting of a Style*, in his first version of the fishing episode at Burguete, Jake relates two stories about Alpine events, the first of which is a piece of fiction while the second focuses on Jake as a skier (19). The final version of the Burguete episode, while it does briefly mention the piece of fiction (120), contains no reference to Jake as a skier. The reason for that excision is not so much the one Svoboda expressly mentions—"Alpine skiing has nothing to do with what happens to the novel's characters in Paris, Pamplona, San Sebastian, Hendaye, or Madrid" (19)—but rather the more general artistic principle which Svoboda discusses a few lines later:

> In a 1958 interview in the *Paris Review*, Hemingway restated one of the primary principles at work in his early fiction—a principle that he consistently followed throughout his career: "I always try to write on the principle of the iceberg. There is seven eighths of it under water for every part that shows. Anything you know you can eliminate and it only strengthens your iceberg . . . If you describe someone, it is flat, as a photograph is, and from my standpoint failure." . . . Within Hemingway's framework of artistic intention, the thing that is left out may be almost as important as that which he left in. (19)

If, after changing the name Duff to Brett, Hemingway had not cut the presentation of Jake as skier, we would have a "flat photograph" showing Brett as ski and Jake as nonskier. Instead, *The Sun Also Rises*, as Svoboda notes, "has the solidity of an iceberg, seven-eighths unseen yet carefully based on that early, unseen foundation" (11). The final version counts on the reader's alertness to foreign words to fathom for himself those portions "under water" that he needs in order to be able to understand a novel about American expatriates in Europe—that is, in this case to fathom the notion of Brett as ski and Jake as nonskier. In fact, I would like to suggest that Hemingway's pun on *Brett* is an in-joke for those of his fellow expatriates who had successfully adjusted to and become appreciative of foreign cultures, and as such a satirical joke on those who had not—including, within the plot of the novel, Robert Cohn. Possessing the astounding "incapacity to enjoy Paris" (42), Cohn possesses the equally astounding incapacity to see Brett for what she is: as an aristocratic British version of the prostitutes roaming the streets of Paris,[1] a ski for many men. That is why, of all the males in the novel, Cohn takes the hardest fall when he gets bounced off the "ski."

But why does Brett have one lover after another bounce off her? Carlos Baker calls her a "nymphomaniac" (91). Yet nowhere does the text suggest that Brett's sexual desire is excessive. Instead it hints that she may have a problem not totally unlike the one which plagues Jake. Hemingway made it clear that, while Jake is sexually incapacitated, he does feel sexual desire (Morrow 55). The textual hint as to what Brett's problem is lies in the statement that she "was built with curves like the hull of a racing yacht" (22). The statement contains two different kinds of allusions, one of which is directed at the tip of the iceberg while the other reaches "under water." The second allusion is caught only after the first one is. The first allusion is to literary contexts which present the woman as a ship to be boarded, most likely to *Much Ado About Nothing* II. ii. 1148–49, where Beatrice says about Benedick: "I am sure he is in the fleet. I wish he had boarded me" (in fact, the *Brett/board* pun may include the verb *to board*). Once Hemingway has introduced the notion of Brett the sex partner as a ship, the statement that she "was built with curves like the hull of a racing yacht" becomes an allusion to a context which is perhaps less well known, a context, however, which outlines the basics of sexual intercourse:

> But neither do you, spreading to full sail, leave your mistress behind, nor let her outstrip your speed; haste side by side to the goal: then is pleasure full when man and woman lie vanquished together. (Ovid 725–28)

Hemingway is alluding to this passage in Ovid's *Art of Love* in order to import into his novel the following idea: Brett is a "racing yacht" which, ironically, is all too often "left behind." Or to express it in terms of the skiing-imagery: Brett is a ski which no man is able to stand on long enough.

Hemingway's allusive transaction with Ovid is downright Popeian. Hemingway is of course no Alexander Pope, the universally recognized champion of allusion (Brower). Yet it is also by applying methods similar to those of the poet of *The Rape of the Lock,* who created most of his text's meanings through allusive filiations which were not readily discernible (Wasserman, Rudat), that the Hemingway of *The Sun Also Rises* builds his icebergs of meaning—out of allusions which most readers would not catch automatically. The novel about the delicate relationship between a man and a woman calls to mind Pope's ironic, misleading statement, in his dedication of *The Rape* to Arabella Fermor, that it is "the Concern of a Poet to have his Works understood, *and particularly by your Sex"* (italics added). Hemingway's novel about a woman named Duff, who in the final version becomes Brett Ashley, is not meant to be understood immediately, least of all by Lady Duff Twysden, lest it embarrass the Lady as well as her acquaintances—or other readers, for that matter.[2]

> . . . Brett moved close to me. We sat close against each other. I put my arm around her and she rested against me comfortably. . . .
>
> "Oh, Jake," Brett said, "we could have had such a damned good time together."
>
> Ahead was a mounted policeman in khaki directing traffic. He raised his baton. The car slowed suddenly pressing Brett against me.
>
> "Yes." I said. "Isn't it pretty to think so?"

When on earlier occasions Jake had sought physical closeness, Brett would usually push him away because she did not want to be reminded of what *could* have been. Here, however, she is the one that is moving close to him. Thus, when she reminds him of what could have been had he not been impotent, she is actually making sexual demands on him that she knows he cannot fulfill.[3]

How can I interpret that Brett is making sexual demands on Jake? The reason is that the final scene is informed by, and has to be read in the light of, an earlier scene where a woman indeed makes sexual advances at Jake and quite physically reminds him of his disability—a scene which significantly is immediately followed by Jake's introduction of Brett into the narrative. Jake is riding in a horse cab with the prostitute Georgette:

> ... She cuddled against me and I put my arm around her. She looked up to be kissed. She touched me with one hand and I put her hand away.
>   "Never mind."
>   "What's the matter? You sick?"
>   "Yes." ...
>   "You're not a bad type," she said. "It's a shame you're sick. We get on well. What's the matter with you, anyway?"
>   "I got hurt in the war." (15–17)

Bringing the earlier scene to bear on the closing lines of the novel, the reader realizes that Brett is doing to Jake intentionally what Georgette had done to him unintentionally. Yet why is Brett rubbing in Jake's impotence? She is doing this in order to force Jake to terminate a relationship whose sexually frustrating nature— for reasons which will be given later—she can no longer endure. And she succeeds: when he replies, "Yes ... Isn't it pretty *to think so*?" (italics added), instead of, say, "Yes, that would have been great," he has already relegated their relationship and what it could have been to the past, to something which he will be able to merely reminisce ("think") about, should he ever choose to do so.

Yet the process of the termination of their relationship is more complex than that. In the first version Jake's final reply had read: "Yes ... It's nice as hell to think so" (Svoboda 93–94). The meaning of this statement is that it is hell for Jake to think of what could have been—and that Brett has brought him to the point where he is no longer willing to subject himself to that hell. In the first draft, then, Jake in his final rejoinder liberates himself of the female. He does this by matching her use of the word *damned* with the word *hell*. He outdoes her in a verbal battle, where he counters a swearword which in this context has lost all religious connotations (*damned*) with a swearword which retains its religious connotations: it is indeed hell for Jake to think of what could have been. Hemingway thus places the final dialogue in the novel into a religious context: that is, when he has Jake terminate the relationship, he has Jake exorcise himself of Duff.

Why did Hemingway change the final line of the novel? The answer is his iceberg principle, for the last line in the final version is the tip of the iceberg: it is the reader's task to fathom the remaining seven-eighths. Bearing in mind the thematically important contrast between Jake's Christianity and Brett's lack thereof (a point which will be elaborated later), the reader suspects that in the closing lines of the novel—a novel, moreover, whose title is taken from the Bible—Jake will find an appropriate comeback for Brett's (mis-)use of the word *damned* and reintegrate it into a religious context. After Jake has told us how much he has had to suffer at the thought of what could have been, we *know* that Brett's reminder is putting him through hell—so that no mention of hell is needed: it can remain under water. Hemingway, therefore, has Jake address Brett's use of the word *damned* only indirectly. Coming from a female British aristocrat, Brett's statement sounds anything but feminine. Jake parries her masculine aggressiveness by verbally adopting the posture of a female, on whom she could not and would not make any sexual demands: Jake's use of the affectedly feminine adjective *pretty* is a cutting rejoinder to Brett's use of the word *damned*—and in the final version, too, Jake exorcises himself of the woman.[4]

In the final version, however, the act of exorcism concentrates on the sexual, leaving the religious under water. In the earlier version the exorcism had also been sexual, but in a different way: Jake had used the word *hell* to counter the woman's masculine aggressiveness as manifested by her use of the word *damned*—that is, to out-macho her, as it were. But then, as Svoboda notes, "Hemingway was already trying alternative phrasings for the last line"—for example, "Isn't it nice to think so" (93). The latter alternative, although it is not quite as affectedly feminine as "Isn't it pretty to think so," already points in that direction, especially since the *question* comes to look "feminine" in the light of her masculinely aggressive *assertion* that they could have had such a damned good time together had he not been impotent. In other words, instead of having Jake out-macho Brett, Hemingway eventually decided to have him do the exact opposite. The change is a vast improvement not only because it "strengthens the iceberg," but also because it presents Jake as having rapidly matured after his seemingly puerile drinking bout in the preceding restaurant scene, where he had unsuccessfully tried to force her to join him in overindulging in food and drink: he has come to realize that machismo is *not* the solution.

But why does Jake eliminate from his life a woman whose promiscuity presumably does not hurt him because he cannot possess her anyway? The answer can be found in Jake's and Brett's discussion of her recent termination of her affair with the nineteen-year-old bullfighter Romero, a termination based on her decision that, thirty-four years old, she is "not going to be one of these bitches that ruins children" (243). A few lines after the announcement of her decision, the following scene takes place in her hotel room:

> . . . Then I saw she was crying. I could feel her crying. Shaking and crying. She wouldn't look up. I put my arms around her.
> "Don't let's ever talk about it. Please don't let's ever talk about it."
> "Dear Brett."
> "I'm going back to Mike." I could feel her crying as I held her close. "He's so damned nice and he's so awful. He's my sort of thing."
> She would not look up. I stroked her hair. I could feel her shaking.
> "I won't be one of those bitches," she said. "But, oh, Jake, please let's never talk about it." (243)

Two pages later, while Jake and Brett are in the hotel bar, she again brings up the topic of Romero. When Jake reminds her, "I thought you weren't going to ever talk about it," she replies, "How can I help it?" (245). The lines I quoted, not only from page 245 but also from page 243, indicate that she is still obsessed with Romero. Her obsession with the bullfighter surprises Jake in view of her promiscuity—but it also hurts his male ego: he senses that there is something special about Romero which has enabled him to replace Jake, whose mere touch, according to her own statement, used to make her, the "board," "simply turn all to jelly" (26). Jake does not know what that "something special" is, but he feels sufficiently betrayed by Brett to get rid of her when, after practically making a show of her obsession with Romero, she reminds Jake of what could have been had he been sexually functional. The author of course knows what that "something special" is: unlike other males, Romero did not "leave the racing yacht behind." It should be noted that Hemingway had alluded to Ovid during the *bal musette* scene, where Jake first introduced Brett into his narrative; the wheel comes full circle for Jake when Brett, in order to force the termination of a relationship whose sexually frustrating nature she can after her experience with Romero no longer endure, makes demands on Jake that, apparently, only Romero could fulfill.

It could be argued that in the final scene Brett also exorcises herself of Jake, and thus that the novel ends with a scene of mutual exorcism. But we are also faced with the following important question: does Brett succeed in exorcising herself of Romero so that she will be able to marry her intended, Mike? While with respect to Jake she is successful because he is more than helpful, she fails with Romero because in that situation she receives no help. For immediately after admitting that she cannot help talking about Romero, she remarks:

> "I just talk around it. You know I feel rather damned good, Jake."
> "You should."
> "You know it makes one feel rather good deciding not to be a bitch."
> "Yes."
> "It's sort of what we have instead of God."
> "Some people have God," I said. "Quite a lot."
> "He never worked very well with me."
> "Should we have another Martini?" (245)

Brett neither obtains nor even deserves Divine help because, in the lines just quoted, she actually replaces God. For when for a change she decides *not* to be a bitch, she claims that her own action and the good feeling resulting from the action are a substitute for having God. Her statement is an act of blasphemy, which Jake counters by pointing out to her that "Some people have God. . . . Quite a lot." The narrator's implication is that *of course* God never worked well with Brett because she has never given God a chance.

The dialogue presently under discussion practically repeats an earlier dialogue which had likewise involved Romero. In Pamplona, Brett had asked Jake to accompany her into San Fermin's Chapel, where she wanted to pray for Romero, who in a few hours would be facing a difficult task in the arena: he was in poor physical shape because he had been brutally beaten up by the jealous Robert Cohn the night before. After a little while Brett becomes so nervous that she has to leave the chapel. She shrugs off this experience claiming that she is not at all worried about Romero, but she does express concern that the wind might not let up in time for the bullfight. Jake uses her voiced concern as an opportunity for getting her to try prayer again:

> "You might pray," I laughed.
> "Never does me any good. I've never gotten anything I prayed for. Have you?"
> "Oh, yes."
> "Oh, rot," said Brett. "Maybe it works for some people, though. You don't look very religious, Jake."
> "I'm pretty religious."
> "Oh, rot," said Brett. "Don't start proselyting to-day. To-day's going to be bad enough as it is." (208–09)

The later scene has to be read in the light of the earlier one, for the wheel has come full circle also for Brett: in Pamplona she had half-heartedly tried religion in an effort to help Romero—half-heartedly because she gave up after a little while and refused to try again—and now she seems in dire need of supernatural help if she is to exorcise herself of the bullfighter.

For this context it might be well to quote Carlos Baker: "Without apology or explanation, Jake Barnes is a religious man. As a professing Catholic, he attends masses at the cathedral before and during fiesta week. On the Saturday before the festival opens, Brett accompanies him: 'She said she wanted to hear me go to confession,' says Jake, 'but I told her that not only was it impossible but it was not as interesting as it sounded, and, besides, it would be in a language she did not know.' Jake's remark can be taken doubly. The language Brett does not understand is Latin; it is also Spanish; but it is especially the language of the Christian religion" (89). In the dialogue following her breakup with Romero, Lady Brett Ashley proves herself to be an impenetrable "board"—impenetrable to the language of the Christian religion. But Brett's situation also has to be viewed from the following perspective: she is unwilling to enter the world of what in this context Jacob Barnes, although he is far from perfect, represents—the world of Christianity. Brett, who is only one lonely board, does not enter that which is made up of innumerable boards, innumerable boards which in their togetherness form a secure shelter. She does not enter Jacob's "barn(e)s"—that is, his churches, where she could have found peace.

Hemingway hints at the narrator's role by giving him for a first name the name of him who, in the Jacob's Ladder dream, found a "house of God" and called it

"Bethel" (Gen. 28.12–22)—it should be noted that the author has Brett say, sig-nificantly in the scene where he first introduces her into the narrative, "You've a hell of a biblical name, Jake" (22)—and for a family name a word which suggests that God has more than one house He can be worshipped in, a word which also connects the houses of worship with the name of the intended worshipper, "Brett Ash-ley."[5] In fact, the place of worship does not even have to be indoors, as Bill Gorton had pointed out in a religious ceremony during the fishing episode at Burguete: "Let no man be ashamed to kneel here in the great out-of-doors. Remember the woods were God's first temples" (122).

Although the ceremony at Burguete had been parodic in form—sucking drum-sticks and drinking wine, Bill had pronounced, "Let us rejoice in our blessings. Let us utilize the fowls of the air. Let us utilize the product of the vine"—it had been serious in spirit: it shows a flexibility akin to the ancient Greek ideal of the *aner spoudogeloios,* the spirit of seriocomic man. In other respects being as flexible as an ash, Brett does not possess this resiliency of spirit, which explains why after a few minutes in the chapel she becomes "uptight" and has to leave. Not only is she unable to resume praying when Jake *laughingly* suggests that she do so, but her tenseness causes her to overreact and interpret Jake's suggestion as an attempt to proselyte. Having once before been accused of proselyting, Jacob Barnes now realizes the futility of trying to discuss religion with Brett and orders another round of Martinis. This gesture is a parody Communion, but, unlike the ceremony at Burguete, it is *purely* parodic.

Jake, who at this point is still perfectly sober, dejectedly substitutes the en-suing drinking bout and its dialogue for what could have been a meaningful type of social intercourse—a discussion of religion. Such a discussion, instead of what Brett quite correctly calls talking *around* Romero, might have helped her find God and exorcise not so much her passion for the bullfighter as that which this passion symbolizes, namely, the eventually self-destructive nature of her sexuality. Instead, she will continue her voyage of meaningless motion and immediate gratification.[6] Brett will continue to be the "hull of a racing yacht," finally to be reduced to a mere "hull."

Or to express it in the terms of Jacob Barnes' position: since Brett, by re-placing Jake with Romero and verbalizing that replacement through her reminder of what could have been but is not, has deliberately undermined Jake's authority as the male who, according to the Bible, is supposed to protect the weaker sex, Jake has no choice but to cut loose as driftwood a Brett who, unwilling to enter one of the many houses of God, rejects the security of a haven. Hemingway himself said that the novel is not "a hollow or bitter satire, but a damn tragedy";[7] what I would like to suggest, then, is that in the final analysis the novel is to be read as a tragedy not only with respect to Jake, but even more so with respect to Brett.

NOTES

[1] For a discussion of Brett as prostitute, see Morrow.

[2] This of course does not mean that Hemingway wants his allusions, literary as well as linguistic, not to be caught at all. I spoke earlier of his pun on *Brett* as an in-joke. In this context I would like to refer to James Hinkle's article. My goal is different from Hinkle's. The latter is not concerned, as I am, with *allusively operative* echoes—that is, echoes which communicate meanings to the reader that are not explicit in the text. Instead, it is Hinkle's "contention that Hemingway made a regular practice of including in his work . . . seemingly gratuitous echoes . . . [and] included them as a sort of private joke *that he was content to let remain private*" (29, italics added).

[3] I initially made this point in my article, "Jake's Odyssey" which I use as a foundation for the present study.

[4] I first interpreted Jake's rejoinder as an act of exorcism in the study listed in note 3, where I view the final line from a somewhat different angle.

[5] Morrow (61) argues that in the concluding lines of the novel "Jake capitulates by joining Brett and her extrinsic values of meaningless motion and immediate gratification."

[6] For symbolism of other proper names see Morrow (63n): "Hemingway may have used the name 'Pedro Romero' not only in honor of the first great Spanish bullfighter, but because Romero is a common Sephardic name. The subtle irony of casting *both* Cohn and Romero as Jews would likely have appealed to young Hemingway's sense of humor."

[7] In a letter dated 19 November 1926, quoted by Morrow (63n).

WORKS CITED

Baker, Carlos. *Hemingway: The Writer as Artist.* Princeton: Princeton UP, 1972.

Brower, Reuben Arthur. *Alexander Pope: The Poetry of Allusion.* Oxford: Clarendon Press, 1959.

Hemingway, Ernest. *The Sun Also Rises.* New York: Scribner's, 1954.

Hinkle, James. "Some Unexpected Sources for *The Sun Also Rises.*" *Hemingway Review* 2 (Fall 1982): 26–42.

Morrow, Patrick D. "The Bought Generation: Another Look at Money in *The Sun Also Rises.*" *Genre* 13 (1980): 51–63.

Rudat, Wolfgang E. H. "Another Look at the Limits of Allusion: Pope's *Rape of the Lock* and the Virgilian Tradition." *Durham University Journal* 71 (1978): 27–34.

———. "Jake's Odyssey: Catharsis in *The Sun Also Rises.*" *The Hemingway Review* 1 (Fall 1984): 33–36.

Svoboda, Frederic Joseph. *Hemingway & The Sun Also Rises: The Crafting of a Style.* Lawrence: UP of Kansas, 1983.

Wasserman, Earl R. "The Limits of Allusion in *The Rape of the Lock.*" *Journal of English and Germanic Philology* 65 (1966): 925–44.

Mark Spilka

JAKE AND BRETT:
WOUNDED WARRIORS

What are we to make ⟨...⟩ of Jake Barnes's sexual wound? Hemingway was certainly not an impotent man when he created that curious condition—a lost portion of the penis—for his first-person narrator. His own wounds had been to the legs and scrotum, the latter a mere infection suggesting perhaps that worse had been barely avoided. In a late letter (December 9, 1951) he explained to a Rinehart editor, as an example of the complications of a writer's involvement in his own fictions, "the whole genesis of The Sun Also Rises":

> It came from a personal experience in that when I had been wounded at one time there had been an infection from pieces of wool cloth being driven into the scrotum. Because of this I got to know other kids who had genito urinary wounds and I wondered what a man's life would have been like after that if his penis had been lost and his testicles and spermatic cord remained intact. I had known a boy that had happened to. So I took him and made him into a foreign correspondent in Paris, and, inventing, tried to find out what his problems would be when he was in love with someone who was in love with him and there was nothing that they could do about it.... But I was not Jake Barnes. My own wound had healed rapidly and well and I was quit for a short session with the catheter.[1]

The last point is interesting in that there is nothing in the novel to indicate if or when Jake was quit with the catheter, or how he urinates now. But more interesting still is the choice of war wounds for an unmarried foreign correspondent in Paris otherwise much like himself. We know that Hemingway's close relations with his friend Duff Twysden, the ostensible model for Jake's beloved Brett Ashley, had much to do with the choice. As Scott Fitzgerald (who knew something about that relation) opined, Jake seems more like a man trapped in a "moral chastity belt"

From *Hemingway's Quarrel with Androgyny* (Lincoln: University of Nebraska Press, 1990), pp. 200–208.

than a sexually wounded warrior: and indeed, it was Hemingway's marital fidelity to Hadley that apparently kept him from having an affair with Duff; so too, Fitzgerald implies, Jake Barnes with Brett, though there is no Hadley in the novel.[2]

There may, however, be an Agnes von Kurowsky. Barnes and Lady Ashley had met each other in a British hospital where Brett worked as a nurse's aide, just as Ernest had met Agnes at a Milan hospital where she worked as an American Red Cross nurse. This prefiguring of the plot of A Farewell to Arms is no more than a background notation in The Sun Also Rises; but it does remind us of the emotional damage Ernest had sustained from his rejection after the war by Agnes Von Kurowsky and his complicity in that rejection. If Jake's sexual wound can be read as an instance of the way in which war undermines the possibilities of "true love," then we begin to understand to some extent why Hemingway chose that curious condition as an index to the postwar malaise, the barrenness of waste-land relations among the expatriates he knew in Paris—and brought with him to Pamplona. It was in a way a self-inflicted wound he was dealing with which had the war's connivance.

Lawrence's Clifford Chatterley, paralyzed from the waist down by a war wound, is a good example of such projected impotence since he functions obviously enough as the bearer of Lawrence's condition while he was writing the novel, the victim by that point in his life of tubercular dysfunction. But Hemingway was there before him with Jake Barnes, as of course Joyce had been there before Hemingway with Leopold Bloom, his imagined Jewish alter ego in Ulysses, and Henry James with Strether in The Ambassadors, and Ford Madox Ford with Dowell in The Good Soldier; and much farther back, Laurence Sterne with Tristram Shandy. The tradition of impotent narration or of impotent heroes, whether comic, serious, or tragic, is an old and honorable one; and our only question is what went into Hemingway's decision to employ it.

Our most recent clue comes from the posthumously published edition of The Garden of Eden (1986), the hero of which engages in androgynous forms of lovemaking with his adventurous young wife in the south of postwar France, and at one point in the original manuscript imagines himself as one of the lesbian lovers in a mysterious statue by Rodin, called variously Ovid's Metamorphoses, Daphnis and Chloe, and Volupté, and deriving from a group called The Damned Women from The Gates of Hell.[3] Since the hero also changes sex roles at night with his beloved, we have one interesting explanation for Hemingway's postwar choice of a symbol for his own unmanning by war wounds and the American nurses who tend them: for if Jake remains "capable of all normal feelings as a man but incapable of consummating them," as Hemingway told George Plimpton in a famous interview, his physical wound suggests also the female genitals as men erroneously imagine them, at least according to Freud.[4] The exact nature of the wound, moreover, is literally nowhere spelled out or explained in the novel; we have only Hemingway's word for the intended condition. It becomes clear nonetheless from the type of mannish heroine he imagines, after Lady Duff Twysden's British example, that an exchange of sexual roles has indeed occurred, prefiguring that of The Garden of Eden, and that it is Jake and not Brett who wears that traditionally female protection, the chastity belt.

What are we to make, then, of Brett Ashley's British mannishness? Her Britishness, as we have seen, goes back to that quasi-British establishment, the Hemingway household in Oak Park presided over by Abba Ernest Hall, a British emigrant in mid-nineteenth century, and his talented daughter Grace, with his wife's brother Tyley Hancock, another mid-century emigrant, as a frequent visitor. These American Fauntleroys, tourers of the British Isles, one of whom almost sang before the queen, others of whom wore mutton chop whiskers and walked tiny dogs, set the at times bantering, smoking, and tippling, at times religiously serious, tones of the household; and the talented Grace's music lessons and concerts helped to further differentiate that home from those of surrounding neighbors like the Hemingways, from whom Grace's husband Clarence, the young doctor whom she met when he tended her dying mother, had gravitated. In Grace and Clarence's favorite Victorian novel, *John Halifax, Gentleman*, one of Dinah Mulock Craik's most striking figures was the Catholic Lady Caroline Brithwood, who came to no good end, and whom we may take as the first fictional harbinger of Lady Ashley in young Ernest's boyhood reading.

Lady Caroline's appeal, in this staunchly moral novel, stems from the mixture in her portraiture of Catholic leniency with European license. In *The Sun Also Rises,* of course, it is Jake Barnes who is the lenient Catholic, Brett Ashley the licensed European; but the combination is striking, especially if we consider Jake for a moment as an aspect of his beloved British lady, or her lesbian lover:

> Brett was damned good-looking. She wore a slipover jersey sweater and a tweed skirt, and her hair was brushed back like a boy's. She started all that. She was built with curves like the hull of a racing yacht, and you missed none of it with that wool jersey. . . .

> I told the driver to go to the Parc Montsouris, and got in, and slammed the door. Brett was leaning back in the corner, her eyes closed. I got in and sat beside her. The cab started with a jerk.
> "Oh darling, I've been so miserable," Brett said. . . .

> The taxi went up the hill . . . We were sitting apart and we jolted close together going down the old street. Brett's hat was off. Her head was back. I saw her face in the lights from the open shops, then it was dark . . . and I kissed her. Our lips were tight together and then she turned away. . .
> "Don't touch me," she said. "Please don't touch me." . . .
> "Don't you love me?"
> "Love you? I simply turn all to jelly when you touch me."
> "Isn't there anything we can do about it? . . .
> "I don't know," she said. "I don't want to go through that hell again." . . .

On the Boulevard Raspail . . . Brett said: "Would you mind very much if
I asked you to do something?"

"Don't be silly."

"Kiss me just once more before we get there."

When the taxi stopped I got out and paid. Brett came out putting on her
hat. She gave me her hand as she stepped down. Her hand was shaky. "I say,
do I look too much of a mess?" She pulled her man's felt hat down and started
in for the bar. . . .

"Hello, you chaps," Brett said. "I'm going to have a drink."[5]

The cab ride is a setup for the ending, when Jake and Brett are in another such
cab in Madrid, pressed together as the cab slows down, with Brett saying, "Oh, Jake
. . . we could have had such a damned good time together," and Jake replying:
"Yes. . . . Isn't it pretty to think so?" A hard-boiled ending, but those early kisses tell
us otherwise. For through them Jake's vulnerability to pain through the essential
feminization of his power to love has been established; like a woman, he cannot
penetrate his beloved but can only rouse and be roused by her through fervent
kisses; nor is he ready, at this early stage of the sexual revolution, for those
oral-genital solutions which recent critics have been willing to impose upon him. His
maleness then is like Brett's, who with her boy's haircut and man's felt hat may be
said to remind us of the more active lesbian lover in the Rodin statue, named
playfully Daphnis in one version to an obvious Chloe. Which again makes us
wonder if Jake is not in some sense an aspect of his beloved—not really her
chivalric admirer, like Robert Cohn, but rather her masculine girlfriend, her admiring Catherine from the novel years ahead who similarly stops her car on the return
from Nice to kiss her lesbian lover, then tells her androgynous husband about it and
makes him kiss her too—or, in Jake's more abject moments, her selfless Catherine
from the novel next in line.

True enough, we see Jake enduring a form of love about which nothing can
be done, working out what could be called a peculiarly male predicament, a sad
form of a common wartime joke, in accord with Hemingway's stated plan; and in
his struggles against his own self-pity we see a standard of male conduct against
which we are asked to measure Robert Cohn's more abject slavishness to his
beloved lady, and Mike Campbell's, and even (more to its favor) young Pedro
Romero's manly devotion. And truer still, we are asked to judge Brett's liberation
as a displacement of male privilege and power in matters of the heart and loins, a
sterile wasteland consequence of postwar change. But what if the secret agenda is
to admire and emulate Brett Ashley? What if Brett is the woman Jake would in
some sense like to be?

"She started all that," he tells us admiringly, and perhaps even predictively.
Brett's style-setting creativity becomes, in *The Garden of Eden,* the leading characteristic of Catherine Bourne, whose smart boyish haircuts, blond hairdyes and
matching fisherman's shirts and pants—all shared with her androgynous husband

David—are plainly expressions of the new postwar mannishness, the new rivalry with men for attention and power, for a larger stake in the socio-sexual pie: new sexual freedoms and privileges, then, new license. They are also forms of artistry, like Catherine's unexpected talent for talk; and if Brett's talent is less for talk than for putting chaps through hell, she is oddly also the same risk-taking character, the same sexual adventurer we ultimately meet in Catherine Bourne, though strictly heterosexual in her conquests—except perhaps with Jacob Barnes. "I suppose she only wanted what she couldn't have," muses the latter, not seeing as yet how well those words describe himself (31).

I do not mean to imply here that Jacob, a soulful wrestler with his own physical condition, would also like to make it with bullfighters and other males—that seems to me misleading—but rather that—in accord with the oddly common attraction for men of lesbian lovemaking, the imagining into it that exercises suppressed femininity, and indeed the need for such imagining, such identification with the original nurturing sources of love—he wants Brett in a womanly way. Hemingway's childhood twinning with his older sister Marcelline may have made him more sensitive to such desires and more strongly liable first to suppress and then ulti- mately to express them; but he was in fact expressing something common, difficult, and quite possibly crucial to coming of age as a man in this century's white bour- geois circles. His admiration for the liberated ladies of the 1920s was widely shared, and his ultimate enslavement by their androgynous powers may tell us more about ourselves and our times than we care to know.

Certainly Jake is enslaved by Brett as are Robert Cohn and Mike Campbell and even Pedro Romero, who escapes her only through her charitable withdrawal of her devastating love. That is the Ulyssean predicament, the Circean circle. But there are worshipful precedents for it in childhood that make it seem less ironic and pitiful (in a novel struggling to get beyond those judgments) than inevitable and rather touching. One thinks of Guy Halifax's boyhood crush on Lady Caroline, in *John Halifax, Gentleman,* as a possible source in this regard of Circe's awful power. Lady Caroline, whom I earlier described as "a handsome charming hedonist hell- bent on adultery," was also "the magic centre of any society wherein she chose to move," an irresistible charmer, like Brett, floating easily "upon and among the pleasantnesses of life," above the ravages of pain. Ultimately, like Brett, she is ravaged by pain, and has done her share of ravaging; but when we first meet her at Longfield, the Halifax estate after which Grace Hemingway would name her farm and music sanctuary across the lake in northern Michigan, the wicked lady receives a curious certification as the preferred romantic mother of little Guy Halifax. This "little gentleman from his cradle" is the first to announce her arrival; he boldly asks her, "Isn't this a pretty view?" as they approach the house, and having touched her green gown (as opposed to his mother's gray), he proceeds to install himself as "her admiring knight attendant everywhere."[6] Later, as a young adult in Paris, he will even strike her seducer and abandoner, Sir Gerard Vermilye, just as Robert Cohn will strike Lady Ashley's rival admirers in Pamplona. Meanwhile in childhood he gathers for her that magnificent arum lily which would eventually appear on the Hemingway family shield, and at bedtime lifts up his face to her to be kissed as by a new and more romantic mother. The kiss is thwarted since Lady Caroline, as we earlier saw, is unable to return it because of sudden distress at her own sinful condition—an earlier version, perhaps, of Lady Ashley's "Don't touch me." At any rate, this confessed adulteress, who resembles Brett in that she defends her sin vigorously on the grounds of her husband's brutality and her lover's kindness and devotion, but who is nonetheless so far gone that she finds the pastoral domestic love of the Halifaxes impossible for herself, even as Brett can't live "quietly in the country . . . with [her] own true love" (55)—this wicked woman is Guy Halifax's "pretty lady," and quite possibly Ernest Hemingway's earliest source of attraction to Brett's prototype, Duff Twysden, his first preferred alternative to real and fictional mothers like Ursula Halifax and Grace Hemingway—the romantic lady, then, of his boyhood reading dreams.

Still another "romantic lady" would figure in the making of Brett Ashley. Critics have long noted the influence of Michael Arlen's heroine Iris March, in *The Green Hat,* possibly because of the fetish made of Brett's man's hat but also because of the modern twist on an old tradition. As Allen Tate observed in criticizing Hemingway for sparing certain characters in *The Sun Also Rises* from equitable judgment, Brett "becomes the attractive wayward lady of Sir Arthur Pinero and Michael Arlen"; whereas "Petronius's Circe, the archetype of all the Bretts, was neither appealing nor deformed" (44). Such observations are useful in that Brett is indeed given special treatment, early on, as "one of us"—that is to say, "one of us" stoical and perhaps Conradian survivors—and is granted a certain nobility at the end for her refusal to destroy the worthy Pedro, to say nothing of her repeated returns to Jake Barnes for support and reassurance, as to the novel's touchstone for stoic endurance. Similarly Arlen's attractively wayward heroine in *The Green Hat* is given more than the usual share of male honor as she protects her suicidal first husband's good name at the expense of her own, assuming to herself the "impurity" (i.e., syphilis) that killed him, and then, in another grand gesture of self-denial, sending her true love back to his wife before roaring off in her yellow Hispano-Suiza to a fiery and quite melodramatic death; and Iris too is characterized as "one of us" and is said to "meet men on their own ground always."[7] Even so, Brett is probably based on still another Arlen heroine in more important ways. Thus, as Carlos Baker reports, Scott Fitzgerald had passed the time on a motor trip with Hemingway in May 1925 "by providing detailed summaries of the plots of the novels of Michael Arlen," one of which—a tale called *The Romantic Lady*—seems to have moved him (though he denied it) to go and do likewise.[8]

"The Romantic Lady" is a Men's Club story told to the narrator by his good friend Noel Anson, whom the narrator has not seen for six years and who has been divorced just six months before, he at once explains, by "a perfect woman." Much later in the evening Anson reserves for his friend the title story, proceeding in a manner our narrator likens to Marlow's as he leads his transfixed hearer "inexorably through the labyrinth of Lord Jim's career, and through many another such intricacy of Conradian imagination."[9] Anson calls it an "ageless tale of the inevitable lady sitting alone in an inevitable [theatre] box" (4)—a story, that is, of a genteel pickup, the twist being that the picker here is in fact himself picked by the lady though he proceeds at first otherwise. Thus, while sitting alone in a stall one night at the old Imperial, Anson suddenly sees in the upper boxes "a marvellous lady in white, amazing and alone and unashamed" (4–5). He at once works out a note inviting this instance of "real, exquisite life" to dinner, receives a reply to call at her box after the revue—and is taken home by her to a table already set for dinner. In other words, he is her guest; she, not he, is the host for dinner, and she actually laughs at him for imagining he has "picked [her] up":

> " 'Don't you know that it was decided this morning that you should come to supper with me, decided quite, quite early? Or some one like you, perhaps not so charming—but then I have been so lucky—. . . . Are you very angry with me?' "
>
> "She was very close to me, smiling, intimate. Pure coquetry of course,—but what perfect *technique!* You knew that she was playing, but that did not prevent the blood rushing to your head; and she was so clean, so much 'one of us'! . . .
>
> " 'Anger isn't exactly one of my emotions at the moment,' I said, stupidly enough. 'But will you please be very gentle with me, because never, never have I met any one like you?' " (12–13)

The Conradian phrase is out; the lady is the right sort, she is "one of us": she is calling the shots, moreover, in what must be candidly recognized as a 1920s Mayfair version of "the zipless fuck," as Erica Jong would later call it—indeed, an anticipation of the new female terms for it as Jong would work them out ("will you please be very gentle with me . . . ?") through her own sexually adventurous ladies.[10]

Our more immediate problem, however, is Hemingway's similar terms for Brett's conquest, and the curious way they bear on modern marriage. For Arlen's lady is not only married; there is a portrait of her husband on the wall, "a very distinguished looking person . . . in the toy uniform of some foreign cavalry, gorgeously decorated," and with "a thin hawk-like face, which with its perfectly poised mixture of ferocity and courtesy would have carried its fortunate owner as easily into the heart of any schoolboy as into the boudoir of the most unattainable "lady" (15). One thinks of Count Mippipopolous, the Greek escort, replete with chauffeur, who drives Lady Brett around Paris in his limousine, brings Jake flowers, exhibits his arrow wounds, values food, wine, and love, and is also characterized by Brett as "one of us." Arlen's romantic lady's husband may have sat for that portrait too, since he turns up later in the story as the coachman who not only takes Anson home, but on being recognized by him, explains the lady's game. Thus he too had first met his wife at the theatre, had himself been picked by her for an evening's romance, and had been told by her upon parting—as Anson has just been told—to forget the address, to settle for one perfect night of love. Instead he had gone back the next day, she had been delighted by his return, had married him—and then tired of him, as she had grown tired of her previous husband to whom he too had then been introduced as his predecessor in the endless game of beautiful one-night stands. Indeed, marriage had been his punishment for insisting upon seeing her again:

> ". . . and I had to acquiesce in her mere affection for me—that affection with which all splendid women enshroud their dead loves. And how much in oneself dies with their dead love! Why, there dies the ritual of love, the sacrament of sex! For sex can be exalted to a sacrament only once in a lifetime, for the rest it's just a game, an indoor sport. . . ."
>
> "You see, such women as she make their own laws. It is not her fault, nor her arrogance, it is ours, who are so consistently susceptible. Physically she belongs to the universe, not to one single man. She never belonged to me, I was just an expression of the world to her. She has never belonged to any one, she never will—for she is in quest of the ideal which even she will never find. And so she will go on, testing out—our quality and breaking our hearts." (34–35)

One thinks of Brett surrounded by wreathed dancers when the fiesta at Pamplona explodes (155); or "coming through the crowd in the square, walking, her head up, as though the fiesta were being staged in her honor" (206); or of the book's epigraph from Ecclesiastes—"the earth abideth forever"—and Hemingway's odd assertion that "the abiding earth" is the novel's hero.[11] If Arlen's romantic lady is any evidence, "abiding heroine" might be more to the point—"earthy" ladies who make their own laws, confine sex to adventurous one-night stands which, in Hemingway's more cynical world, do not mean anything, but which are in fact cynical enough in Arlen's formulation—his Marlovian narrator having been divorced six months before, he now reminds us, for having himself gone back for the punishment of marriage. "Be very gentle with me" indeed: those oddly passive, now androgynous remarks remind us all too tellingly that it was Pauline who pursued and won Ernest away from Hadley in 1926, the year in which *The Sun Also Rises* was first published.

NOTES

[1] Hemingway, *Selected Letters, 1917–1961*, ed. Carlos Baker (New York: Scribner's, 1961), p. 745.
[2] See Fitzgerald's long letter to Hemingway on cutting the early chapters, in Frederic Joseph Svoboda's *Hemingway and* The Sun Also Rises: *The Crafting of a Style* (Lawrence: University Press of Kansas, 1981), 140: "He isn't *like an impotent man. He's like a man in a sort of moral chastity belt*" (italics mine). See also Carlos Baker, *Ernest Hemingway: A Life Story* (New York: Bantam, 1970), 203: "The situation between Barnes and Brett Ashley, as Ernest imagined it, could very well be a projection of his own inhibitions about sleeping with Duff."

[3] *The Garden of Eden* manuscript, bk. 1, chap. 1, pp. 17, 23–24, in Hemingway Collection, Kennedy Library, Boston, Mass. For reproductions of bronze and plaster versions of the statues in question, see especially *The Sculptures of Auguste Rodin*, ed. John Tancock (Philadelphia: Philadelphia Museum of Art, 1976).

[4] George Plimpton, "An Interview with Ernest Hemingway," in *Writers at Work: The* Paris Review *Interviews*, 2nd ser. (New York: Viking Press, 1963).

[5] Hemingway, *The Sun Also Rises* (New York: Scribner's, 1954), 22, 24–28. Page references in the text are to this 1954 edition.

[6] Dinah Mulock Craik, *John Halifax, Gentleman* (London: A. & C. Black, 1922; London: Dent, 1961), 175, 249–53.

[7] Michael Arlen, *The Green Hat* (London: Cassell, 1968), 95, 229, 231.

[8] Baker, *Ernest Hemingway*, 189. See also *Selected Letters*, 238. For Fitzgerald's acute observation that the original opening chapters are indeed written in the effusive style of Michael Arlen (to which Fitzgerald strongly objected), see Svoboda, *Hemingway*, 138: "You've done a lot of writing that *honestly* reminded me of Michael Arlen." See also chapter 14 of *The Torrents of Spring* (New York: Scribner's, 1972), where Yogi Johnson tells a version of Arlen's *The Romantic Lady* in which a beautiful woman uses him for voyeuristic purposes (79–81). In *Along with Youth: Hemingway, The Early Years* (New York: Oxford University Press, 1985), 65, Peter Griffin mistakes this obvious borrowing for autobiographical truth.

[9] Michael Arlen, *The Romantic Lady* (New York: Dodd, Mead, and Co., 1921), 4. Page references in the text are to this 1921 New York edition.

[10] See Erica Jong, *Fear of Flying* (New York: Holt, Rinehart, and Winston, 1973), and the novels that follow, especially *Fanny*, in which she more or less appropriates for her sex the previously male world of sexual adventure and conquest.

[11] Hemingway to Maxwell Perkins, 19 November 1926, in *Selected Letters*, 229.

CONTRIBUTORS

HAROLD BLOOM is Sterling Professor of the Humanities at Yale University and Henry W. and Albert A. Berg Professor of English at the New York University Graduate School. He is a 1985 MacArthur Foundation Award recipient, served as the Charles Eliot Norton Professor of Poetry at Harvard University (1987–88), and is the author of nineteen books, the most recent being *The Book of J* (1990). Currently he is editing the Chelsea House series Modern Critical Views and The Critical Cosmos, and other Chelsea House series in literary criticism.

ROBERT W. LEWIS is Professor of English at the University of North Dakota. He is the author of *Hemingway on Love* (1965) and the editor of *Hemingway in Italy and Other Essays* (1990).

JACKSON J. BENSON is Professor of English and Comparative Literature at San Diego State University. He is coeditor (with Richard Astro) of *Hemingway in Our Time* (1974) and *The Fiction of Bernard Malamud* (1977), and is the editor of *The Short Novels of John Steinbeck: Critical Essays* (1990).

BERTRAM D. SARASON is the editor of *Hemingway and The Sun Set* (1972) and was a former editor of *The Connecticut Review*. He is a former professor at Southern Connecticut State University (New Haven, CT).

CAROLE GOTTLIEB VOPAT is Associate Professor of English at the University of Wisconsin–Parkside.

SAM S. BASKETT is Professor of English at Michigan State University. He has written articles on Thoreau, T. S. Eliot, Jack London, and Hemingway.

PATRICK D. MORROW is Professor of English at Auburn University and is the author of *Bret Harte* (1972) and *Bret Harte: Literary Critic* (1979).

LINDA WAGNER-MARTIN is Professor of English at the University of North Carolina at Chapel Hill and consulting editor for UMI Research Press. She is the author of *Hemingway and Faulkner: Inventors/Masters* (1975), *Ernest Hemingway: A Reference Guide* (1977), and *The Modern American Novel 1914–1945: A Critical History* (1990).

ROGER WHITLOW is Professor of English at Eastern Illinois University (Charleston, IL) and author of *Black American Literature: A Critical History* (1973).

MILTON A. COHEN is Associate Professor of English and Education at the University of Texas–Richardson. He has written *Poet and Painter: The Aesthetics of e. e. cummings' Early Work* (1987).

WOLFGANG E. H. RUDAT is Professor of English at the University of Houston. He is the author of numerous articles on Hemingway and has written *The Mutual Commerce: Masters of Classical Allusion in English and American Literature* (1985).

MARK SPILKA is I. J. Kapstein Professor of English at Brown University and author of *The Love Ethic of D. H. Lawrence* (1955), *Dickens and Kafka* (1963), and *Hemingway's Quarrel with Androgyny* (1990).

BIBLIOGRAPHY

Adair, William. "Hemingway's *The Sun Also Rises.*" *Explicator* 45, No. 3 (Spring 1987): 48–49.

Adams, Richard P. "Sunrise out of *The Waste Land.*" *Tulane Studies in English* 9 (1959): 119–31.

Aldridge, John W. "Hemingway: Nightmare and the Correlative of Loss." In *After the Lost Generation: A Critical Study of the Writers of Two Wars.* New York: Noonday Press, 1958, pp. 23–43.

Anderson, David D. "Ernest Hemingway, The Voice of an Era." *Personalist* 48 (1966): 234–47.

Baker, Carlos. *Hemingway: The Writer as Artist.* Princeton: Princeton University Press, 1952.

Bass, Eban. "Hemingway's Women of Another Country." *Markham Review* 6, No. 1 (Winter 1977): 35–39.

Beach, Joseph Warren. "Ernest Hemingway: Empirical Ethics." In *American Fiction 1920–1940.* New York: Macmillan, 1941, pp. 69–93.

Bloom, Harold, ed. *Ernest Hemingway's* The Sun Also Rises. New York: Chelsea House, 1987.

Brenner, Gerry. "A 'Vulgar' Ethic: *The Sun Also Rises.*" In Concealments in Hemingway's Works. Columbus: Ohio State University Press, 1983, pp. 42–61.

Budick, Emily Miller. "*The Sun Also Rises:* Hemingway and the Art of Redemption." *University of Toronto Quarterly* 56 (1987): 319–37.

———. "*The Sun Also Rises:* Hemingway's New Covenant of History." In *Fiction and Historical Consciousness: The American Romance Tradition.* New Haven: Yale University Press, 1989, pp. 164–84.

Canby, Henry Seidel. "Introduction." In *The Sun Also Rises.* New York: Modern Library, 1930, pp. v–ix.

Cargill, Oscar. "The Primitivists." In *Intellectual America: Ideas on the March.* New York: Macmillan, 1841, pp. 311–98.

Casillo, Robert. "The Festival Gone Wrong: Vanity and Victimization in *The Sun Also Rises.*" *Essays in Literature* 13 (1986): 115–33.

Charters, James. "Pat and Duff, Some Memories." *Connecticut Review* 3, No. 2 (April 1970): 24–27.

Cochran, Robert W. "Circularity in *The Sun Also Rises.*" *Modern Fiction Studies* 14 (1968): 297–305.

Cody, Morrill. "*The Sun Also Rises* Revisited." *Connecticut Review* 4, No. 2 (April 1970): 5–8.

Curtis, Mary Ann. "*The Sun Also Rises:* Its Relation to *The Song of Roland.*" *American Literature* 60 (1988): 274–77.

Farquhar, Robin H. "Dramatic Structures in the Novels of Hemingway." *Modern Fiction Studies* 14 (1968): 271–96.

Geismar, Maxwell. "Earnest Hemingway: You Could Always Come Back." In *Writers in Crisis: The American Novel between Two Wars.* Boston: Houghton Mifflin, 1942, pp. 39–85.

———. "Hemingway: At the Crossroads." In *American Moderns: From Rebellion to Conformity.* New York: Hill and Wang, 1958, pp. 55–57.

Grenberg, Bruce L. "The Design of Heroism in *The Sun Also Rises*." *Fitzgerald/Hemingway Annual 1971,* pp. 247–89.

Hanneman, Audre. *Ernest Hemingway: A Comprehensive Bibliography.* Princeton: Princeton University Press, 1967.

———. *Supplement to* Ernest Hemingway: A Comprehensive Bibliography. Princeton: Princeton University Press, 1975.

Harrell, David. "A Final Note on Duff Twysden." *Hemingway Review* 5 (1986): 45–46.

Hart, Jeffrey. "*The Sun Also Rises:* A Revalution." *Sewanee Review* 86 (1978): 557–62.

Hays, Peter L. "Creation of a New Prose." In *Ernest Hemingway.* New York: Ungar, 1990, pp. 38–53.

Hemingway Review 6, No. 1 (Fall 1986). Special *The Sun Also Rises* issue.

Higgs, Robert J. "Apollo." In *Laurel & Thorn: The Athlete in American Literature.* Lexington: University Press of Kentucky, 1981, pp. 22–90.

Hinkle, James. "Some Unexpected Sources for *The Sun Also Rises*." *Hemingway Review* 2, No. 1 (1982): 26–42.

Krell, Norman. "Impotence and Frigidity." In *Varieties of Sexual Experience: Psychosexuality in Literature.* New York: International Universities Press, 1976, pp. 394–442.

Kunar, Sukrita Paul. "Woman as Hero in *The Sun Also Rises*." *Literary Endeavor* 6, Nos. 1–4 (1985): 102–8.

Lee, Brian. "Modernism: Stein, Hemingway, West, Roth, Fitzgerald." In *American Fiction 1865–1940.* New York: Longman, 1987, pp. 189–225.

Lennox, Sarah. " 'We Could Have Had Such a Damned Good Time Together': Individual and Society in *The Sun Also Rises* and *Mutmassungen über Jakob.*" *Modern Language Studies* 7 (1977): 82–90.

Linebarger, J. M. "Eggs as Huevos in *The Sun Also Rises*." *Fitzgerald/Hemingway Annual 1970,* pp. 237–39.

Loeb, Harold. "Hemingway's Bitterness." *Connecticut Review* 1, No. 1 (October 1967): 7–25.

McAlmon, Robert. *Being Geniuses Together 1920–1930.* Garden City, NY: Doubleday, 1968.

Merrill, Robert. "Demoting Hemingway." *American Literature* 60 (1988): 255–68.

Moreland, Kim. "Hemingway's Medievalist Impulse—Its Effect on the Presentation of Women and War in *The Sun Also Rises*." *Hemingway Review* 6, No. 1 (Fall 1986): 30–41.

Nichols, Kathleen L. "The Morality of Asceticism in *The Sun Also Rises:* A Structural Reinterpretation." *Fitzgerald/Hemingway Annual 1978,* pp. 321–30.

Reynolds, Michael S. The Sun Also Rises: *A Novel of the Twenties.* Boston: Twayne, 1988.

Ross, Morton L. "Bill Gorton, the Preacher in *The Sun Also Rises*." *Modern Fiction Studies* 18 (1972): 517–27.

Rovit, Earl, and Gerry Brenner. "*The Sun Also Rises:* An Essay on Applied Principles." In *Ernest Hemingway.* Boston: Twayne, 1986, pp. 128–29.

Rudat, Wolfgang E. H. "Cohn and Romero in the Ring: Sports and Religion in *The Sun Also Rises*." *Arizona Quarterly* 41 (1985): 311–18.

———. "Hemingway's Brett: Linguistic Manipulation and the Male Ego in *The Sun Also Rises*." *Journal of Evolutionary Psychology* 7, Nos. 1–2 (March 1986): 76–82.

———. "Mike Campbell and 'These Literary Chaps': Palimpsestic Narrative in *The Sun Also Rises*." *Studies in the Novel* 20 (1988): 302–15.

———. "Sexual Dilemmas in *The Sun Also Rises:* Hemingway's Count and the Education of Jacob Barnes." *Hemingway Review* 8, No. 2 (Spring 1989): 2–13.

Schneider, Daniel J. "The Symbolism of *The Sun Also Rises*." *Discourse* 10 (1967): 337–42.

Schonhorn, Manuel. "*The Sun Also Rises:* I. The Jacob Allusion; II. Parody as Meaning." *Ball State University Forum* 16, No. 2 (Spring 1975): 49–55.

Snell, George. "Ernest Hemingway: And the Fifth Dimension." *Fitzgerald/Hemingway Annual 1969*, pp. 77–103.

Spilka, Mark. "The Death of Love in *The Sun Also Rises:* Hemingway, 1926." In *Twelve Original Essays on Great American Novels*, ed. Charles Shapiro. Detroit: Wayne State University Press, 1958, pp. 238–56.

Sprague, Claire. "*The Sun Also Rises:* Its 'Clear Financial Basis.'" *American Quarterly* 21 (1969): 259–66.

Stallman, R. W. "*The Sun Also Rises*—But No Bells Ring." In *The Houses That James Built and Other Literary Studies*. East Lansing: Michigan State University Press, 1961, pp. 173–93.

Steinke, Jim. "Brett and Jake in Spain: Hemingway's Ending for *The Sun Also Rises*." *Hemingway Review* 4 (1984): 33–36.

Stewart, Donald Ogden. "An Interview." *Fitzgerald/Hemingway Annual 1972*, pp. 83–89.

Strychacz, Thomas. "Dramatizations of Manhood in Hemingway's *In Our Time* and *The Sun Also Rises*." *American Literature* 61 (1989): 245–60.

Stuckey, W. J. "*The Sun Also Rises* on Its Own Ground." *Journal of Narrative Technique* 6 (1976): 224–32.

Takigawa, Motoo. "The Relationship between God and Human Beings in American Literature." *Studies in English Literature* 53 (1976): 59–73.

Tavernier-Courbin, Jaqueline. "Ernest Hemingway et le clan des expatriés americains à Paris." *Canadian Review of American Studies* 8 (1977): 116–30.

Thorn, Lee. "*The Sun Also Rises:* Good Manners Make Good Art." *Hemingway Review* 8, No. 1 (Fall 1988): 42–49.

Torchiana, Donald T. "*The Sun Also Rises:* A Reconsideration." *Fitzgerald/Hemingway Annual 1969*, pp. 77–103.

Wagner-Martin, Linda. "Hemingway's Search for Heroes. Once Again." *Arizona Quarterly* 44 (1988): 58–68.

———, ed. *New Essays on* The Sun Also Rises. New York: Cambridge University Press, 1987.

Wedin, Warren. "Trout Fishing and Self-Betrayal in *The Sun Also Rises*." *Arizona Quarterly* 37 (1981): 63–74.

White, William, ed. *The Merrill Studies in* The Sun Also Rises. Columbus, OH: Merrill, 1969.

Wilentz, Gay. "Re(teaching) Hemingway: Anti-Semitism as a Thematic Device in *The Sun Also Rises*." *College English* 52 (1990): 186–88.

Williams, Wirt. "*The Sun Also Rises:* Passivity as a Tragic Response." In *The Tragic Art of Ernest Hemingway*. Baton Rouge: Louisiana State University Press, 1981, pp. 40–64.

Wilson, Edmund. "The Sportman's Tragedy." In *A Literary Chronicle 1920–1950*. Garden City, NY: Doubleday, 1950, pp. 96–101.

Young, Philip. "Death and Transfiguration." In *Ernest Hemingway: A Reconsideration.* University Park: Pennsylvania State University Press, 1966, pp. 79–133.

Zehr, David Morgan. "Paris and the Expatriate Mystique." *Arizona Quarterly* 33 (1977): 156–64.

ACKNOWLEDGMENTS

"The Unpublished Opening of *The Sun Also Rises*" by Ernest Hemingway from *Antaeus* 33, No. 1 (Spring 1979), © 1926 by Ernest Hemingway. Reprinted by permission of Charles Scribner's Sons, an imprint of Macmillan Publishing Company, and Hemingway Foreign Rights Trust.

"Hard-Boiled" by Allen Tate from *Nation,* December 15, 1926, © 1926 by Nation Enterprises, Inc. Reprinted by permission.

"The Background of a Style" by Mark Schorer from *Kenyon Review* 3, No. 1 (Winter 1941), © 1940 by Kenyon College. Reprinted by permission.

"The Women" by John Atkins from *The Art of Ernest Hemingway* by John Atkins, © 1952 by John Atkins. Reprinted by permission.

"Circe and Company" by Carlos Baker from *Hemingway: The Writer as Artist* by Carlos Baker, © 1952, 1956, 1963, 1972 by Carlos Baker. Reprinted by permission of Princeton University Press.

"Primitivism and Masculinity in the Work of Ernest Hemingway" by Tom Burnam from *Modern Fiction Studies* 1, No. 3 (August 1955), © 1955 by *Modern Fiction Studies.* Reprinted by permission.

"Hemingway in Paris" by Malcolm Cowley from *A Second Flowering: Works and Days of the Lost Generation* by Malcolm Cowley, © 1956, 1967, 1968, 1970, 1973 by Malcolm Cowley. Reprinted by permission of Viking Penguin, a division of Penguin USA Inc., and Andre Deutsch Ltd.

"Ernest Hemingway: The River and the Hawk" by W. M. Frohock from *The Novel of Violence in America* by W. M. Frohock, © 1950, 1957 by W. M. Frohock. Reprinted by permission of Natalie B. Frohock.

"Ernest Hemingway: Man on His Moral Uppers" by Cleanth Brooks from *The Hidden God: Studies in Hemingway, Faulkner, Yeats, Eliot, and Warren* by Cleanth Brooks, © 1963 by Yale University. Reprinted by permission of Yale University Press.

"Fitzgerald's *Sun Also Rises:* Notes and Comment" by Philip Young and Charles W. Mann from *Fitzgerald/Hemingway Annual 1970,* © 1970 by the National Cash Register Company, Dayton, Ohio. Reprinted by permission of Matthew J. Bruccoli.

"The Great American Bitch" by Dolores Barracano Schmidt from *College English* 32, No. 8 (May 1971), © 1971 by the National Council of Teachers of English. Reprinted by permission of the National Council of Teachers of English.

"Symbolic Hats in *The Sun Also Rises*" by J. M. Linebarger from *Fitzgerald/Hemingway Annual 1972,* © 1972 by the National Cash Register Company, Dayton, Ohio. Reprinted by permission of Matthew J. Bruccoli.

The Life and Writings of Ernest Hemingway by Robert Brainard Pearsall, © 1973 by Editions Rodopi BV. Reprinted by permission.

"Of Women and Bitches: A Defense of Two Hemingway Heroines" by Sunita Jain from *Journal of the School of Languages* 12, No. 2 (Winter 1975–76), © 1975 by Jawaharlal Nehru University. Reprinted by permission.

"Hemingway Reads Huxley: An Occasion For Some Observations on the Twenties and the Apostolate of the Lost Generation" by Jerome Meckier from *Fitzgerald/Hemingway Annual 1976,* © 1976 by Indian Head Inc. Reprinted by permission of Matthew J. Bruccoli.

"Hemingway" by Mimi Reisel Gladstein from *The Indestructible Woman in Faulkner, Hemingway, and Steinbeck* by Mimi Reisel Gladstein, © 1986 by Mimi Reisel Gladstein. Reprinted by permission of UMI Research Press, Ann Arbor, MI.

"Tristan or Jacob?" by Robert W. Lewis from *Hemingway on Love* by Robert W. Lewis, © 1965 by Robert W. Lewis. Reprinted by permission of The University of Texas Press.

"Roles and the Masculine Writer" by Jackson J. Benson from *Hemingway . . . The Writer's Art of Self-Defense* by Jackson J. Benson, © 1969 by the University of Minnesota. Reprinted by permission of the University of Minnesota Press.

"Lady Brett Ashley and Lady Duff Twysden" by Bertram D. Sarason from *Connecticut Review* 2, No. 2 (April 1969), © 1969 by the Board of Trustees of Connecticut State College. Reprinted by permission.

"The End of *The Sun Also Rises:* A New Beginning" by Carole Gottlieb Vopat from *Fitzgerald/Hemingway Annual 1972,* © 1972 by the National Cash Register Company, Dayton, Ohio. Reprinted by permission of Matthew J. Bruccoli.

"Brett and Her Lovers" (originally titled "An Image to Dance Around: Brett and Her Lovers in *The Sun Also Rises*") by Sam S. Baskett from *Centennial Review* 22, No. 1 (Winter 1978), © 1978 by *The Centennial Review.* Reprinted by permission of *The Centennial Review.*

"The Bought Generation" (originally titled "The Bought Generation: Another Look at Money in *The Sun Also Rises*") by Patrick D. Morrow from *Genre* 13, No. 1 (Spring 1980), © 1980 by *Genre.* Reprinted by permission of *Genre.*

"Women in Hemingway's Early Fiction" (originally titled " 'Proud and Friendly and Gently': Women in Hemingway's Early Fiction") by Linda Wagner-Martin from *College Literature* 7, No. 3 (Fall 1980), © 1980 by West Chester University. Reprinted by permission of *College Literature.*

"Bitches and Other Simplistic Assumptions" by Roger Whitlow from *Cassandra's Daughters: The Women in Hemingway* by Roger Whitlow, © 1984 by Roger Whitlow. Reprinted by permission of Greenwood Press.

"Circe and Her Swine" (originally titled "Circe and Her Swine: Domination and Debasement in *The Sun Also Rises*") by Milton A. Cohen from *Arizona Quarterly* 41, No. 4 (Winter 1985), © 1985 by Arizona Board of Regents. Reprinted by permission of *Arizona Quarterly.*

"Brett's Problem" (originally titled "Brett's Problem: Ovidian and Other Allusions in *The Sun Also Rises*") by Wolfgang E. H. Rudat from *Style* 19, No. 3 (Fall 1985), © 1985 by *Style*. Reprinted by permission of *Style*.

"Jake and Brett: Wounded Warriors" (originally titled "Three Wounded Warriors") by Mark Spilka from *Hemingway's Quarrel with Androgyny* by Mark Spilka, © 1990 by the University of Nebraska Press. Reprinted by permission of the University of Nebraska Press.

INDEX